HOME-MADE BEVERAGES

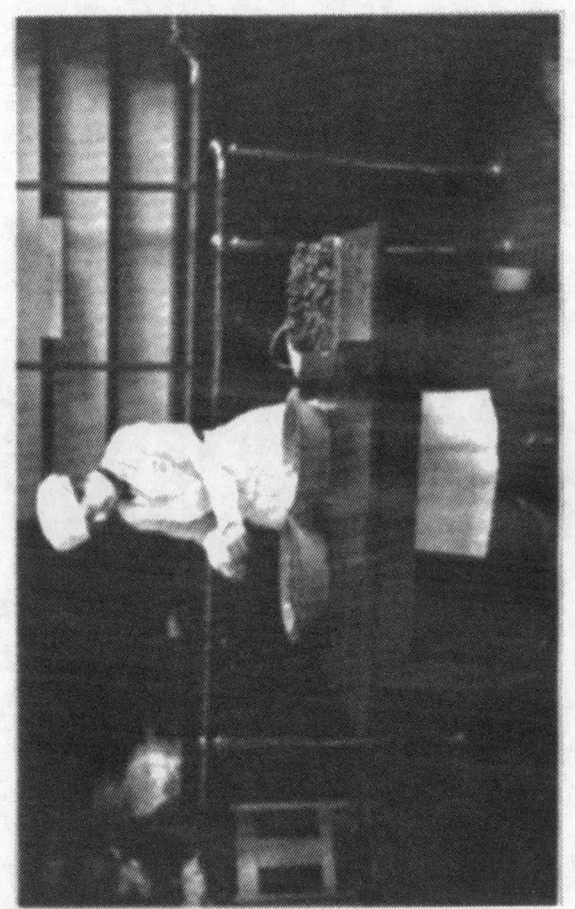

STEMMING THE GRAPES.

HOME MADE BEVERAGES

*The Manufacture of
Non-Alcoholic and Alcoholic Drinks
in the Household*

BY

ALBERT A. HOPKINS
EDITOR OF THE "SCIENTIFIC AMERICAN CYCLOPEDIA OF
FORMULAS," TRANSLATOR OF DE BREVANS' "MANU-
FACTURE OF LIQUORS AND PRESERVES," ETC.

Creative Cookbooks
Monterey, California

Home Made Beverages:
The Manufacture of Non-Alcoholic and Alcoholic
Drinks in the Household

by
Albert A. Hopkins

ISBN: 1-58963-531-0

Copyright © 2001 by Fredonia Books

Reprinted from the 1919 edition

Creative Cookbooks
An Imprint of Fredonia Books
Monterey, California
http://www.creativecookbooks.com

All rights reserved, including the right to reproduce this book, or portions thereof, in any form.

In order to make original editions of historical works available to scholars at an economical price, this facsimile of the original edition of 1919 is reproduced from the best available copy and has been digitally enhanced to improve legibility, but the text remains unaltered to retain historical authenticity.

TABLE OF CONTENTS

CHAP.		PAGE
I.	Essences and Extracts	1–23
II.	Syrups	24–54
III.	Non-alcoholic Beers	55–60
IV.	Eggs and Milk or Cream Drinks	61–65
V.	Frappés	66–68
VI.	Ginger Ales, Beers, Pop, Etc	69–74
VII.	Glacés	75
VIII.	Grape Juice	76–82
IX.	Ice Cream Beverages for Fountains	83–86
X.	Lemon, Lime, Mint, Etc.	87–93
XI.	Malt Beverages	94–95
XII.	Malted Milk and Mead	96–99
XIII.	Phosphates	100–106
XIV	Punches	107–111
XV.	Sundaes	112–114
XVI.	Hot Beverages	115–127
XVII.	Beverages for the Sick	128–130
XVIII.	Ciders	131–144
XIX.	Wines and Wine Making	145–196
XX.	Mixed Drinks	197–212
XXI.	Punches	213–221

PREFACE

THE Persian astronomer, sage, and one-time tent maker for other people—Omar Khayyam—was one of the first to extol the merits of vinous beverages:

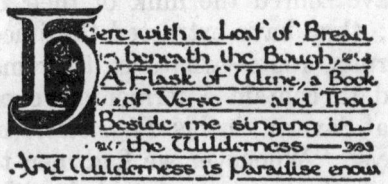

Here with a Loaf of Bread
beneath the Bough,
A Flask of Wine, a Book
of Verse — and Thou
Beside me singing in
the Wilderness —
And Wilderness is Paradise enow

We probably owe the first "household" wine manufactured to that able Naval Constructor named Noah; for he planted and cultivated the vine. Bacchus was the reputed inventor of fermented wine; Osiris was the originator of beer in the torrid clime of Egypt, and for many centuries the world had to exist on what we have heard so much of lately—"Light wines and beer." It was reserved for those hoary Arabian chemists and alchemists, it makes little difference which, to discover the process of extracting the spirituous part in which the strength lies, namely, by distilla-

Preface

tion. Alcohol for beverage purposes was really a by-product with them; for they were looking for perfume extraction, but their researches soon carried them far afield; and thus we have—"Spirits-of-Wine"—or brandy. This knowledge of the extraction of alcohol has benefited the world greatly; for by analogous processes quinine, morphine, and strychnine have been made.

In all ages, even among what we have agreed to call savages, men have succeeded in making drinks of various kinds at home. They have soured the milk of their domestic animals; they have extracted the juice of different fruits, roots—whatever they may have imagined to contain a fermentative principle. As Brillat-Savarin, in his *Physiologie du Goût*, aptly says: "Whenever we find men together, we also find they are provided with strong liquors, which they make use of at their banquets, their religious ceremonies, their marriages, their funerals—in short, on every festive or solemn occasion." The gastronomic *avocat* and judge further says: "In any case, this thirst for a liquid which Nature has wrapped up in mystery—an extraordinary desire, influencing all races of men, under all climates and in all latitudes—well deserves to fix the attention of the philosophic observer."

The French peasant almost universally has his still; his English brother his kitchen brewing plant; if he is away from the large city;

Preface

the Italian has his cheap and healthy wine; while the beverages of other countries are used and seldom abused by the natives. Of course very high proof beverages with poisonous flavorings like absinthe, or vodka, should be prohibited by the State. In the United States the distilling industry has been dealt a heavy blow, and it is doubtful if these plants will not be altogether too extensive for the manufacture of alcohol for technical and "scientific" purposes. Wine may still be had for medical and sacramental purposes, however.

Without holding a brief for either the prohibitionist or those who wish to manufacture innocuous beverages at home, this little book is offered in the hope that its catholicity will appeal at once to the "pros" and the "antis;" for herein will be found everything from strong wine to lemonade. In any event, the information contained will be of interest even in this seemingly dry northern half of our hemisphere of the world.

HOME-MADE BEVERAGES

HOME-MADE BEVERAGES

Chapter I.

ESSENCES AND EXTRACTS

ESSENCE.—An oil distilled at a comparatively low temperature from a plant in which it already exists; as *essence* of peppermint.—*Century Dictionary*.

EXTRACT.—Anything drawn from a substance by distillation, heat, solution, or other chemical process, as an essence or tincture.—*Century Dictionary*.

Allspice

1.—Allspice, coarsely ground, 4 oz.; diluted alcohol, 1 pt.

2.—Deodorized alcohol, 500 parts; proof spirits, 300 parts; oil of allspice, 100 parts; carbonate of magnesia, 100 parts. Color with caramel.

Almonds

1.—One fl.oz. essential oil of almonds, 1 pt. spirit; proceed as allspice.

2.—Essence of bitter almonds, essence of peach kernels, almond flavor. Essential oil of almonds, 1 fl.oz.; rectified spirit (56 o.p.), 19 fl.oz. Mix and agitate them together until united.

3.—Concentrated essence of almonds, double strength. Take of essential oil of almonds, 1 fl.oz.; alcohol, strongest,

1

Beverages—Non-Alcoholic

9 fl.oz. Mix. Used chiefly to impart the nutty aroma and flavor of bitter almonds and peach kernels to other preparations. The first is the common essence of the shops. Essences of other essential oils may be prepared in a similar manner. Many of them are now much used by confectioners and cooks as well as in perfumery and cosmetics. It should be remembered that essence of almonds is poisonous.

4.—Oil of bitter almonds, 1 oz.; alcohol, 13 oz.; water 6 oz. Some color it with half an ounce of tincture of turmeric.

Angelica

1.—Angelica root, 2 oz.; rectified spirit, 2½ oz.; water, 9 oz. Digest, strain and evaporate.

2.—Angelica root, 2 lb.; rectified spirit, 1 gal.; make a tincture; to the marc add 1 gal. proof spirit and repeat the digestion; filter the two tinctures separately, mix, distil off the spirit, and evaporate.

Anise

1.—Aniseed, 2 oz.; oil of star anise, 1 oz.; alcohol, 2 pt.

2.—Deodorized alcohol, 500 parts; proof spirits, 300 parts; oil of anise, 100 parts; carbonate of magnesia, 100 parts. Color with caramel.

Apples

1.—Peel and reduce to pulp, 6 lb. unripe crab apples; add 1 lb. iron wire in small coils; digest in a vapor bath for about a week, express, strain, decant and evaporate in a porcelain vessel, with constant stirring, to the consistency of a soft extract; dissolve the residue in 4 parts water, strain and evaporate as before.

2.—Deodorized alcohol, 500 parts; pure apple brandy, 400 parts; apple ether, 100 parts. Color with tincture of red sanders.

3.—Glycerine, 1 oz.; amyl valerianate, 4 drams;

linalyl formate, 45 m.; fld. ext. orris, 1 oz.; alcohol, 11 oz.; water q. s. ad., 1 pt.

4.—Conc. ess. of apple peel, 720 parts; valerianate of amyl, 120 parts; acetic ether, C. P., 80 parts; nitric ether, 80 parts.

Apricot

1.—Butyric ether, 10 parts; valerianic ether, 5 parts; glycerine, 4 parts; amylic alcohol, 2 parts; amyl-butyric ether, chloroform, enanthic ether, and tartaric acid, each 1 part.

2.—Linalyl formate, 90 m.; glycerine, 1 oz.; amyl valerianate, 4 drams; alcohol, 11 oz.; fld. ext. orris, 1 oz.; water, q. s. ad., 1 pt.

3.—Alcohol, 400 parts; conc. ess. of apricot peel, 360 parts; butyric of amyl, 200 parts; oil of bitter almond, 40 parts.

Banana

1.—Banana essence, 2 oz.; citric acid, 1 oz.; alcohol, 70°, 2 pt.

2.—Deodorized alcohol, 500 parts; proof spirits, 200 parts; pure banana juice, 190 parts; banana ether, 100 parts; tincture of vanilla, 10 parts. Color with tincture of curcuma.

3.—Acetate of amyl, 1 oz.; valerianate of ethyl, 1 dram; diluted alcohol, 15 oz.

4.—Amyl acetate, 4 drams; alcohol, 10 oz.; water, enough to make 16 oz. Some add butyric ether, which, however, is of questionable utility.

5.—Alcohol, 430 parts; conc. ess. of banana peel, 400 parts; butyrate of amyl, 100 parts; butyric ether, 50 parts; chloroform, 10 parts; aldehyde, 10 parts.

Bergamot

Alcohol 780 parts; pineapple ether, 200 parts; oil of bergamot, 20 parts.

Birch

1.—First cut the oil. The essence is made as follows:

Beverages—Non-Alcoholic

Oil of birch or wintergreen, 1½ oz.; alcohol, 95°, 12 oz.; water, 12 oz.

2.—Sassafras, 1 oz.; wild cherry bark, ½ oz.; pimento, 1 oz.; wintergreen, 1 oz.; hops, ¼ oz.; coriander seed, ½ oz. Percolate with diluted alcohol until 10 ounces of tincture are obtained. The "extract" is added to plain mineral water when drawn, in the proportion of a half a teaspoonful more or less to an ordinary glass.

Blackberry

1.—Apple oil, 1 oz.; quince oil, 1 oz.; tincture of orris, 1 oz.; tartaric acid, 1 oz.; alcohol, 70°, 2 pt.

2.—Tincture of orris root (1 to 8), 1 pt.; acetic ether, 30 drops; butyric ether, 60 drops.

3.—Blackberry.—Deodorized alcohol, 500 parts; proof spirits, 200 parts; pure blackberry juice, 170 parts; blackberry ether, 100 parts; essence of cinnamon, 10 parts; essence of coriander, 10 parts; essence of nutmeg, 10 parts.

4.—Alcohol, 500 parts; conc. ess. of blackberry, 400 parts; acetic ether, C. P., 50 parts; formic ether, 20 parts; butyrate of amyl, 20 parts; acetate of amyl, 10 parts.

Blueberry

Alcohol, 420 parts; conc. ess. of blueberry, 400 parts; acetic ether, C. P., 60 parts; benzoic ether, 60 parts; enanthic ether, 40 parts; pelargonic ether, 20 parts.

Cacao

Deodorized alcohol, 500 parts; proof spirits, 100 parts; powdered cacao, 300 parts; powdered vanilla, 50 parts; powdered cinnamon, 45 parts; ambergris, 5 parts. Macerate for two weeks, express and filter.

Calamus

Deodorized alcohol, 500 parts; proof spirits, 300 parts; oil of calamus, 100 parts; carbonate of magnesia, 100 parts.

Essences and Extracts

Caraway

Deodorized alcohol, 500 parts; proof spirits, 300 parts; oil of caraway, 100 parts; carbonate of magnesia, 100 parts. Color with tincture of grass.

Cardamom

1.—Cardamom seeds, 600 gr.; alcohol at 85°, 10.5 liters; water, 5 liters. Product, 10 liters.

2.—Deodorized alcohol, 500 parts; proof spirits, 400 parts; oil of cardamom, 50 parts; carbonate of magnesia, 50 parts.

Cassia

Deodorized alcohol, 500 parts; proof spirits, 300 parts; oil of cassia, 100 parts; carbonate of magnesia, 100 parts. Color with tincture of red sanders.

Catechu

(Cachou.) Catechu, 600 grams; alcohol, 85°, 10.5 liters; water, 5 liters. Product, 10 liters.

Cedrat

Rinds of 60 fresh citrons; alcohol, 12 liters. Macerate for twenty-four hours; at the time of distilling add 5 liters of water and distil; draw off 11 liters. Rectify with 5 liters of water. Product, 10 liters.

Celery

1.—Bruised celery seed, 4½ oz.; proof spirit, 1 pt.; digest 14 days, strain.

2.—Celery seed, 7 oz.; rectified spirit, 1 pt.; digest and strain as 1.

3.—Deodorized alcohol, 500 parts; proof spirits, 300 parts; oil of celery, 100 parts; carbonate of magnesia, 100 parts.

Cherry

1.—Oil of bitter almonds, 2 drams; apple oil, 1 oz.; citric acid, 1 oz.; alcohol, 70°, 2 pt.

Beverages—Non-Alcoholic

2.—**Black.**—a.—Benzoic ether, 5 parts; acetic ether, 10 parts; oil of persico (peach kernels) and benzoic acid, each 2 parts; citric acid, 1 part.

b.—Alcohol, 550 parts; conc. ess. of black cherry, 400 parts; acetate of amyl, 25 parts; oil of bitter almond, 10 parts; butyrate of amyl, 8 parts; oil of citron, 2 parts; oil of cinnamon, 2 parts; oil of clove, 2 parts; oil of sweet orange, 1 part.

3.—**Morella Cherry.**—Deodorized alcohol, 500 parts; proof spirits, 200 parts; pure morella cherry juice, 160 parts; morella cherry ether, 100 parts; carbonate of magnesia, 20 parts; oil of bitter almond, 10 parts; oil of lemon, 4 parts; oil of sweet orange, 2 parts: oil of cinnamon, 2 parts; oil of cloves, 2 parts.

4.—**Wild Cherry.**—a.—Wild cherry in fine powder, 16 oz.; glycerine, 4 oz.; water, 8 oz.; mix the glycerine and the water, and digest the wild cherry in 8 oz. of the mixture for four days; pack in a percolator and pour on the remaining 4 oz. glycerine and water; when this has disappeared from the surface, pour on rectified spirit (0.817) until 12 oz. of fluid have been obtained, and set this portion aside. Then percolate with spirit until 20 oz. more have been obtained; evaporate to 4 oz. and mix with the reserved portion.

b.—Deodorized alcohol, 500 parts; proof spirits, 250 parts; powdered wild cherry bark, 250 parts. Macerate for two weeks, express and filter. Color with caramel.

c.—Acetic ether, 5 fl.dr.; benzoic ether, 5 fl.dr.; enanthic ether, 1 fl.dr.; oil of bitter almonds (deprived of hydrocyanic acid), 2 fl.dr.; saturated alcoholic solution of benzoic acid, 1 fl.dr.; glycerine, 4 fl.dr.; deodorized alcohol, enough to make 16 fl.oz.

Cinchona

Yellow cinchona bark in coarse powder, 16 oz.; sufficient distilled water; rectified spirit, 1 oz. Macerate the bark in 40 oz. water for twenty-four hours, pack in a percolator and add water until 240 oz. have passed through, or until the bark is exhausted; evaporate the liquor to 20 oz. at a temperature not exceeding 160° F. (71 C.); filter and continue the evaporation to 3 oz., or until the sp. gr. of the liquid is 1.200; when cold add the spirit gradually, constantly stirring.

Cinnamon

1.—Oil of cinnamon, 2 drams; Ceylon cinnamon, bruised, 4 oz.; diluted alcohol, 2 pt.

2.—Cinnamon, pulverized, 300 grams; alcohol, 85°, 10.5 liters; water, 5 liters. Macerate for twenty-four hours, distil over open fire. Rectify the product with 5 liters water over an open fire. Product, 10 liters.

Citron

Alcohol, 700 parts; pineapple ether, 200 parts; oil of citron, 100 parts.

Cloves

1.—Deodorized alcohol, 500 parts; proof spirits, 300 parts; oil of cloves, 100 parts; carbonate of magnesia, 100 parts. Color with caramel.

2.—Powdered cloves, 4 oz.; diluted alcohol, 1 pt.

Cocoa

Dissolve 1 lb. of chocolate in a quart of boiling water, let it cool; take out the cocoa butter and add to it 4 oz. of glycerine and bottle. For flavoring ice cream.

Coffee

1.—Pour upon a pound of the best fresh roasted coffee 1 qt. of cold water, heat gently for half hour, then let it come to a boil, cool for two hours, strain and add 4 oz. of glycerine.

2.—For Dispensing (Liebig's).—Pour 1 qt. boiling water on 2 lb. of best ground coffee; allow it to stand one hour, place in a percolator; add enough water to obtain 32 fl.oz. of extract; add 2 oz. of alcohol to preserve, or more alcohol if intended to keep a long time.

3.—For Dispensing.—Ground Java coffee, 8 oz.; sliced vanilla bean, 2 drams; diluted alcohol, q. s.

4.—Ground roasted coffee, 2 to 8 oz.; cinnamon, bruised, 60 gr.; vanilla, sliced, 60 gr.; diluted alcohol, q. s. Moisten the ingredients with some of the liquid and pack in percolator. Put in enough diluted alcohol to leave a stratum above it. Macerate for forty-eight hours, covered; percolate, pour on enough diluted alcohol until 32 fl.oz. of extract is obtained.

5.—From 1 part of ground coffee and the necessary quantity of boiling water make a decoction that after filtration consists of ½ part by weight of fluid. This with the addition of 0.2 part sugar is evaporated in a shallow dish at a temperature of at the highest 140° F. to such an extent that a sample dropped on a glass plate on cooling becomes a solid mass. The fluid is then poured into molds that give the solidified pieces the form of tablets and these are wrapped in tinfoil or paraffined paper.

6.—Mocha coffee, ¾ lb.; Java coffee, ½ lb.; hot water, sufficient to make 2 qt. Grind the coffee to a moderately fine powder. Moisten with the hot water and pack in a glass funnel or preferably in a cylindrical percolator and percolate by pouring on boiling water in divided portions until two quarts of percolate are obtained.

7.—Mocha coffee, 4 parts; "Old Government Java" coffee, 8 parts; Rio coffee, 4 parts; glycerine, 3 parts; water, enough. The coffee should be freshly roasted and reduced to a moderately fine powder. Put into a vessel provided with a tightly fitting cover, and pour over it 10 parts of boiling water to which the glycerine has been added. Put on the cover and close tightly. Now wrap the vessel in a blanket or felt, to preserve the heat as long as possible, and set away in a warm place one hour and a half. At the expiration of this time pack into a per-

Currant

1.—Acetic ether, tartaric acid, each 5 parts; benzoic acid, succinic acid, benzoic ether, aldehyde and enanthic acid, each 1 part.

2.—Black.—Raspberry ether, 500 parts; conc. ess. of black currant, 400 parts; acetic ether, C. P., 100 parts.

3.—Red.—a.—Raspberry ether, 900 parts; acetic ether, 80 parts; French wine vinegar, 20 parts.

b.—Acetic ether, 5 parts; benzoic ether, 1 part; aldehyde, 1 part; acetic acid, 1 part; benzoic acid, 1 part; enanthic ether, 1 part; raspberry essence, 10 parts; deodorized alcohol, q. s. to make 100 parts. Mix. The above is rendered much finer by the addition of 20 parts of pure fresh currant juice.

Foam Extract

Crushed soap bark, ½ lb.; alcohol, ½ pt.; glycerine, ½ pt.; water, 1 pt. The bark should be saturated with 3 oz. of the mixture of alcohol, glycerine and water. Pack in a percolator, close the lower orifice; add enough liquid to leave a stratum above the bark; then macerate for twenty-four hours, and percolate; add of alcohol, glycerine and water in the above proportions enough to obtain 1 qt. of extract.

The proportions are from 1 dram to ½ oz. to 2 qt. of syrup, according to the foam desired on the beverage.

Fruit Essences

Dingler's Polytechnic Journal gives the following table of the composition of artificial fruit essences, showing the number of parts of each ingredient to be added to 100 parts of alcohol—all chemically pure. Glycerine is found in all—it appears to blend the different odors, and to harmonize them:

Beverages—Non-Alcoholic

COMPOSITION OF ARTIFICIAL FRUIT ESSENCES

	Peach	Apricot	Plum	Cherry	Black Cherry	Lemon	Pear	Orange	Apple	Grape	Gooseberry	Raspberry	Strawberry	Melon	Pineapple
Glycerine	5	4	8	3	..	5	10	10	4	10	..	4	2	3	3
Chloroform	..	1	..	..	..	1	..	1	2	..	..	..	..	..	1
Nitric Ether	..	..	..	..	..	1	..	..	1	..	..	..	..	..	..
Aldehyde	2	..	5	..	..	2	..	2	2	2	..	1	1	2	1
Acetate of Ethyl	5	..	5	5	10	10	5	5	1	..	5	5	5	..	..
Formiate of Ethyl	5	..	1	..	..	..	..	1	..	2	..	1	1	1	..
Butyrate of Ethyl	5	10	2	..	..	..	..	1	..	..	..	1	5	4	5
Valerianate of Ethyl	5	5	..	..	..	..	..	1	..	..	..	..	1	5	..
Benzoate of Ethyl	..	..	..	5	5	..	..	1	..	..	1	1	..	..	..
Enanthylate of Ethyl	5	1	4	1	2	..	..	..	..	10	1	1	..	..	..
Sebacic Ether	1	..	..	..	..	..	..	..	..	..	..	1	..	10	..
Salicylate of Methyl	2	2	..	..	..	..	1	..	1	..	..	1	1	..	..
Acetate of Amyl	..	..	..	..	..	10	10	..	..	..	..	1	3	..	..
Butyrate of Amyl	..	1	..	..	..	..	..	..	..	..	..	1	2	..	10
Valerianate of Amyl	..	..	..	..	10	..	..	..	10	..	..	..	..	..	..
Essence of Orange	..	..	..	..	..	..	10	..	..	..	..	..	..	..	..
Alcoholic solutions saturated in the cold of— Tartaric Acid	..	..	..	..	..	10	..	1	..	..	5	5	5	..	..
Succinic Acid	..	..	..	..	..	..	1	..	..	..	3	1	1	..	..
Benzoic Acid	..	..	..	1	2	..	..	..	..	..	..	1	..	..	..

Ginger

1 (Creuse's Process).—Fluid extract of ginger, 1½ pt.; water, 3 pt.; carbonate of magnesia, 3 oz. Mix, shake often for 24 hours, filter, evaporate to ¾ pt. and add ¾ pt. alcohol.

2.—Jamaica ginger, fine powdered, 6 oz.; alcohol, 2 pt. Moisten powder with ½ pt. of alcohol and allow it to macerate for 24 hours. Pack in percolator and gradually pour menstruum on it until 2 pt. are obtained of this extract. Use 3 oz. to 1 gal. simple syrup and 1 oz. foam.

3.—Ginger, unbleached, 4 oz.; calamus, 2 drams; Canada snake root, 2 drams; cinnamon, mace and cloves, of each 2 drams; alcohol, 85 per cent., sufficient to make 16 oz. Dextrin syrup is the article familiarly known as "glucose." Its use is deemed preferable to cane sugar in mixture, owing to the gum it contains and the body given to the preparation without excessive sweetness.

4.—Deodorized alcohol, 500 parts; proof spirits, 250

Essences and Extracts

parts; powdered Jamaica ginger, 250 parts. Macerate for two weeks, express and filter.

5.—Grated ginger, 3 oz.; fresh lemon peel, 2 oz., digested in 1½ pt. brandy for ten days.

6.—Equal parts best unbleached Jamaica ginger in coarse powder, and silicious sand, sprinkled with enough rectified spirit of wine to perfectly moisten; after 24 hours the mass is placed in a percolator, and after returning the first runnings two or three times, the receiver is changed and more rectified spirit is poured on gradually and at intervals as required until as much essence is obtained as there has been ginger employed.

7.—Twelve lb. best unbleached Jamaica ginger in coarse powder digested in 2½ gal. rectified spirit for fourteen days; the expressed and strained tincture is reduced by distillation in a stream or water bath to 1 gal., cooled, transferred rapidly to stoppered bottles and filtered.

8.—Twenty-four lb. ginger as in 7, 6 gal. rectified spirit; make a tincture as before, and distil down to 1 gal.; cool as quickly as possible out of contact with the air and add 1 gal. strongest rectified alcohol; filter if necessary.

9.—Causes no turbidity with water of syrup. One lb. finest Jamaica ginger in powder, macerated in 8 oz. rectified spirit for several hours; add more spirit and percolate to 16 oz.; add 2 oz. heavy carbonate of magnesia, agitate and add 24 oz. water; shake well and filter. If the filtrate is turbid, shake up with more magnesia and filter again. It becomes turbid again after a few days' rest, but on filtering continues clear.

Gooseberry

Aldehyde, 1 part; acetic ether, 5 parts; benzoic ether, 1 part; enanthic ether, 1 part; tartaric acid, saturated solution, 1 part; benzoic acid, saturated solution, 1 part; alcohol (deodorized), q. s. to make 100 parts.

Grape

1.—Chloroform, 2 parts; aldehyde, 2 parts; formic ether, 2 parts; enanthic ether, 10 parts; methyl-salicylic ether, 1 part; tartaric acid, saturated solution, 5 parts; succinic acid, saturated solution, 3 parts; glycerine, 10 parts; alcohol (deodorized), q. s. to make 100 parts. Mix.

2.—Deodorized alcohol, 500 parts; proof spirits, 300 parts; pure Catawba grape juice, 140 parts; acetic ether, 30 parts; butyric ether, 15 parts; oil of bitter almond, 10 parts; cognac oil, 5 parts.

3.—Enanthic ether, glycerine, each 10 parts; tartaric acid, 5 parts; succinic acid, 3 parts; aldehyde, chloroform and formic ether, each 2 parts, and methyl-salicylic ether, 1 part.

Lemon

1.—Oil of lemon, acetic ether and tartaric acid, each 10 parts; glycerine, 5 parts; aldehyde, 2 parts; chloroform, nitrous ether and succinic ether, each 1 part.

2.—One-half lb. yellow peel of fresh lemons, ½ gal. boiling water; infuse one hour, express the liquor, boil

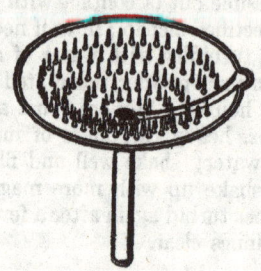

The Ecuelle, for rupturing the oil vessels of citrus fruits

down to ½ pt., cool and add ¼ oz. oil of lemon dissolved in 1½ pt. alcohol; mix and filter.

3.—Citral, 1 oz.; oil of lemon, 15 oz.; cologne spirit, 3 gal.; water, 2 gal.

4.—Deodorized alcohol, 500 parts; proof spirits, 250 parts; oil of lemon, 100 parts; carbonate of magnesia,

100 parts; pineapple ether, 50 parts. Color with tincture of curcuma.

5.—White sugar, 600 grams; distilled water, 400 grams; citric acid, 40 grams; orange flower water, 100 grams; alcohol, 100 grams; oil of lemon, 10 grams. Dissolve the sugar in the water and to the syrup add the citric acid dissolved in the orange flower water. Filter and add the oil of lemon dissolved in the alcohol. To make lemonade add 100 grams of this essence to 1 liter of water or carbonated water.

Lime

1.—Deodorized alcohol, 500 parts; proof spirits, 250 parts; oil of lime fruit, 100 parts; carbonate of magnesia 100 parts; pineapple ether, 50 parts. Color lightly with tincture of curcuma.

2.—Dissolve ½ oz. of oil in 15½ oz. of alcohol, making just a pint of finished product.

Mace

Deodorized alcohol, 500 parts; proof spirits, 350 parts; powdered mace, 150 parts. Macerate for two weeks, express and filter.

Malt

1.—An infusion of malt is made in water at 160 to 170° F. (71 to 77° C.), drained off without pressure and evaporated to a honey-like consistency. The quantities are 1 pt. crushed malt in 3 pt. hot water and the infusion occupies about four hours.

2.—47½ oz. extract of malt, mixed with 1 oz. iron pyrophosphate and ammonia citrate dissolved in 1½ oz. water.

Mead

Oil of lemon, 1 oz.; oil of cloves, 2 drams; oil of cinnamon, 2 drams; oil of nutmeg, 1 dram; oil of allspice, 30 drops; oil of sassafras, 40 drops; oil of ginger, 1 dram. Cut the oils with pumice and sugar; dissolve 16 or 32 oz. alcohol. Add gradually an equal quantity of water. Clarify.

Beverages—Non-Alcoholic

Melon

Sebacylic ether, 10 parts; valerianic ether, 5 parts; glycerine, 3 parts; butyric ether. 4 parts; aldehyde, 2 parts; formic ether, 1 part.

Nectarine

Extract of vanilla, 2 parts; essence of lemon, 2 parts; essence of pineapple, 1 part.

Nutmeg

1.—Oil of nutmeg, 2 drams; mace, powder, 1 oz.; alcohol, 95 per cent., deodorized, 32 oz. Dissolve the oil in the alcohol by agitation, add the mace, agitate, then stopper tightly and macerate 12 hours. Filter through paper.

2.—Deodorized alcohol, 500 parts; proof spirits, 400 parts; oil of nutmeg, 50 parts; carbonate of magnesia, 50 parts. Color lightly with caramel.

Orange

1.—Oil of orange and glycerine, each 10 parts; aldehyde and chloroform, each 2 parts; acetic ether, 5 parts; benzoic ether, formic ether, butyric ether, anylacetic ether, methysalicylic ether and tartaric acid, each 1 part.

Peach

1.—Oil of almonds, 3 dr.; pineapple oil, 3 dr.; tartaric acid, 3 dr.; alcohol, 80°, 1½ pt.

2.—Deodorized alcohol, 500 parts; proof spirits, 200 parts; pure peach juice, 200 parts; peach ether, 100 parts. Color with tincture of red sanders.

3.—Formic ether, valerianic ether, butyric ether, acetic ether, glycerine, and oil of persico, each 5 parts; aldehyde and amylic alcohol, each 2 parts; sebacylic ether, 1 part.

4.—Linalyl formate, 120 m.; amyl valerianate, 8 dr.; fld. ex. orris, 2 oz.; enanthic ether, 2 dr.; oil rue 30 m.;

Essences and Extracts

chloroform, 2 dr.; glycerine, 2 oz.; alcohol, 70 per cent., to 3 pt.

5.—Amylic alcohol, 2 parts; aldehyde, 2 parts; acetic ether, 5 parts; butyric ether, 5 parts; formic ether, 5 parts; sebacic ether, 1 part; valerianic ether, 5 parts; glycerine, 5 parts; oil peach kernels, 5 parts; alcohol, 100 parts (all by measure).

Pear

1.—Acetic ether, 5 oz.; acetate of amyl, 10 oz.; glycerine, 10 oz.; alcohol, 100 oz.

2.—Amyl acetate, 1 oz.; pear juice, 2 oz.; glycerine, 2 oz.; cologne spirit, 11 oz. Mix them and filter.

3.—Deodorized alcohol, 500 parts; proof spirits, 200 parts; pure pear juice, 200 parts; pear ether, 100 parts. Color lightly with tincture of red sanders.

Peppermint

1.—Oil of peppermint (Mitcham), 1 fl.oz.; rectified spirit, 1 pt.; mix by agitation. White. This is the usual strength of that sold in the shops. The corresponding preparation of the new Br. Ph., "spiritus menthæ piperitæ," has more than double this strength, being made with 1 fl.oz. of oil to 9 fl.oz. of rectified spirit.

2.—To the product of No. 1 (above) add about ½ oz. of herb peppermint, parsley leaves, spinach leaves, and digest for a week, or until sufficiently tinged; or agitate the essence with 10 or 12 gr. of sap green, previously rubbed down with about a teaspoonful of hot water. A delicate light green. The ignorant do not conceive it to be good and pure unless it has a pale greenish tint.

Used in toothache and to disguise foulness of the breath, but chiefly as a flavoring ingredient by confectioners, cooks and druggists. Peppermint (essence, water) is a great favorite in domestic and popular medicine as a remedy in flatulence, colic, nausea, sickness, etc., and to disguise the flavor of nauseous substances. The dose of the essence is 10 to 30 drops on sugar, or mixed up with

Beverages—Non-Alohcolic

a little water or wine; of the water a teacupful or more, at will. A few drops of the essence, well agitated with ½ pint of cold water, form an extemporaneous peppermint water equal to that obtained by distillation. This water is an excellent mouth wash for smokers.

3.—One oz. oil of peppermint, 4 oz. rectified spirit; mix.

4.—To 3 add ½ oz. herb of peppermint, or parsley or spinach leaves (preferably one of the first two), digest for a week, or until sufficiently colored; 10 or 12 gr. sap green rubbed up with a teaspoonful of hot water is also used for coloring.

5.—Two fl.oz. of oil of peppermint, 16 fl.oz. rectified spirits.

Pineapple

1.—Pineapple essence, 2 oz.; citric acid, 1 oz.; alcohol, 80°, 2 pt.

2.—Amyl butyric ether, 10 parts; butyric ether, 5 parts; glycerine, 3 parts; aldehyde and chloroform, each 1 part.

3.—Deodorized alcohol, 500 parts; proof spirits, 200 parts; pure pineapple juice, 190 parts; pineapple ether, 100 parts; tincture of vanilla, 10 parts. Color with tincture of curcuma.

4.—Oil of lemon, 2 drams; butyric ether, 4 drams; acetic ether, 2 oz.; spirit of nitrous ether, 1 oz.; glycerine, 1 oz.; alcohol, 1 pt.; water, enough to make 2 pt.

5.—Amyl acetate, 1 part; amyl butyrate, 10 parts; ethyl butyrate, 5 parts; glycerine, 3 parts; oil lemon, 0.1 part; oil orange, 0.2 part; alcohol, 100 parts.

6.—Amyl butyrate, 4 drams; butyric ether, 2 oz.; sebacic ether, 4 drams; acetic ether, 2 drams; amyl acetate, 2 drams; pineapple juice, 2 oz.; glycerine, 2 oz.; cologne spirit, 12 oz. Mix then and filter. A very fair essence of pineapple is made by mixing 2 oz. of butyric ether with 12 oz. of cologne spirit. Mix them and filter.

7.—Pineapple Punch Essence.—Alcohol, 2 qt.; rum, 1 qt.; artificial pineapple essence, ½ fl.dr.; essence enanthic ether, 20 gr.; citric acid solution, 1 to 1½ fl.oz.; syrup, 2 qt.

Essences and Extracts

Pistachio

1.—Essence of almond, 2 fl.oz.; tincture of vanilla, 4 fl.oz.; oil of neroli, 1 drop.

2.—Oil of orange peel, 4 fl.dr.; oil of cassia, 1 fl.dr.; oil of bitter almond, 15 m.; oil of calamus, 15 m.; oil of nutmeg, 1½ fl.dr.; oil of clove, 30 m.; alcohol. 12 fl.oz.; water, 4 fl.oz.; magnesium carbonate, 2 drams. Shake together, allow to stand 24 hours and filter.

3.—Oil orange, 45 m.; amyl acetate, 4 drams; oil bitter almonds, 5 drams; butyric ether, 5 drams; acetic ether, 9 drams; alcohol, 16 oz.; water to make 24 oz.

Plums

1.—Glycerine, 8 parts; acetic ether and aldehyde, each 5 parts; oil of persico, 4 parts; butyric ether, 2 parts, and formic ether, 1 part.

2.—Deodorized alcohol, 500 parts; proof spirits, 200 parts; plum ether, 300 parts.

Pomegranate

Oil sweet orange, 3 parts; oil cloves, 1 part; tincture vanilla, 15 parts; tincture ginger, 10 parts; maraschino liqueur, 150 parts; tincture coccionella, 165 parts; distilled water, 150 parts; phosphoric acid, dilute, 45 parts; alcohol, 95 per cent., q. s. to make 1,000 parts. Mix and dissolve.

Quince

1.—Fluid ext. orris, 2 oz.; enanthic ether, 1½ oz.; linalyl formate, 90 m.; glycerine, 2 oz.; alcohol, 70 per cent., to 3 pt.

2.—Alcohol, 460 parts; conc. ess. of quince peel, 400 parts; pelargonic ether, 100 parts; chloroform, 20 parts; aldehyde, 20 parts.

3.—Deodorized alcohol, 500 parts; proof spirits, 200 parts; pure quince juice, 160 parts; quince ether, 100 parts; carbonate of magnesia, 20 parts; oil of cinnamon, 10 parts; oil of cloves, 10 parts. Color with tincture of saffron.

Beverages—Non-Alcoholic

Raspberry

1.—Raspberry essence, 3 drams; tincture of orris, ¼ oz.; citric acid, ¼ oz.; liq. carmine, 15 drops; extract rose (from pomade), ¼ oz.; alcohol, 85°, ½ pt.

2.—Butyric ether, 5 parts; acetic ether, 3 parts; nitrous ether, 1 part; glycerine, 2 parts; alcohol (deodorized), q. s. to make 100 parts. The addition of from 25 to 30 parts of fresh raspberry juice is recommended.

3.—Fresh raspberries, 200 grams; distilled water, 100 grams; vanilla essence, 2 grams; alcohol, sufficient. Pulp the raspberries, let stand at a temperature of about 70° for 48 hours, and then add 100 grams of water. Fifty grams are then distilled off, and alcohol 90 per cent., 25 grams, in which 0.01 vanillin has been previously dissolved, is added to the distillate.

4.—Fresh raspberries, 16 oz.; Angelica (California), 6 oz.; brandy (California), 6 oz.; alcohol, 8 oz.; water, q. s. Mash the berries to a pulp in a mortar or bowl and transfer to a flask, along with the Angelica, brandy, alcohol and about 8 ounces of water. Let macerate overnight, then distill off until 32 ounces have passed over. Color red. The addition of a trifle of essence of vanilla improves this essence.

5.—Deodorized alcohol, 500 parts; proof spirits, 200 parts; pure raspberry juice, 170 parts; raspberry ether, 100 parts; tincture of orris, 20 parts; triple extract of roses, 10 parts. Color with tincture of alkanet.

6.—Acetic ether and tartaric acid, each 5 parts; glycerine, 4 parts; aldehyde, formic ether, benzoic ether, butyric ether, amyl butyric ether, acetic ether, enanthic ether, methylsalicylic ether, nitrous ether, sebacylic ether and succinic acid, each 1 part.

Rhubarb

1.—Sliced or bruised rhubarb, 8 oz.; rectified spirit, 5 oz.; distilled water, 50 oz. Macerate four days; strain and set to subside; decant the clear, strain, mix and evap-

Essences and Extracts

orate to a proper consistency over a water bath at 160° F. (71° C.).

2.—Compound.—Extract rhubarb, 3 drams; extract of aloes, softened with 4 drams water, 1 dram; evaporate to an extract; dry in a warm place and powder.

3.—Rhubarb powder, 5 oz.; silicious sand, 5 oz.; proof spirit, 1 oz.; extract by displacement.

Root Beer

Sassafras, 4 oz.; yellow dock, 4 oz.; allspice 4 oz.; wintergreen, 4 oz.; wild cherry bark, 2 oz.; coriander seed, 2 oz.; hops, 1 oz. Reduce to powder and percolate with a menstruum composed of 3 volumes of alcohol and 5 volumes of water until 48 fl.oz. of liquid have passed. Of this half-strength fluid extract 2 fl.oz. are sufficient to make 1 gal. of root beer. Or exhaust the above drugs with the menstruum indicated, add enough water to make 6 gal., and start fermentation with 1 pt. of yeast.

Percolate the following ingredients with 2 parts of water to 1 part of alcohol until the drugs are exhausted: Sarsaparilla, 5 lb.; spikenard, 2 lb.; wintergreen, 1 lb.; birch bark, 1 lb.; sassafras bark, 1 lb.; wild cherry, 8 oz.; prickly ash, 1 lb.; Jamaica ginger root, 4 oz.; nutmeg, 4 oz.

Rose

1.—Red rose leaves, 2 oz.; oil of rose, 1 dram; alcohol, 2 pt.

2.—Deodorized alcohol, 500 parts; proof spirits, 300 parts; extract of rose geranium, 190 parts; otto of roses, 5 parts; carbonate of magnesia, 5 parts. Color with tincture of alkanet.

Sarsaparilla

Oil of anise, 1 dram; oil of wintergreen, 2 drams; oil of sassafras, 3 drams; alcohol, enough to make 4 oz.

Sassafras

1.—Deodorized alcohol, 500 parts; proof spirits, 400

parts; oil of sassafras, 100 parts; carbonate of magnesia, 100 parts. Color with caramel.

2.—Oil of sassafras, 1 oz.; sassafras in coarse powder, 2 oz.; alcohol, 2 pt.

Spearmint

Deodorized alcohol, 500 parts; proof spirits, 400 parts; oil of spearmint, 50 parts; carbonate of magnesia, 50 parts. Color with tincture of grass.

Spice

Deodorized alcohol, 500 parts; proof spirits, 300 parts; carbonate of magnesia, 100 parts; oil of cassia, 40 parts; oil of bitter almond, 20 parts; oil of cloves, 20 parts; oil of lemon, 10 parts; oil of neroli, 10 parts. Color with caramel.

Spruce

Deodorized alcohol, 500 parts; proof spirits, 400 parts; oil of spruce, 50 parts; carbonate of magnesia, 50 parts. Color with caramel.

Strawberry

1.—Pineapple oil, 1½ oz.; tincture of orris, ¾ oz.; tartaric acid, ¾ oz.; alcohol, 80°, 1½ pt.

2.—Butyric ether and acetic ether, each 5 parts; amyl-acetic ether, 3 parts; amyl-butyric ether and glycerine, each 2 parts; formic ether, nitrous ether and methyl-salicylic ether, each 1 part.

3.—Deodorized alcohol, 500 parts; proof spirits, 200 parts; pure strawberry juice, 140 parts; strawberry ether, 100 parts; pineapple ether, 45 parts; tincture of orris, 10 parts; tincture of vanilla, 5 parts. Color with tincture of alkanet and saffron.

4.—Raspberry ether, 840 parts; pineapple ether, 150 parts; tincture of orris, 5 parts; extract of vanilla, 5 parts.

5.—Oil of strawberry, ½ oz.; glycerine, ½ oz.; alcohol, 8 oz.; water, 7 oz. Dissolve oil in the alcohol, add the glycerine and then the water; mix well and filter.

6.—Oil of wintergreen, 1 part; nitrous ether, 1 part;

acetic ether, 5 parts; butyric ether, 5 parts; glycerine, 2 parts; deodorized alcohol, 45 parts; distilled water, q. s. to make 100 parts.

7.—Acetic ether, 5 parts; butyric ether, 5 parts; nitrous ether, 5 parts; formic ether, 1 part; amyl acetate, 3 parts; amyl butyrate, 2 parts; tincture of orris root, 5 parts; oil of wintergreen, 1 part; acetic acid, 1 part; raspberry essence (see above), 10 parts; pineapple essence (see above), 5 parts; pure, fresh strawberry juice, 20 parts; deodorized alcohol, q. s. to make 100 parts. Mix.

Tea

Extract the crushed tea-leaves with water and then distil the liquid in a vacuum. The first portion of the distillate, which contains the essential oil and other volatile flavor, is extracted with ether, and the oils are afterward mixed with the extract which remains in the still. Both the delicate and the heavier flavors are preserved in the extract in this way.

Tonic Beer Essence

Oil of wintergreen, 6 drams; oil of sassafras and oil of orange, 6 drams of each; oil of anise, 30 gr.; oil of cloves, 30 gr. Cut the oils, dissolve in 20 fl.oz. alcohol, 95°; add gradually 20 fl.oz. water.

Tonka

1.—Tonka bean, coarsely ground, 4 oz.; diluted alcohol, 1 pt.

2.—Tonka, 1 oz.; balsam peru, 2 drams; sugar, alcohol, water, of each a sufficient quantity. Reduce the beans and balsam of peru to a powder with magnesium carbonate and gradually add sugar to absorb the juice. Transfer to a percolator and cover with dilute alcohol. When the liquid appears at the exit cork the percolator and allow the maceration to progress for a period of 24 hours. Then remove the stopper and allow percolation to continue until 1 pint of extract has been obtained.

Beverages—Non-Alcoholic

Vanilla

1.—Cut up fine 1 oz. vanilla bean, grind with 2 oz. of loaf sugar, in a mortar, mix 8 oz. of rose water and 2¼ oz. of alcohol, 95°, add a portion to the vanilla and sugar, put in a displacer and pour on the balance of diluted alcohol. Add a few drops of caramel if not dark enough.

2.—Vanilla beans, sliced Mexican, 1 lb.; alcohol, 90°, 1 gal. Pack in percolator after thoroughly moistening; let stand one week, and percolate to 1 gal.

3.—Pure.—Vanilla bean, 1 oz.; pumice stone, 3 oz.; diluted alcohol, q. s. Cut the vanilla into small pieces, and beat in an iron mortar with the pumice until reduced to fine powder; moisten thoroughly with diluted alcohol, and allow to stand for three days in a warm place. Then transfer to a percolator, and add diluted alcohol until one pint of extract is obtained. The extract may also be made by maceration, of course. When so made add to the beans a pint of the menstruum, and when filtered off pass enough more through the filter to bring the finished preparation to the measure of one pint.

4.—Vanilla bean, ¾ oz.; tonka bean, ¼ oz.; pumice stone, 3 oz.; diluted alcohol, q. s. to make 1 pt. Proceed as in the foregoing formula.

5.—3.75 parts of Peruvian balsam and 1.75 parts of oil of orange are rubbed down with 250 parts of rectified alcohol and 10 parts of magnesia; 125 parts of essence of orris root, 62 parts of tonka beans, and 30 drops of tincture of castoreum mixed in. The whole is allowed to stand for four weeks in a warm place and it is then colored with caramel and filtered.

6.—Vanilla, in fine bits, 250 parts is put into 1,350 parts of mixture of 2,500 parts of 95 per cent. alcohol and 1,500 parts of distilled water. Cover tightly, put in the water-bath and digest for one hour at 140° F. Pour off the liquid and set aside. To the residue in the bath add one-half of the remaining water, treat in the same manner, and repeat. Now pack the vanilla in an extraction apparatus and treat with 250 parts of alcohol and water,

Essences and Extracts

mixed in the same proportions as before. Mix the results of three infusions first made, filter and wash the filter paper with the results of the percolation, allowing the filtered percolate to mingle with the filtrate of the mixed infusions.

7.—Vanilla.—Deodorized alcohol, 500 parts; proof spirits, 300 parts; sugar, 100 parts; vanilla, 100 parts. Slit the beans and cut them very fine; then mix them with the sugar, and bruise till moderately fine; add the alcohol and spirits, and macerate for two weeks, occasionally shaking; filter. Color with caramel.

8.—a.—Vanillin, 20 parts; absolute alcohol, 600 parts; water, 450 parts. Dissolve the vanillin in the alcohol and add the water.

b.—Musk, 1 part; potassium carbonate, 1 part; vanilla beans, 60 parts; boiling water, 240 parts; alcohol, 720 parts. Mix the vanilla, cut fine, the musk and potassium salt, and pour over them the boiling water. Let them stand until quite cold, then add the alcohol and set aside for 14 days. Finally strain, express and filter the percolate.

9.—Vanillin, 45 gr.; coumarin, 3 gr.; alcohol, 3 fl.oz.; glycerine, 2 fl.oz.; simple syrup, 2 fl.oz.; comp. tincture cudbear, 2 fl.dr.; water enough to make 16 fl.oz. Dissolve the vanillin and coumarin in the alcohol, add the glycerine, syrup and tincture, and lastly enough water to make 16 fl.oz.

Wintergreen

1.—Oil of wintergreen, 1 oz.; alcohol, 1 pt.; cudbear or cochineal, 10 gr.

2.—Wintergreen, 2 oz.; sassafras, 2 oz.; sarsaparilla, 4 oz.; burdock root, 4 oz.; dandelion, 1½ oz.; calamus, 4 dr.; dilute alcohol, 1 pt.; water, q. s. Grind all the drugs to a coarse powder and mix. Moisten the drugs with the dilute alcohol and macerate for two days and percolate with the dilute alcohol and water till 32 oz. of product are obtained, then add oil wintergreen, ½ dr.; oil sassafras, ½ dr., previously dissolved in 2 oz. of alcohol, and then filter. Use 4 oz. of this extract to a gallon of simple syrup and color with caramel to suit.

Chapter II.

SYRUPS

Preparation

IN the preparation of syrups, which are solutions of sugar, more or less strong according to the object for which they are used, care should be taken to employ only the best refined sugar, and either distilled or filtered rain water, as they will be rendered much less liable to spontaneous decomposition and become perfectly transparent without the trouble of clarifying. When, however, impure sugar is employed, clarification is always necessary. This is best done by dissolving the sugar in the water or fruit juices cold, and then beating up a little of the cold syrup with some white of egg and one or two ounces of cold water, until the mixture froths well. This must be added to the syrup in the boiler, and when the whole is frisked up to a good froth, heat should be applied and the scum which forms removed from time to time with a clean skimmer. As soon as the syrup begins to simmer it must be removed from the fire and allowed to stand until it has cooled a little, when it should again be skimmed, if necessary, and then passed through a clean flannel. By using refined sugar, however, all this trouble of clarification can be avoided.

When vegetable infusions or solutions enter into the compositions of syrups, they should be rendered perfectly transparent by filtration or clarification before being added to the sugar.

The proper quantity of sugar for syrups will, in general,

Syrups

be found to be two pounds avoirdupois to every pint of water or thin aqueous fluid. These proportions allow for the water that is lost by evaporation during the process and are those best calculated to produce syrup of proper consistency and possessing good keeping qualities. They closely correspond to those recommended by Guibourt for the production of a perfect syrup, which, he says, consists of 30 parts of sugar to 16 parts of water.

In the preparation of syrup it is of great importance to employ as little heat as possible, as a solution of sugar, even when kept at a temperature of boiling water, undergoes slow decomposition. The best plan is to pour the water (cold) over the sugar and to allow the two to lie together for a few hours in a covered vessel, occasionally stirring, and to apply a gentle heat, preferably that of steam or of a water bath, to finish the solution. Syrups are sufficiently boiled when some, taken up in a spoon, pours out like oil, or a drop cooled on the thumb nail gives a proper thread when touched. When a thin skin appears on blowing the syrup, it is judged to be completely saturated. These rude tests, however, often lead to errors, which might be easily prevented by employing the proper proportions or determining the specific gravity by immersing in the syrup one of Baumé's saccharometers or syrup gauges, as indicated in the following table:

Sugar in 100 parts.	Sp. Gr.	Deg. Baumé.
0	1.000	0
5	1.020	3
10	1.040	6
15	1.062	8
20	1.081	11
25	1.104	13.5
30	1.128	16.3
35	1.152	19
40	1.177	21.6
45	1.204	24.5
50	1.230	27
55	1.257	29.5
60	1.284	32
67	1.321	35

A fluid ounce of saturated syrup weighs 577½ grains; a gallon weighs 13½ pounds; its specific gravity is 1.319

Beverages—Non-Alcoholic

to 1.321, or 35° Baumé; its boiling point is 220° F., and its density at the temperature of 212° is 1.260 to 1.261, or 30° Baumé. The syrups prepared with the juices of fruits mark about two or three degrees more on Baumé scale than the other syrups. According to Ure, the decimal part of the number denoting the specific gravity of a syrup multiplied by 26 gives very nearly the number of pounds of sugar it contains per gallon.

The preservation of syrups, as well as of all saccharine solutions, is best promoted by keeping them in a moderately cool, but not a very cold place. Let syrups be kept in vessels well closed and in a situation where the temperature never rises above 55° F. They are kept better in small than in large vessels, as the longer a bottle lasts the more frequently will it be opened and the syrup consequently exposed to the air. By bottling syrups while boiling hot, and immediately corking down and tying the bottles over with a bladder, perfectly airtight, they may be preserved even at a summer heat for years, without fermenting or losing their transparency.

The candying of syrups may be prevented (unless the syrup be oversaturated with sugar) by the addition of acetic or citric acid, two or three drams per gallon. Confectioners add a little cream of tartar to the syrup to prevent granulation. Syrup may be effectually prevented from fermenting by the addition of a little sulphite of potassa or lime; also by the use of salicylic acid in small quantities. Fermenting syrups may be immediately restored by exposing the vessel containing them to the temperature of boiling water. The addition of a little spirit is also good, say about 10 per cent.

A solution of sugar prepared by dissolving two parts of double refined sugar in one of water, and boiling this a little, affords a syrup which neither ferments nor crystallizes.

The best way to keep fruit syrups from fermenting is by bottling while hot into suitable bottles or larger vessels and to prevent access of air. This is the principle,

Syrups

and it may be carried out in various ways. For instance, fill the syrup while hot in quart bottles, previously warmed, and fill them almost full. Cover or cork the bottles temporarily until the syrup cools a little and contracts in volume; then, having heated a small quantity of the syrup, refill the bottles, cork them securely and wax them.

A great variety of syrups are made by the addition of proper flavoring ingredients to simple syrup, but in other cases, especially when the juices of fruits are employed, the syrup is not first prepared and then flavored, but the processes go hand in hand. In such instances specific instructions will be given. It is always advisable, when fresh fruit can be obtained, to use it in preference to the essence. One general recipe, which answers for nearly all fresh fruit, is as follows: Use nothing but the very best fresh fruit, which must be freed from stocks, etc., and crushed with a wooden instrument (not metal). When well mashed, let it stand in a room of even temperature (about 68° F.) for 4 days, which will give sufficient time for fermentation to take place; press out the juice from the fruit and let it settle in a cool cellar for 2 days, after which 5 pounds of the clear juice is to be simmered with 9 pounds of loaf sugar. While warm strain through flannel. The color may be improved by a solution of some coloring agent.

It is advisable to add to the fresh fruit, before setting it for fermentation, about 2 pounds of powdered loaf sugar for every 100 pounds of fruit. When cold, it is ready for bottling. Cleanliness should be strictly observed in all the utensils used. When bottling for storing, skim the top of any floating matter from the syrups in the large pan, and see that no residue at the bottom goes into the bottles. Most of the syrups not made of fruit may have a little mucilage of gum arabic added, in order to produce a rich froth. The following recipes comprise syrups made from the fruit and also from essences. These may be varied to suit taste and requirements. A variety of syrups have been brought into use by adding the

Beverages—Non-Alcoholic

various wines, such as claret, hock, sherry, etc., to simple syrup; others, by the addition of spirits, as milk punch, by adding to vanilla cream Jamaica rum and nutmeg. Almost any syrup may be made by the addition of a sufficient quantity of flavoring essence to simple syrup, but these artificially prepared syrups are inferior to those made from fresh fruits.

Red Coloring for Soda Water Syrups

The most convenient is probably tincture of cudbear, as it affords a good, substantial and natural-looking color, miscible with syrups without cloudiness. It may be made as follows: 2 to 4 oz. powdered cudbear, 1 pt. diluted alcohol. Exhaust by maceration or displacement. Used alone, the tincture gives a shade of red closely imitating the color of raspberries or currants. For deeper red, like blackberries, the addition of some caramel is all that is necessary. The strawberry color is best imitated with tincture of cochineal. Aniline red, owing to its cheapness, is often used for coloring syrups, but it produces a glaring, artificial-looking bluish red and is liable to the objection that it sometimes contains arsenic.

TABLE SHOWING AMOUNT OF SYRUP OBTAINED:

1.—The addition of pounds of sugar to 1 gallon of water, and
2.—Amount of sugar in each gallon of syrup resulting therefrom:

Lbs. sugar added to 1 gal. cold water.	Syrup actually obtained.			Lbs of sugar in 1 gal. of syrup.
	Gals.	Pints.	Fl ozs.	
1	1	0	10	.93
2	1	1	4	1.73
3	1	1	14	2.43
4	1	2	8	3.05
5	1	3	2	3.6
6	1	3	12	4.09
7	1	4	6	4.52
8	1	5	0	4.92
9	1	5	10	5.28
10	1	6	4	5.62
11	1	6	14	5.92
12	1	7	8	9.18
13	2	0	2	6.38
14	2	0	12	6.7
15	2	1	6	6.91

Syrups

SYRUP FORMULAS

Apple Syrup

Proceed with apples as for pineapple syrups.

Apricots

1.—Strain and rub 2 qt. of apricot pulp through a fine hair sieve into a bright and clean tinned basin; add to this 2 gal. of simple syrup, boiling hot; mix well and add a little dissolved citric acid; stir occasionally until it becomes perfectly cold. When serving it add a little plain cream or ice cream to each glass of soda drawn.

2.—Apricot pulp (bottled), 1 pt.; solution of citric acid, 1 oz.; rock candy syrup, 3 pt.; orange flower water (best), 1 pt. Two ounces to 14-ounce glass; crushed ice and straws.

3.—Three qt. of simple syrup, 1 qt. of apricot juice, 2 oz. of soda foam, ½ oz. of citric acid solution. Color orange.

Banana

1.—Oil of banana, 2 drams; tartaric acid, 1 dram; simple syrup, 6 pt.

2.—Proceed with bananas as for pineapple syrups.

3.—Cut the fruit in slices and place them in a jar. Sprinkle with sugar and cover the jar, which is then enveloped in straw and placed in cold water and the latter is heated to the boiling point. The jar is then removed, allowed to cool and the juice is poured into bottles.

4.—Bananas, 2; simple syrup (10 lb. to gal.), 2 pt. Slice the bananas and bray them in a mortar until all lumps are reduced, and add the syrup in small quantities, mixing thoroughly after each addition. Care should be taken to employ ripe fruit and to peel it thoroughly. This syrup should be made fresh every day.

Beverages—Non-Alcoholic

Blackberry

1.—Prepared from ripe fruit the same as raspberry syrups. Blackberry syrup is improved by adding 1 oz. best French brandy to each quart.

2.—Prepare like either strawberry or mulberry syrup.

Calisaya Tonic

Brown calisaya, 4 av.oz.; gentian 1 av.oz.; orange peel, 1½ av.oz.; cinnamon, 1 av.oz.; alcohol, 65 per cent., enough to make 32 fl.oz. For use at the soda fountain mix one measure of this tincture with two measures of syrup.

Capillaire (Maidenhair) Syrup

1.—Maidenhair, 8 oz.; boiling water, 5 pt.; orange flower water, 4 oz. Sugar, sufficient. Infuse the maidenhair in the boiling water. When nearly cold, press out and filter the liquid, add to it the orange flower water and dissolve it with sugar in the proportion of 7 oz. to each 4 fl.oz. of liquid.

2.—Nine lb. loaf sugar, 4 lb. orange flower water. Boil till the sugar is dissolved and the syrup is clear. While hot, strain through flannel, add to the cool syrup 2 drams of tartaric acid, previously dissolved in 8 oz. of the strongest orange flower water; lastly add 4 oz. of the best Rhine wine.

3.—Florida orange wine, 1 pt.; water, 1 pt.; granulated sugar, 6 lb. Dissolve by agitation or percolation and add liquid phosphate, 1 oz.

Celery

Tincture celery seed, 2 oz.; juice of two lemons, pineapple juice, 16 oz.; syrup, enough to make 1 gal. A "gamey" flavor is obtained by bruising the fresh lemon peels in the syrup, afterward straining them out.

Cherry

1.—Take sour cherries, a convenient quantity, bruise them in a porcelain, stone or wood mortar, to break the

Syrups

stones or pits of the fruit; express the juice, set it aside for three days to undergo fermentation, and proceed according to the directions given for strawberry syrup.

2.—Crush the cherries, pits and all, in a stone or wooden mortar. Express the juice, add about a pound of sugar for each pint of it, heat to the boiling point and strain. While the syrup is still hot, pour it into bottles which have been boiled and are of about the same temperature as the syrup and cork or plug the bottle's mouth with antiseptic cotton. When wanted for use, dilute with plain syrup and add about an ounce of a saturated solution of citric acid to each gallon of the diluted syrup.

3.—It is best to use as far as possible the black varieties, which are of fine flavor and good color. Stone the cherries, pound about one-tenth of the stones to a paste, mash and mix well together, let stand for a short time, stirring it occasionally, and strain.

4.—Essence of cherries, 4 oz.; citric acid, $3\frac{1}{2}$ oz.; cane sugar, 6 oz.; distilled water, 10 pt.; liquid cochineal, sufficient. Dissolve the sugar in the water, and, when cold, add the other ingredients.

5.—Stem and wash 1 qt. of cherries. Stone the cherries and pass through the chopper and add syrup to make 2 qt. Cleanliness should be observed in all the processes. Utensils and machine should be washed before the next fruit is prepared, and when the work is finished all utensils and machines should be carefully washed and dried.

6.—Cherry Phosphate Syrup.—Cherry juice, 3 pt.; sugar, 6 lb.; water, 1 pt.; acid phosphate, 4 oz. Bring to boil and when cool add acid phosphate.

7.—Wild Cherry Syrup.—a.—Ground wild cherry, 2 lb.; water, 1 gal. Infuse for 24 hours, express and add sugar, 9 lb.

b.—Wild cherry bark (in coarse powder), 5 oz. Moisten the bark with water and let it stand for 24 hours in a close vessel. Then pack it firmly in a percolator and pour water upon it until 1 pt. of water is obtained. To this add sugar, 28 oz.

8.—Wild Cherry Phosphate Syrup.—Syrup of wild cherry, U. S. P., 10 fl.oz.; cherry juice, black, 8 fl.oz.; glucose syrup, 12 fl.oz.; diluted phosphoric acid, 2 fl.oz.; oil bitter almond, 4 drops. Mix.

Chocolate

1.—Best chocolate, 8 oz.; water, 2 pt.; white sugar, 4 lb. Mix the chocolate in water and stir thoroughly over a slow fire. Strain and add the sugar.

2.—Bark of roasted cacao bean, 2 oz. Reduce to a moderately fine powder, mix with simple syrup, 2 oz. Pack in a percolator and exhaust with the following menstruum at a boiling temperature: Sugar, 12 oz.; water, 8 oz., so as to obtain 1 pt. of syrup. To the percolate add, when cold, extract of vanilla, 2 fl.dr.

3.—Cocoa, soluble, 2 oz.; water, 32 fl.oz.; sugar, 52 oz.; vanilla extract, about 4 fl.dr. Triturate the cocoa in a mortar with a portion of the water to a smooth paste, add the remainder of the water, then the sugar, heat the whole in a suitable vessel with constant stirring, until it nearly reaches the boiling point, then strain through a fine sieve, and when cold add the vanilla extract.

4.—Chocolate, powder, 4 oz.; sugar 52 oz.; vanilla extract, about 6 fl.dr.; water, boiling, 24 fl.oz. Mix the chocolate and sugar, triturate the mixed powders with the boiling water added slowly and strain. When cool, add the vanilla extract.

5.—B——'s chocolate, 8 oz.; powdered borax, ½ oz.; powdered boric acid, ½ oz.; starch, 1 oz.; water, 64 fl.oz.; sugar, 6 lb.; vanilla extract, about 1 fl.oz. Grate the chocolate, triturate with the borax, boric acid and starch, add slowly, with stirring, the water, bring to a boil, strain, allow to cool and add the extract. In view of the popular outcry against the use of boric acid, this formula is open to objection.

6.—Chocolate, 4 oz.; granulated sugar, 24 oz.; water, 48 fl.oz. Put the chocolate in an enameled pot, and add about 8 avoirdupois ounces of sugar, stirring well

Syrups

with a porcelain pestle until all the lumps in the chocolate are reduced to powder and are well mixed with the sugar. Add the remainder of the sugar, mixing well. Heat the water to boiling, pour it on the mixture of chocolate and sugar, stir well with a wooden ladle and boil the whole for a few minutes.

7.—Cocoa, 8 oz.; hot water, 2 pt.; gelatine, Cooper's, ½ sheet; sugar, 1 lb. Boil together for a few minutes and then strain.

8.—Cocoa, light, soluble, 4 oz.; granulated sugar, 2 lb.; boiling hot water, 1 qt.; extract vanilla, 1 oz. Dissolve the cocoa in hot water by stirring, then add the sugar and dissolve. Strain and when cold add the vanilla extract.

9.—B——'s chocolate, plain, 4 oz.; boiling water, 4 oz.; water, 28 oz.; sugar, 50 oz.; extract of vanilla, ½ oz. Cut the chocolate into small pieces, then add the boiling water and stir briskly until the mixture forms into a thick paste and assumes a smooth and uniform appearance. Then slowly add the remainder of the water, stirring at the same time, and set aside until cold. Then remove carefully by skimming the layer of solid fat which consists of almost pure cocoa butter; add the sugar, dissolve it by the aid of a gentle heat and allow the whole to come to a boil. Then strain and add the extract of vanilla.

10.—Confectioners' chocolate, ½ lb.; hot water, 2 qt.; condensed milk, 1 can; granulated sugar, 5 lb.; extract of vanilla, 1 oz.; gum foam, 1 oz.; whites of 2 eggs. Cut the chocolate fine, place in an evaporating dish and rub with the water (which must be boiling hot), gradually added, until a smooth paste is obtained; then stir in the milk and sugar, and when the latter is dissoved set aside to cool. When cold, skim off any particles of grease, etc., which may have arisen to the top, add the white of egg previously well beaten, the extract of vanilla and the gum foam. Strain through muslin and it is ready for use.

Beverages—Non-Alcoholic

11.—Fruit Chocolate.—Strawberry syrup, 10 fl.oz.; vanilla syrup, 10 fl.oz.; raspberry syrup, 8 fl.oz.; chocolate syrup, 4 fl.oz. In serving draw 2 fluid ounces of this syrup into a 12-ounce glass, add 1 or 2 fluid ounces of cream, nearly fill the glass with the coarse stream of carbonated water and then top off with the fine stream.

Cinchona Syrup

1.—Tincture cinchona, detannated (N.F.), 3 fl.oz.; tincture vanilla, 1 fl.oz.; essence orange, 2 fl.dr.; alcohol, 3 fl.oz.; water, 6 fl.oz.; syrup, 6 fl.oz.; red coloring, enough; syrup lemon, enough to make 32 fl.oz. Mix the first five ingredients, filter through a small amount of purified talc and color red to suit. Serve "solid."

2.—Tincture of detannated cinchona, 6 oz.; extract of vanilla, 2 oz.; alcohol, 6 oz.; rock candy syrup, 8 oz.; spirits of curaçoa, 2 dr.; distilled water, enough to make 1 qt. Mix and filter through carbonate of magnesia and then color a deep red with carmine solution. Then add 1 quart of lemon syrup and shake. Pour 1 ounce of cinisaya syrup into a mineral glass and draw carbonated water in another glass. Mix thoroughly by pouring from one glass to the other and serve.

Cinnamon

Oil of cinnamon, 30 m.; carbonate of magnesia, 60 gr.; water, 2 pt.; granulated sugar, 56 oz. Rub the oil first with the carbonate of magnesia, then with the water gradually added, and filter through paper. In the filtrate dissolve the sugar without heat.

Coca

Wine coca, 1 pt.; cane sugar or rock candy syrup, 7 pt. This has a pleasant, very slightly bitterish taste.

Coca-Vanilla

Wine of coca, 1 pt.; strong extract of vanilla, 2 oz.; cane sugar or rock candy syrup, 7 pt.

Syrups

Coffee

1.—Coffee syrup, 2 pt.; cream, 1 pt.

2.—Coffee, roasted, ½ lb.; boiling water, 1 gal. Enough is filtered to make ½ gal. of the infusion, to which add granulated sugar, 7 lb.

3.—Ground Java coffee, 2 oz.; simple syrup, 2 fl.oz. Mix and pack in a percolator and add, boiling hot, a mixture of loaf sugar, 12 av.oz.; distilled water, 8 fl.oz. To percolate 1 pt. of syrup.

4.—Take of ground, roasted coffee, 4 oz.; boiling water, 2 pt.; sugar (com.), 4 lb. Infuse the coffee in the water until cold, strain, add the sugar and make a syrup.

5.—Take 1 lb. of fresh roasted Java or Mocha coffee and percolate according to the directions of the Pharmacopœia with the following mixture: Alcohol, 8 oz.; glycerine, 4 oz.; water, 4 oz., and continue the percolation with diluted alcohol until 14 ounces have passed. Set this aside and continue the percolation until the coffee is exhausted. Evaporate to 2 ounces and mix with the 14 ounces reserved. This makes a fluid extract of which 1 ounce is sufficient for 1 pint of syrup.

6.—Java coffee, 1 oz.; Mocha coffee, 1 oz.; Rio coffee, 4 oz.; glycerine, 1 fl.oz.; simple syrup, extra heavy, 4½ pt.; hot water, a sufficient quantity. Roast the coffee, reduce at once to fine powder, moisten with about 7 ounces of hot water with which the glycerine has been mixed. Let stand for 1½ hours in a very warm place and then percolate until 24 fluid ounces of liquid are obtained. Add to this the syrup.

Crab Apple Tonic

Sweet cider, 1 gal.; sugar, 7 lb.; extract malt, 4 fl.oz.; solution citric acid, 1½ fl.oz. Evaporate the cider to 4 pints. In this dissolve the sugar, strain and add the remaining ingredients. Serve either "solid" or with foam. This syrup is said to yield a drink quite similar to some proprietary syrups, such as *champagne mist* and *kylo*.

Beverages—Non-Alcoholic

Cream

1.—Fresh cream, ½ pt.; fresh milk, ½ pt.; powdered sugar, 1 lb. Mix by shaking and keep in a cool place. The addition of a few grains of bicarbonate of soda will for some time retard souring.

2.—Oil of sweet almonds, 2 oz.; powdered gum arabic, 2 oz.; water, 4 oz. Make an emulsion and add simple syrup enough to complete 2 pt.

3.—One pt. condensed milk, 1 pt. water, 1¼ lb. sugar. Heat to boiling and strain. This will keep for over a week in a cool place.

4.—Imitation.—Make an emulsion with 3 oz. fresh oil of sweet almonds, 2 oz. powdered gum arabic, and 2 oz. water; then dissolve 1 lb. white sugar by gentle heat, strain, and when cool add the whites of 2 eggs. It should be put up in small bottles, well corked, in a cool place. This is not only an excellent imitation and substitute for cream syrup, but will keep for a considerable time.

Currant

1.—Refined sugar, 5 kilos; conserve of currants, 2.6 liters. Put the sugar in a pan, add the conserve and heat rapidly. Remove the syrup from the fire as soon as it boils. Skim and pass through woolen cloth.

2.—Six pt. simple syrup, 2 pt. water, 2 oz. tartaric acid, 3 dr. fruit essence. Mix, color with red carmine for red currants and with burnt sugar for black.

3.—One pt. red currant juice, 1 gal. simple syrup.

4.—Proceed as for strawberry syrup.

5.—Framboisé Currant Syrup.—Raspberry syrup, 1 pt.; currant syrup, 4 pt.

6.—French Currant Syrup.—French currant juice, 1 bottle; citric acid, 2 dr.; caramel, 1 dr.; tincture of cochineal, 3 dr.; syrup, enough to make 2 gal.

Fancy Syrup

Vanilla syrup, 2 pt.; pineapple syrup, 8 oz.; raspberry syrup, 8 oz.

Syrups

Foam

1.—If it is thought desirable to give an extra foam or "head" this formula will do: Take soap bark in coarse powder, 2 oz.; animal charcoal, 1 oz. Macerate 2 days in alcohol, 2 oz.; glycerine, 2 oz.; distilled water, 4 oz. Percolate to obtain 8 oz. of finished product. Quantity to be used, 2 drams to the gallon of concentrated ginger ale.

2.—To each gallon of syrup add from 2 to 4 oz. of gum arabic dissolved in its own weight of water.

3.—Quillaya bark, 4 oz.; alcohol, 4 oz.; glycerine, 4 oz.; water, 8, oz. Exhaust by percolation so as to make one pint of tincture. From 2 to 5 drams of this tincture to every gallon of syrup will be found sufficient to give every glass of soda drawn that creamy appearance so universally liked. At the same time it has the advantage of being cheap, is used in such minute quantities that it cannot be discovered by taste, is always ready for use and will never spoil.

4.—Irish Moss.—Take of Irish moss 1 oz. and water enough to make 1 pt. Wash the Irish moss in water, to free from impurities; add 1 pt. of water and boil for 5 minutes, or heat in a water bath for 15 minutes, or macerate in cold water for 24 hours, with occasional stirring; filter through purified cotton, on a muslin strainer, in a hot water funnel. This mucilage, it is calimed, has no more taste than mucilage of gum arabic and is said to keep better. It can be used with soda syrup in the proportion of from 2 to 4 oz. to 1 gal. of the syrup.

Fruit Juices, Preservation Of

Express the juice of any fruit, filter and pour into champagne bottles; fill them up to the bend of the necks; cork tightly and fasten the corks down with cord or wire; then put the bottles into a kettle; set them on a double sheet of coarse paper, placed on the bottom of the kettle, and pack the bottles loosely in with hay or cloths; then fill the kettle up to the necks of the bottles with cold water; place over a moderate fire and let boil for 20 minutes, then remove the kettle from the fire, allowing the bottles to remain in the kettle until the water becomes cold; then seal the corks and pack the bottles sideways in a cool, dry cellar. Prepared in this way, they will keep in a perfect state for a very long time. Fruit pulps are preserved in precisely the same way, except that they have about an ounce of finely powdered sugar added for each bottle of pulp so put up.

De Brevans, in "Manufacture of Liquors and Preserves," gives the following formulas:

Huckleberries, Barberries, Cherries and Grapes.—Crush the fruit and pass the pulp through a horsehair sieve; crush the marc and unite and carry to the cellar. After 24 hours of fermentation filter and preserve. The juice of cherries is better when a mixture of black and red cherries is used.

Orange and Lemon Juice.—Remove skin and seeds, crush the pulp and press and mix with rye straw washed and cut fine to assist the separation of the juice. Clarify by repose, filter and preserve.

Quince, Pear and Apple Juice.—Peel and rasp the fruit, taking care not to touch the seeds. Press the pulp, mixed with rye straw, washed and cut fine. Clarify by repose, filter and preserve. The quinces should be fully ripe.

Raspberry Juice—Crush the fruit and press. The liquid is allowed to repose for 1 to 2 days, after which filter. One-fifth of the weight of red cherries may be added. Another process reported to have given excellent results is this one: The clarified juice is heated to boiling in a copper vessel and then poured into a dish. Meanwhile the bottles are provided with stoppers and are then gradually filled, a space of about 2 centimeters in the

Syrups

neck being left empty; some alcohol is then poured upon the hot liquid and the bottle is quickly stoppered, the cork being further secured as the liquid cools. The alcohol which evaporates into the empty space is sufficient for the preservation of the juice. The juice of fresh herbs may be preserved in the same manner. This process seems to be an entirely unobjectionable one. It is generally believed that many of the fruit juices as found in the market are usually preserved by means of antiseptics and anti-ferments, such as salicylic acid, boric acid, boroglyceride, sodium sulphite, peroxide of hydrogen, formaldehyde, etc.

Fruit Punch

Strawberry syrup, 10 oz.; orange syrup, 10 oz.; pineapple syrup, 10 oz.; lemon juice, 2 oz. Mix. Use 2 ounces of this syrup to a large glass one-third full of shaved ice, then fill with carbonated water and add a slice of pineapple and some strawberries.

Ginger

1.—Soluble essence of ginger (N.F.), 3 oz.; tincture of ginger, 1 oz.; syrup, 6 pt.; water, 2 pt.

2.—Take of tincture of ginger, 2 oz.; white sugar, 7 lb. (com.); water, ½ gal. Heat the sugar and water until the sugar is dissolved, raise to the boiling point, then gradually add the tincture of ginger, stirring briskly after each addition.

3.—Six pt. simple syrup, 2 pt. water, 1 oz. tartaric acid, 2 oz. ginger. Burnt sugar to color.

4.—Four oz. extract of Jamaica ginger, 1 gal. syrup. Shake well. A few drops of tincture curcuma to color.

5.—Nine lb. loaf sugar, 5 lb. water, 12 oz. essence ginger, 4 oz. white wine. Boil sugar and water until dissolved and clear. When cool add ginger and wine. Mix well and let settle.

6.—Tincture of ginger, 2 fl.oz.; simple syrup, 4 pt.

7.—Soluble extract of ginger, 2 oz.; tincture of capsicum,

Beverages—Non-Alcoholic

4 dr.; simple syrup, 1 gal. Mix. For a good many people ginger is scarcely warm enough without the addition of Cayenne pepper.

8.—Syrup of ginger, 2 pt.; syrup of lemon, 1 pt.; tincture of capsicum, 1 dr.

Grape

1.—Brandy, ½ pt.; tincture of lemon, 1 oz.; simple syrup, 1 gal.; tincture red sanders, 1 qt.

2.—Brandy, ½ pt.; spirits of lemon, ¼ oz.; tincture of red sanders, 2 oz.; simple syrup, 1 gal.

3.—A grape syrup, not an artificial syrup, or one for fountain use, but a syrup from the fruit, for domestic or table use, etc. Take 20 lb. ripe freshly picked and selected tame grapes, put them into a stone jar and pour over them 6 qt. of boiling soft water. When sufficiently cool to allow it, well squeeze them thoroughly with the hand, after which allow them to stand 3 days on the furnace with a cloth thrown over the jar, then squeeze out the juice and add 10 lb. of crushed sugar; let it remain a week longer in the jar; then take off the scum, strain and bottle, leaving a vent until done fermenting, when strain again and bottle tight and lay the bottles on the side in a cool place.

4.—Brandy, ½ pt.; extract of lemon, ½ oz.; tincture of cudbear, 1 oz.; simple syrup, 1 gal.

5.—Bottle grape juice, 1 qt.; sugar, 1 lb.; simple syrup, 2 qt.; sol. citric acid, 1 oz. Dissolve the sugar in the grape juice and add the acid and syrup.

6.—Grape juice, 2 pt.; acid solution, 1 oz.; gum foam, 1 oz.; simple syrup, q. s. 1 gal. Mix thoroughly. To serve a grape phosphate use 1 oz. of the syrup to an 8-oz. mineral glass.

Grenadine

Extract grenadine, 2 oz.; liquid foam, 1 oz.; red fruit coloring, 1 dr.; syrup, 1 gal. Mix, then add fruit acid, 2 oz.

Syrups

Hock and Claret
Hock or claret wine, 1 pt.; simple syrup, 2 pt.

Imperial
Equal parts of raspberry and orange syrups.

Java Tonic
Compound tincture of cinchona, 6 fl.dr.; coffee syrup, 8 fl.oz.; vanilla syrup, 4 fl.oz.; glucose syrup, 8 fl.oz.; syrup, enough to make 32 fl.oz. Serve "solid" in 8-oz. glasses, like the phosphates.

Lemon

1.—Dissolve 6 dr. of tartaric acid and 1 oz. of gum arabic, in pieces, in 1 gal. of simple syrup; then flavor with 1½ fl.dr. of best oil of lemon, or flavor with the saturated tincture of the peel in cologne spirits.

2.—Grate off the yellow rinds of lemons and beat them with a sufficient quantity of granulated sugar; express the lemon juice; add to each pt. of juice 1 pt. of water, 3½ lb. granulated sugar, including that rubbed up with the rind; warm until the sugar is dissolved and strain. Under no circumstances must the syrup be allowed to boil, and the less heat that can be used to effect the complete solution of the sugar the better will be the syrup.

3.—Add to 1 gal. simple syrup, when cold, 20 drops fresh oil lemon and ½ oz. citric acid, previously dissolved in 3 oz. water; mix by shaking well in a bottle; add 4 oz. gum solution, made by dissolving 2 oz. of fine white gum arabic in 2 oz. warm water.

4.—Simple syrup, 6 pt.; distilled water, 2 pt.; essence lemon, 2 oz.; citric acid, 2 oz., dissolved in boiling water. Mix and, if required, color with saffron.

5.—Simple syrup, 1 gal.; oil of lemon, 25 drops; citric acid, 10 dr. Rub the oil of lemon with the acid, add a small portion of syrup and mix.

6.—Lemons, 8; alcohol, 4 oz.; citric-acid solution, 50

Beverages—Non-Alcoholic

per cent., 2 oz.; sugar 150 oz.; water, 10 pt. Peel the lemons, chop the peeling fine and exhaust with the alcohol. Press out the juice of the lemons and add it to the alcoholic extract. Make a syrup of the sugar and water, by the aid of a mild heat, let cool and add the citric-acid solution. Beat up the white of 8 eggs to a stiff foam, stir it into the syrup and apply a slow heat, just sufficient to coagulate the albumen. Now strain and finally add the alcoholic extract and lemon juice.

Licorice Syrup

To 45 parts water add 7½ parts licorice root, cut in pieces. Boil for 15 minutes. Pour the liquid off and evaporate to 26 parts. Add 30 parts white sugar and 30 parts purified honey. Boil up once.

Malted Milk

Malted milk, 8 oz.; hot water, 8 oz.; simple syrup, 4 pt.

Maple

1.—Maple syrup, 4 lb.; water, 2 pt.

2.—Maple sugar, 3½ lb.; water, 1 qt. Dissolve, and, if desired, add a small proportion of gum solution to produce a rich froth.

3.—Maple sugar, 3½ lb.; water, 1 qt.; solution of citric acid, ½ oz.; extract of vanilla, 1 dr.; soda foam, ½ oz. Dissolve the sugar in the water by the aid of a gentle heat; strain and add the solution of acid, extract and foam. The extract may be omitted if desired.

4.—Maple sugar, 3 lb.; water, 30 oz.; solution of citric acid, 4 dr.; vanilla extract, 1 dr.; soda foam, sufficient.

5.—Maple sugar syrup, 7 pt.; fine old sherry wine, 13 oz.; soluble ess. vanilla, 2 oz.; lactic acid, 1 oz. Mix well together and filter. For dispensing, put into a 12-oz. tumbler 2 oz. of this syrup, add 1 fresh egg and fill up with iced cold rich milk. Shake thoroughly and dress with whipped cream.

6.—Artificial.—a.—This is said to be given to simple

Syrups

syrup or glucose by the addition of aqueous extract of guaiac wood. The wood, finely rasped, is boiled down to the condition of an extract. This is shaken up with ether, or a mixture of alcohol and ether, to get rid of the resinous matters taken up in boiling. Some manufacturers attain the desired end, though not so completely, by adding cold water to the aqueous extract while still hot, which causes the resinous matter to precipitate. After standing a little the clear extractive is poured off and is ready for use. It is said that when a proper mixture of cane syrup and glucose is used the imitation of the maple flavor is so near as to puzzle an expert.

b.—Make a solution of white sugar, two in one; bring to a boil and remove from the fire; then add to it strips of the inner bark of hickory (carya alba) or white heart hickory (carya tomentosa), ½ oz. to each pint of syrup; let stand 10 minutes and strain.

c.—Red corn cobs, 4; water, 2 pt.; enough light brown sugar. Boil the cobs in the water until the latter is quite red, strain and add sufficient sugar to make a heavy syrup. When cold the flavor is very pleasant to the taste.

Marshmallow Syrup

1.—Orange flower water, 4 oz.; gum arabic, 12 dr.; extract vanilla, ½ oz.; syrup simp., 8 pt.

2.—Rock candy syrup, 7 pt.; powdered gum acacia, 10 dr.; orange flower water, 4 pt.; citric acid, 4 dr.; water, enough to make 1 gal.

3.—Althea root, cut 20 grams; sugar, 480 grams; distilled water, q. s. 1,000 grams. The althea, previously washed with cold water, is macerated for 2 hours in 400 grams cold distilled water. In the strained liquid 480 grains of sugar are dissolved and then sufficient water added to make 1,000 grams of syrup.

Mint

1.—Make syrup of 1½ oz. peppermint essence, 4 dr. vanilla extract, 1 oz. solution citric acid, ½ gal. syrup, sufficient water and soda foam and enough tincture of grass to impart a green tint. Mix essence with 2 ounces of water and filter through powdered magnesium carbonate, passing enough water through to make 2 ounces filtrate. Add the remaining ingredients. Serve solid in 8-oz. glass.

2.—Spirits of peppermint, 1 oz.; soda foam, 1 oz.; simple syrup, 1 gal.

3.—Peppermint water (fresh), 4 pt.; sugar, 6 lb.; enough vegetable green color.

Nectar

1.—Take of vanilla syrup, 5 pt.; pineapple syrup, 1 pt.; strawberry, raspberry or lemon syrup, 2 pt. Mix.

2.—Extract vanilla, 1 oz.; extract rose, 1 oz.; extract lemon, 1 oz.; extract bitter almonds, 1 oz. Mix and add 1 gal. simple syrup; color pink with cochineal.

3.—Mix 3 parts vanilla syrup with 1 part each of pineapple and lemon syrups.

4.—Vanilla syrup, 3 parts; pineapple syrup, 1 part; cream syrup, 1 part. The cream syrup is made by dissolving in the cold 3 parts of sugar in 2 of rich milk, fortified with some additional cream.

Nuts

Blanch 1 lb. of the kernels of hickory nuts, or walnuts, in the usual way, then powder in a Wedgewood or porcelain mortar, a few at a time, adding a few drops of lemon juice to prevent the separation of the oil, and sufficient water, gradually, to make a pasty emulsion. As each batch of kernels is emulsified, says a foreign publication, empty the contents of the mortar on a linen cloth, and by gathering the corners and twisting, squeeze out all that will pass into a proper receptacle. The residue on the cloth, after squeezing, is to be returned to the mortar, to be again treated, along with the next batch. Proceed in this manner until the kernels have all been exhausted. The accumulated emulsion is to be passed through a

Syrups

strainer, and the colate, which should make about 2 pt., is to be added to and thoroughly incorporated with 3 qt. of cream syrup. This formula may be varied and perhaps improved upon by the addition of vanilla extract or other flavoring extracts. Other nuts may be used, notably the pecan and filbert, the former making an especially rich emulsion.

Nut Fruit Syrup

Roasted almonds, 1 lb.; whole cherries, 8 oz. Grind or chop quite fine, then add simple syrup, 1 qt. Boil for 10 minutes. When cold add simple syrup, to make 1 gal.; almond extract, 5 drops; rose extract, 3 drops. Mix and stir thoroughly.

Orange

1.—Oil of orange, 30 drops; citric acid, 4 dr.; simple syrup, 1 gal. Rub the oil with the acid and mix. Instead of the essential oil, a tincture of the fresh peel of Florida orange can be used with advantage.

2.—Sicilian oranges, a convenient quantity. Express the juice; to each pint of it add ½ pt. of water, filter or strain, and in the liquid dissolve 38 oz. of sugar. Flavor with some of the fresh peel crushed with the sugar, or still better, with Florida orange peel.

3.—Take 6 select oranges, grate off the yellow part only into a good-sized mortar. Add ½ lb. of sugar, rub thoroughly with a pestle and let stand for 2 or 3 hours. Extract the juice from the oranges and add. Stir until all the sugar is dissolved, adding a little water if necessary, and strain through cheese cloth into a gallon bottle. Add syrup to make 1 gallon and mix thoroughly. No artificial coloring, fruit acid or foam is necessary.

4.—Fresh oil of orange, ½ dr.; citric acid, 1 oz.; water, 2 oz.; simple syrup, 1 gal.; tincture of curcuma, a sufficient quantity. Rub the oil and acid crystals in a mortar until the latter have been reduced to a fine powder, add the water, and, when the acid has been dissolved, the syrup. A few drops of tincture of curcuma will give a good color.

5.—Blood Orange.—Orange juice, 1 pt.; raspberry juice, 1 oz.; claret wine, ½ oz.; fruit acid, ½ oz.; foam extract, 1 oz.; cochineal color, ½ dr.; simple syrup, 1 gal. The kind of fruit acid used in this formula consists of 2 oz. of citric acid dissolved in 4 oz. of water; the cochineal color is 2½ oz. of cochineal in 20 oz. of water, macerated for several days and filtered.

6.—Orange Flower Syrup.—Orange flower water, 1 pt.; granulated sugar, 28 oz. Dissolve without heat.

7.—Orange Peel. Fresh orange peel, 2 oz.; alcohol, 2 oz.; aqua pura, q. s. to percolate 9 oz.; sugar, 14 oz. Cut the peel in small pieces, put in mortar and add the alcohol. Thoroughly bruise to a pulp, put in a glass percolator, add the aqua pura until 9 oz. have percolated. Put the sugar in percolator and percolate the menstruum through the sugar until dissolved.

8.—Orange Phosphate.—Dispensers who use a large quantity of orange phosphate will find it convenient to previously prepare a special syrup for the purpose. To 1 gal. of fruity orange syrup add about 6 oz. of solution of acid phosphate. The syrup so made is ready for use and dispensing with it is much more rapid than using a squirt bottle.

Orgeat Syrup

1.—Cream syrup, ½ pt.; simple syrup, ½ pt.; vanilla syrup, 1 pt.; oil bitter almonds, 5 drops.

2.—Beat to an emulsion in a mortar 8 oz. blanched sweet almonds and 4 oz. bitter ones, adding a little water; when smooth add 3 pt. water; mix and strain. Dissolve in this without heat 6 lb. sifted white sugar and 4 oz. fresh orange flower water. An excellent imitation of orgeat syrup is made by flavoring cream syrup, made with eggs and milk, with a few drops of oil of bitter almonds.

3.—Sweet almonds, 8 oz.; bitter almonds, 2½ oz.; sugar, 3 lb.; water, 26 oz.; orange flower water, 4 oz. Blanch the almonds, rub them in a mortar to a fine paste

Syrups

with 12 oz. of the sugar and 2 oz. of the water. Mix the paste with the remainder of the water, strain with strong expression, add the remainder of the sugar and dissolve it with the aid of a gentle heat. Lastly, add the orange flower water and strain the syrup again.

4.—Cream syrup, ½ pt.; vanilla syrup, 1 pt.; simple syrup, ½ pt.; oil bitter almonds, 5 drops.

Pear Syrup

Proceed with it same as pineapple syrup.

Peach Syrup

Proceed in the same manner as for strawberry syrup.

Phosphated Syrup

Syrup phosphoric acid, 50 per cent., 2 oz.; phosphate of soda, 1 oz.; simple syrup, 1 gal. Flavor with either lemon or vanilla.

Pineapple Syrup

1.—Proceed as for raspberry, but the hard nature of this fruit requires pounding with a heavy billet of wood (not metal) in a tub with a strong bottom; when well mashed it will require great pressure to extract all the juice from this fruit. A cider press will answer the purpose, and 14 lb. of sugar to a gallon of juice and a little pure acetic acid. Put it on a slow fire and stir until the sugar dissolves. When cold, bottle and tie down.

2.—Use pineapples of good flavor, cut or chop them up, and set aside from 24 to 36 hours; press and proceed as directed for strawberry syrup.

3.—Take a convenient number of the fruit; pare and mash them in a marble or porcelain mortar, with a small quantity of sugar; express the juice; for each quart of juice take 1½ pt. of water and 6 lb. of sugar; boil the sugar and water and add the juice; remove from the fire; skim and strain.

Beverages—Non-Alcoholic

4.—Oil of pineapple, 1 dr.; tartaric acid, 1 dr.; simple syrup, 6 pt.

5.—Select a choice pineapple of good quality and ripe. One costing about 30 cents in proper season will make a gallon of syrup. Wash it thoroughly; then with a sharp knife remove the outer skin in a thin peeling. This is discarded. Now take a thicker slice from the outside of the fruit, just deep enough to include the eyes, and retain these in one of the pitcher containers. Now slice the remainder of the fruit down to the core and retain these slices in another pitcher. The slices containing the eyes and the core are now passed through the chopper, using the fine knives. A large amount of juice and pulp is obtained. Place in cheese cloth to strain, squeeze the pulp until it is free from juice and reject it. The second slicing is passed through the fine knives of the chopper and mixed with the juice already obtained. To the whole is then added enough rock candy syrup to make a gallon.

6.—Carbonated Pineapple Champagne.—Plain syrup, 42°, 10 gal.; essence of pineapple, 8 dr.; tincture of lemon, 5 oz.; carbonate of magnesia, 1 oz.; liquid saffron, 2½ oz.; citric-acid solution, 30 oz.; caramel, 2½ oz. Filter before adding the citric-acid solution and lime juice. Use 2 oz. to each bottle.

Pistachio for Dispensing

To ½ gal. syrup add ½ oz. extract pistachio, ¼ oz. essence bitter almond. Condensed milk should be added for dispensing.

Prunes

Set aside 1 lb. of the best prunes, with water enough to cover them, for several hours and repeat the washing several times. When they are completely washed add 1½ pt. of distilled water and gradually heat the whole on sand bath. When the ebullition point is reached boil from 20 to 30 minutes and allow to cool. Place in a suitable vessel, and with the aid of a spatula make into a

Syrups

pulpy mass. When of the proper consistency remove to a half-gallon salt-mouthed glass jar and add 1 pt. of 95 per cent. alcohol. Set aside for 2 weeks, shake at intervals and press the juice out through a strong wet muslin strainer and filter. Two parts of this extract to 4 parts of syrup will be sufficient for making *Prune Syrup*.

Raspberries

1.—Simple syrup, 6 pt.; water, 2 pt.; tartaric acid, 2 oz.; essence raspberry, 2 oz. Coloring sufficient. Coloring for raspberry, blackberry, etc., syrups may be made by boiling 1 oz. cochineal with ½ teaspoonful cream of tartar; filter.

2.—Take any quantity of fully ripe fruit; free them from stalks; place them in a tub and crush them with a wooden spatula; after they have been mashed, let them remain for 3 or 4 hours, and strain the crushed berries through a strong flannel bag or strainer into a suitable vessel. Dissolve ½ oz. citric acid in 3 oz. water and add this quantity to each gallon of juice; mix 14 lb. broken sugar to every gallon of juice; put on a slow fire and stir until all the sugar is dissolved (not boil); take off the fire and when cold bottle and cork for future use. If too thick when cold, it may be brought to a proper consistency by the addition of water.

3.—Take fresh berries and inclose them in a coarse bag; press out the juice, and to each quart add 6 lb. white sugar and 1 pt. of water; dissolve, raising it to the boiling point; strain; bottle and cork hot, and keep in a cool place. Raspberry syrup is improved by adding 1 part of currants to 4 parts of raspberries.

4.—Raspberries, 5 qt.; white sugar, 12 lb.; water, 1 pt. Sprinkle some of the sugar over the fruit in layers, allowing the whole to stand for several hours; express the juice and strain, washing out the pulp with the water; add the remainder of the sugar and water; bring the fluid to the boiling point and then strain. This will keep for a long time.

Beverages—Non-Alcoholic

5.—Black raspberry juice, 8 oz.; gum foam, 1 dr.; simple syrup, enough to make 32 oz. It may be necessary to add a little cochineal coloring to have the glass of soda the right shade.

6.—Raspberry juice, 32 oz.; granulated sugar, 3½ lb. Dissolve the sugar in the juice with the aid of heat. For use add 20 oz. of this to 40 oz. of simple syrup and tint to required color with a raspberry coloring.

7.—Proceed as directed for strawberry syrup.

8.—Artificial.—a.—Orris root (best), 1 oz.; cochineal, 2 dr.; tartaric acid, 2 dr.; water, 2 pt. Powder the orris root coarsely together with the cochineal; infuse in the water with the acid for 24 hours; strain, add 4 lb. of sugar, raise to the boiling point and strain again.

b.—Bruised orris root, 3 oz.; acetic acid, 2 oz.; acetic ether, 1 oz.; alcohol, 1 pt. Cochineal to color. Mix and allow to stand a few days; filter and use to flavor simple syrup.

Rose Syrup

Simple syrup, 1 gal.; essence rose, 1 oz. Color pink with prepared cochineal and acidulate lightly with a solution of citric acid.

Royal Muscadine

Raspberry syrup, 1 pt.; grape juice syrup, 1 pt.; raspberry vinegar, 2 oz. Mix. Pour 2 oz. into a mineral water glass, fill with carbonated water and serve.

Sangaree

Make a syrup of 1 oz. tartaric acid, 1 dr. acetic acid, 8 oz. claret, 2 pt. port, enough syrup to make 1 gal. Serve 1 oz. solid in 8-oz. glass, filling with carbonated water.

Sarsaparilla

1.—Oil of wintergreen, 10 drops; oil of anise, 10 drops; oil of sassafras, 10 drops; fluid ext. of sarsaparilla, 2 oz.; simple syrup, 5 pt.; powdered ext. of licorice, ½ oz.

Syrups

2.—Simple syrup, 4 pt.; comp. syrup sarsaparilla, 4 fl.oz.; caramel, 1½ oz.; oil of wintergreen, 6 drops; oil of sassafras, 6 drops.

3.—Essence of sarsaparilla, 3 dr.; solution of caramel, 1 oz.; gum foam, 2 dr.; simple syrup, enough to make 32 oz.

4.—Sassafras bark, bruised, 1 lb.; licorice root, bruised, 7 oz.; water, 2½ gal.; oil of sassafras, 1½ dr.; oil of wintergreen, 2 dr.; alcohol, 95 per cent., 2 oz. Boil the sassafras and licorice in the water half an hour. Strain through flannel, then add the syrup. Dissolve the oils in the alcohol and add them to the syrup. Agitate the mixture freely.

Sherbet Syrup

1.—Lemon essence, 2 dr.; orange essence, 2 dr.; pineapple juice, 4 oz.; solution citric acid, 2 oz.; syrup, ½ gal. Color with solution of cochineal.

2.—Vanilla syrup, 3 pt.; pineapple syrup, 1 pt.; lemon syrup, 1 pt.

Simple Syrup

Take of white sugar (com.), 14 lb.; water, 1 gal. Dissolve with the aid of a gentle heat, strain and when cold add the whites of 2 eggs, previously rubbed with a portion of the syrup, and mix thoroughly by agitation. (The egg albumen is added to produce froth.)

Strawberry

1.—Put 2 parts of strawberries deprived of the calyx, without crushing them, into a large-mouthed jar; add to them 2½ parts of sugar and frequently shake, keeping the vessel in a cool place. The sugar absorbs the juice, leaving the fruit shriveled and tasteless, the latter being removed by means of a strainer without pressure. Mix the clear syrup with 20% of alcohol.

2.—Proceed as for Raspberry Syrup 3, but the fruit, being more stubborn, will require a good beating with the spatula to mash them; when they have stood 3 or

Beverages—Non-Alcoholic

4 hours, strain and press the juice out by squeezing the strainer between the hands. Add to the juice the same quantity of citric acid; dissolve in each gallon 1¼ lb. of loaf sugar; simply warm the juice sufficiently to dissolve the sugar; take from the fire, and when cold bottle and cork till required.

3.—Take of fresh ripe strawberries, 10 qt.; white sugar, 24 lb.; water, ¼ gal. Spread a portion of the sugar over the fruit, in layers, let it stand 4 or 5 hours, express the juice, strain, washing out the marc with water; add remainder of sugar and water, raise to the boiling point and strain.

4.—Use strawberries of a good flavor. Do not forget that if the berries possess no flavor, you cannot expect to obtain a syrup of fine flavor. Avoid also rotten berries, because, unless you do, you may be sure to find as flavor the smell of the rotten berries in your syrup. Mash the fruit in a barrel or other suitable vessel, by means of a pounder, and leave the pulp for 12 or 24 hours at a temperature between 70 and 80°; stir occasionally, press, set the juice aside for one night, add for every pound avoirdupois of juice 1 oz. avoirdupois of cologne spirit or deodorized alcohol; mix, set aside for another night and filter through paper.

For 1 lb. of the filtered juice take 1½ lb. of sugar and heat to the boiling point, taking care to remove from the fire or turn off the steam as soon as the mixture begins to boil; remove the scum and bottle in perfectly clean bottles, rinsed with a little cologne spirit.

This syrup, as well as those made by the same process, is strong enough to be mixed with two or three times its weight of simple syrup for the soda fountain.

5.—Strawberry juice, 8 oz.; cochineal coloring, 2 dr.; gum foam, 1 dr.; simple syrup, enough to make 32 oz. A good strawberry flavor is one of the hardest to get, and one of the most unsatisfactory. Still it is not advisable to be without even a poor article.

6.—Remove the hulls from a quart of strawberries and

Syrups

wash the berries in a strainer. Pass them through the chopper, using the coarse knives, and add rock candy syrup to make 2 qt.

Tea

1.—Black tea, 3 oz.; green tea, 5 oz.; granulated sugar, 36 oz.; boiling water, 16 oz.

2.—Choice young Hyson tea, 8 oz.; hot water, 2 pt.; sugar, 4 lb. Infuse the tea, rolled or bruised into a coarse powder, for 2 hours in a tightly closed vessel. Strain and add to the sugar, dissolving the latter by agitation. Then add pure extract of vanilla, 1 oz.; pure cognac, 4 oz.; pure fruit juice (pineapple), 1 pt.; cane syrup or rock candy syrup, enough to make 1 gal.

3.—English breakfast tea, 1½ oz.; sugar, 1 lb.; boiling water, 2 pt. Infuse for 15 minutes; filter and dissolve the sugar in the filtrate. This drink is served in mineral glasses, with plenty of milk.

4.—Best green tea, 1 to 2 oz.; boiling water, 2 pt.; citric acid, ½ oz.; sugar, 56 oz. Infuse the tea in boiling water; strain the liquid, add enough water to complete 2 pt. and with the aid of a gentle heat dissolve in it the citric acid and the sugar. Strain the syrup through flannel and keep it in a cool place. Dispensed with soda water, this syrup makes a drink resembling *Iced Tea*.

Vanilla Syrup

1.—White syrup, 2 gal.; citric acid, 1 oz.; extract vanilla, 2 fl.oz. The acid should be dissolved in a small quantity of the syrup before adding to the other ingredients.

2.—Fluid extract of vanilla, 1 oz.; simple syrup, 3 pt.; cream (or condensed milk), 1 pt. May be colored with carmine.

3.—Simple syrup, 1 gal.; extract vanilla, 1 oz.; citric acid, ½ oz. Stir the acid with a portion of the syrup, add the extract of vanilla; mix.

4.—Simple syrup, 4 pt; extract of vanilla, 2 oz.

Beverages—Non-Alcoholic

5.—Tincture of vanilla, 4 dr.; solution of caramel, 4 dr.; gum foam, 2 dr.; simple syrup, enough to make 32 oz.

Violet Syrup

Refined sugar, 5 kilos; fresh violets, tops of the flowers only, 0.525 kilo; water, 2,600 liters. Bruise the violets in a mortar; put in a water bath with 1.5 liter at 60° C. Agitate for some minutes and press out the flowers. Put them back in the water bath; add the rest of the boiling water; infuse for 12 hours; allow it to settle; add the sugar and dissolve by heat.

Whipped Cream

1.—Secure cream as fresh as possible. Surround the bowl in which the cream is being whipped with cracked ice and perform the work in a cool place. As fast as the whipped cream rises, skim it off and place it in another bowl, likewise surrounded with ice. Do not whip the cream either too long or too violently. The downward motion of the beater should be more forcible than the upward motion, as the first tends to force the air into the cream, while the second tends, on the contrary, to expel the air. A little powdered sugar should be added to the cream *after* it is whipped, in order to sweeten it. Make the whipped cream in small quantities and keep it on ice. The object of keeping the cream cool and avoiding too much beating is to prevent the formation of butter. The beating of the cream can be easily effected by means of the egg beater.

2.—Artificial.—Gelatine, 4 oz.; whites of 8 eggs; vanilla extract, 2 oz.; syrup, 1 gal. Dissolve the gelatine in water, beat the eggs, mix both with syrup, then with 9 gal. of water and charge at a pressure of about 100 lb.

Wintergreen Syrup

Oil of wintergreen, 25 drops; simple syrup, 5 pt.; burnt sugar (to color), q. s.

Chapter III.

NON-ALCOHOLIC BEERS

Beer Tonic

PLAIN syrup, 22° Baumé, 5 gal.; oil of wintergreen, 2 dr.; oil of sassafras, 2 dr.; oil of allspice, ½ dr.; oil of sweet orange, 2 dr. Mix the oil with 12 oz. of alcohol and add to the plain syrup. Then add 35 gal. of water at blood heat and ferment with sufficient yeast. To this add 1 dr. of salicylic acid dissolved in conjunction with 1 dr. of baking soda in a small glass of water. After it has ceased effervescing, add to the fermenting beer. The object of using this minute quantity is to prevent putrefactive fermentation. The natural vinous ferments will not be obstructed by it.

Birch Beer

1.—Black birch bark, ½ lb.; hops, 1 oz.; pimento, ¼ lb.; ginger, ¼ lb.; yellow syrup, 6 pt.; yeast, ½ pt., or 2 oz. of compressed yeast. Boil the bark in 3 or 4 pt. of water, and, when considerably reduced, strain and boil rapidly until the liquor is as thick as molasses. Meanwhile boil the hops, pimento and ginger in 6 qt. of water for 20 minutes, then strain it on the bark extract. Stir until it boils, add the yellow syrup, and, when quite dissolved, strain the whole into a cask. Add 10 gal. of water previously boiled and allowed to cool, and as soon as it becomes lukewarm stir in the liquid yeast. Let it remain loosely bunged for 2 or 3 days or until fermentation has ceased, then strain into small bottles, cork them tightly and store in a cool place.

Beverages—Non-Alcoholic

2.—Essence of wintergreen, ¼ oz.; essence of sassafras, ¼ oz.; essence of birch, 1 oz.; cinnamon (in powder), 1 teaspoonful; hops, 1 teacupful; yeast, 1 teacupful; sugar, a sufficiency; water, to make 1 gal. Macerate the essence, cinnamon and hops in the water for 12 hours, then add sugar to taste and the yeast. Set aside for a day or two to ferment; then strain and bottle.

Dandelion Root Beer

1.—Tincture of ginger, 8 oz.; oil of wintergreen, 2 dr.; oil of sassafras, 1 dr.; fluid extract of dandelion, 1 oz.; fluid extract of wild cherry, 1 oz.; fluid extract of sarsaparilla, 1 oz.; diluted alcohol, enough to make 1 pt.

2.—Dandelion, 2 oz.; burdock root, 4 oz.; sarsaparilla, 4 oz.; sassafras, 2 oz.; caramel, 2 dr.; calamus, 4 dr.; oil of wintergreen, 30 m.; oil of sassafras, 30 m.; diluted alcohol, 1 pt.; alcohol, 2 oz.; water, a sufficient quantity. Mix the drugs, and, if not already powdered, reduce them to a coarse powder, moisten with the diluted alcohol, macerate and pack in the percolator and percolate with the remainder of the diluted alcohol and then with the water until the drugs are exhausted. Reserve the first 28 oz.; evaporate the weak percolate to 4 oz. and add to the reserved portion. Dissolve the oils in the alcohol, add to the percolate and filter, if necessary, through purified talcum or calcium phosphate.

Hop Beer

1.—Percolate the following with a menstruum of 3 volumes of alcohol to 5 volumes of water until exhausted: Sassafras, 1 oz.; yellow dock, 1 oz.; wild cherry bark, ½ oz.; allspice, 1 oz.; wintergreen, 1 oz.; hops, ¼ oz.; coriander seed, ½ oz. To the percolate add 1 pt. of yeast and sufficient water to make 6 gal. and allow to ferment in a warm place. Or a fluid extract of the above can be made of one-half the strength of the drug and 2 oz. of the extract used for preparing a gallon of beer.

2.—Water, 5 qt.; hops, 6 oz. Boil 3 hours, strain the

Non-Alcoholic Beers

liquor, add water, 5 qt., bruised ginger, 4 oz., and boil a little longer, strain and add 4 lb. of sugar, and when milk warm, 1 pt. of yeast. Let it ferment; in 24 hours it is ready for bottling.

3.—Hops, 5 oz.; water, 8 gal.; brown sugar, 2½ lb.; yeast, 3 or 4 tablespoonfuls. Boil hops and water together for 45 minutes, add the sugar, and, when dissolved, strain into a bowl or tub. As soon as it is lukewarm add the yeast, let it work for 48 hours, then skim well, and strain into bottles or a small cask. Cork securely and let it remain for a few days before using it.

Lemon Beer

1.—Boiling water, 1 gal.; lemon, sliced, 1; bruised ginger, 1 oz.; yeast, 1 teacupful; sugar, 1 lb. Let it stand 12 to 20 hours and it is ready to be bottled.

2.—Put in a keg 1 gal. of water, 1 sliced lemon, 1 tablespoon ginger, 1 pt. syrup, ½ pt. yeast. Ready for use in 24 hours. If bottled, tie down the corks.

Maple

1.—To 4 gal. of boiling water add 1 qt. of maple syrup, ½ oz. of essence of spruce; add 1 pt. of yeast and proceed as with ginger pop.

2.—To 4 gal. of boiling water add 1 qt. of maple syrup, ½ oz. essence of spruce and 1 pt. of yeast. Let it ferment for 24 hours and then strain and bottle it. In a week or more it will be ready for use.

3.—Boiling water, 6 gal.; maple syrup, 1½ qt.; essence of spruce, ¾ oz.; add 1½ pt. yeast.

Molasses Beer

Take 14 lb. molasses, 1½ lb. hops, 36 gal. water, 1 lb. yeast. Boil the hops in the water, add the molasses and ferment.

Ottawa Beer

Sassafras, allspice, yellow dock, wintergreen, 1 oz. each; wild cherry bark and coriander, 1½ oz.; hops, ¼ oz.; molasses, 3 qt. Put boiling water on the ingredients and let them stand 24 hours. Filter and add ½ pt. of brewer's yeast. Leave again 24 hours, then put it in an ice cooler, and it is ready for use. It is a wholesome drink if it is used in moderation.

Root Beer

1.—To 5 gal. of boiling water add 1½ gal. of molasses. Allow it to stand for 3 hours, then add bruised sassafras bark, wintergreen bark, sarsaparilla root, of each ¼ lb., and ½ pt. of fresh yeast, water enough to make 15 to 17 gal. After this has fermented for 12 hours it can be drawn off and bottled.

2.—Pour boiling water on 2½ oz. sassafras, 1½ oz. wild cherry bark, 2½ oz. allspice, 2½ oz. wintergreen bark, ½ oz. hops, ½ oz. coriander seed, 2 gal. molasses. Let the mixture stand 1 day. Strain, add 1 pt. yeast, enough water to make 15 gal. This beer may be bottled the following day.

3. Sarsaparilla, 1 lb.; spicewood, ¼ lb.; guaiacum chips, ½ lb.; birch bark, ⅛ lb.; ginger, ¼ oz.; sassafras, 2 oz.; prickly ash bark, ¼ oz.; hops, ½ oz. Boil for 12 hours over a moderate fire with sufficient water, so that the remainder shall measure 3 gal., to which add tincture of ginger, 4 oz.; oil of wintergreen, ½ oz.; alcohol, 1 pt. This prevents fermentation. To make root beer, take of this decoction, 1 qt.; molasses, 8 oz.; water, 2½ gal.; yeast, 4 oz. This will soon ferment and produce a good, drinkable beverage. The root beer should be mixed, in warm weather, the evening before it is used, and can be kept for use either bottled or drawn by a common beer pump. Most people prefer a small addition of wild cherry bitters or hot drops to the above beer.

Sarsaparilla Beer

Decoction of sarsaparilla compound, 2 oz.; sassafras root, bruised, ¼ oz.; honey, ¾ lb.; cane sugar, 1 lb.; fresh yeast, 4 oz.; distilled water, boiling, 1 gal. Dissolve the sugar and honey in the water, add the sassafras, and when cooled down the sarsaparilla and yeast. Set aside in a warm place for a few days and then strain and bottle.

Spruce Beer

1.—Sarsaparilla, 4 oz.; pipsissewa, 4 oz.; licorice root, 3 oz.; sassafras bark, 3 oz.; ginger root, 1 oz. Mix the drugs and grind to a coarse powder and extract by percolation with a menstruum of 3 parts of alcohol and 1 of water until 24 fl.oz. of product are obtained, and add the following: oil lemon, 2 dr.; oil sassafras, 2 oz.; oil spruce, 2 oz.; oil wintergreen, 1 dr.; magnesia, 4 dr. Dissolve the oils in 6 oz. of alcohol and rub with magnesia and add 2 oz. of water and mix well. Now mix both solutions and filter. Use 4 or 5 oz. to 1 gal. of simple syrup and color with caramel.

2.—Hops, 2 oz.; chip sassafras, 2 oz.; water, 10 gal. Boil half an hour, strain; add brown sugar, 7 lb.; essence of spruce, 1 oz.; essence of ginger, 1 oz.; ground pimento, ½ oz. Put in a cask and cool, add 1½ pt. of yeast, let it stand 24 hours, fine, draw it off to bottle.

3.—Hops, 8 oz.; chip sassafras, 2 oz.; water, 10 gal. Boil half an hour, strain and add brown sugar, 7 lb.; essence of spruce, 1 oz.; essence of ginger, 1 oz. ground pomento, ½ oz. Put into a cask and cool, add 1½ pt. yeast, let it stand 24 hours, fine, draw it off to bottle.

4.—To 6 gal. of water add 1 pt. essence of spruce, 10 oz. of pimento, 10 oz. ginger, 1 lb. hops. After boiling about 10 minutes, add 24 lb. of moist sugar and 22 gal. of warm water. When the ingredients are well mixed and lukewarm, add 1 qt. yeast. Let it ferment 24 hours. Strain and bottle.

5.—Sugar, 1 lb.; essence of spruce, ½ oz.; boiling water, 1 gal.; mix well and when nearly cold add ½ wineglass of yeast and the next day bottle.

6.—Essence of spruce, ½ pt.; pimento and ginger (bruised), of each 5 oz.; hops, ½ lb.; water 3 gal.; boil the whole for 10 minutes, then add of moist sugar, 12 lb.;

Beverages—Non-Alcoholic

water, 11 gal.; mix well and when lukewarm add 1 pt. of yeast. After the liquor has fermented for about 24 hours, bottle it.

7.—Water, 16 gal.; boil half, put the water thus boiled to the reserved cold half, which should be previously put into a barrel or other vessel; then add 16 lb. molasses, with a few spoonfuls of the essence of spruce, stirring the whole together; add ½ pt. of yeast, and keep it in a temperate situation with the bunghole open for 2 days, or till fermentation subsides; then close it up or bottle it off, and it will be fit to drink in a few days.

White Spruce Beer

Five lb. loaf sugar are dissolved in 5 gal. of boiling water, then 2 fl.oz. of spruce are added. When almost cold add a gill of yeast. Place in warm place and after 24 hours strain through a piece of flannel and bottle.

Chapter IV.

EGGS AND MILK OR CREAM DRINKS

Mostly for the Fountain

Egg Drinks

DRAW desired syrup or syrups into glass; into shaker put q. s. crushed ice, break egg into shaker with one hand by holding egg in fingers, the thumb being made to give upward pressure on one end and third and forth fingers on the other. Strike the egg on edge of shaker and pull apart in above manner. Put syrup into shaker with egg and ice and shake well, holding both thumbs against bottom of glass and fingers around shaker, moving arms outward from body. Strain into clean glass, wash ice out of shaker, then add soda, using fine stream freely.

Calisaya.—White and yolk of 1 egg; ½ tumblerful of cracked or shaved ice; 3 dashes of elixir calisaya; 1¼ oz. lemon syrup. Shake well, strain, and add 1 tumblerful of plain soda. Pour from tumbler to shaker alternately several times, then grate nutmeg on top and serve.

Egg Sour.—Juice of 1 lemon; simple syrup, 12 dr.; 1 egg. Shake, strain and fill with soda. Mace on top.

Golden Fizz.—One egg yolk; Catawba syrup, 1 oz.; juice of ¼ lemon; powdered sugar, 1 teaspoonful; cracked ice. Shake together and strain; then fill the glass with seltzer. A good morning drink.

Grape Egg Phosphate.—Orange syrup, 2 oz.; grape juice, 1 oz.; 3 dashes of phosphate; 1 egg; a little fine ice. Shake, fill with soda and strain.

Beverages—Non-Alcoholic

Lemon Sour.—Lemon syrup, 12 dr.; juice of 1 lemon; 1 egg.

Lemonade.—1.—Break 1 egg in mixing glass, use 1 or 2 lemons, simple syrup to taste, shake well with ice, use fine stream of soda and serve in bell glass with nutmeg or cinnamon.

2.—In 1 pt. of water dissolve ½ lb. granulated sugar; squeeze in the juice of 4 large lemons and add a cupful cracked ice. Have ready the yolks and whites of 4 fresh eggs, well beaten, separately, the whites until stiff and dry; stir in the yolks with the lemonade, and, lastly, the whites; if necessary, add more sugar.

Phosphate.—1.—Put some cracked ice into a shaker, break in a fresh egg, add 1 oz. of American orange syrup and a dash of phosphate. Shake well, then strain into glass. Draw fine stream to make the drink creamy, then pour back and forth from a shaker to glass. Sprinkle top with grated nutmeg and serve with a straw.

2.—Small quantity cracked ice, lemon syrup, 1½ oz.; 1 egg; liquid phosphate, 30 drops. Shake together with hand shaker and add enough plain soda to fill the glass. Mix well by pouring from glass to shaker and serve, after adding a little grated nutmeg.

3.—Orange syrup, 1 oz.; pineapple syrup, 1 oz.; 1 egg; acid phosphate, 6 dashes; lemon juice, 6 dashes. Shake, strain and add soda water, using a fine stream freely. Sprinkle mace on top.

Pineapple.—Break a fresh egg into a 12-oz. soda-tumbler, add 1½ oz. pineapple syrup, 2 dashes phosphate, 1 oz. plain water; shake thoroughly; fill shaker with fine stream soda, strain carefully into tumbler and serve.

Raspberry Sour.—Raspberry syrup, 12 dr.; 1 egg; juice of 1 lemon.

Silver Fizz (non-alcoholic).—Catawba syrup, 2 oz.; lemon juice, 8 dashes; white of 1 egg.

Vichy à la Egg.—One whole egg, ½ glass shaved ice, 1 oz. pure water. Shake thoroughly, then add slowly,

Eggs and Milk or Cream Drinks

Egg and Milk or Cream

while contantly stirring, enough vichy water to fill the glass.

1.—One egg, ½ oz. of lemon and vanilla syrup. 1 oz. pure cream, 2 teaspoonfuls shaved ice. Shake and strain.

2.—Evaporated cream, 4 oz.; egg yolks, 4; extract vanilla, 1 oz.; syrup, 12 oz.

3.—One egg; vanilla or Catawba syrup, 1 oz.; other syrups may be used; glass ¼ full fine ice. Fill with milk and shake up well. Sprinkle nutmeg on top and serve.

4.—Cream, 6 oz.; pulverized sugar, 2 tablespoonfuls; 1 egg; shaved ice. Shake, strain and add soda water.

Chocolate—1.—Chocolate syrup, 2 oz.; 1 egg; shaved ice; milk to fill glass; whipped cream. Shake egg, syrup, milk and ice together and strain; draw fine stream of soda to fill glass; use whipped cream on top.

2.—Chocolate syrup, 2 oz.; cream, 4 oz.; white of 1 egg.

Claret.—Claret syrup, 2 oz.; cream, 3 oz.; 1 egg.

Cocoa Mint.—Chocolate syrup, 1 oz.; peppermint syrup, 1 oz.; white of 1 egg; cream 2 oz.

Coffee.—1.—Cream, 3 qt.; sugar, 1½ oz.; port wine, ½ oz.; 1 egg. Add a little ice, using a 12-oz. glass, fill with milk shake, strain into a clean glass and add a few dashes of nutmeg.

2.—Coffee syrup, 2 oz.; cream, 3 oz.; 1 egg; shaved ice.

Currant Cream.—Red currant syrup, 2 oz.; cream, 3 oz.; 1 egg.

Fruit Blend.—Pineapple syrup, ½ oz.; vanilla syrup, ½ oz.; orange syrup, ½ oz.; 1 egg; plain cream, 2 oz.; sherry wine, 2 dashes: ice, ¼ glass. Shake, strain, toss and serve.

Orange.—1.—Orange syrup, 1 oz.; Catawba or pineapple syrup, 1 oz.; cream, 2 oz.; 1 egg.

2.—Orange syrup, 2 oz.; ice cream, 1 tablespoonful; 1 egg; milk, 3 oz.; cracked ice, q. s. This is put into a shaker and thoroughly mixed. It is served with cracked

Beverages—Non-Alcoholic

ice and enough plain soda to fill the glass. Served with straws.

Punch.—1.—Orange syrup, 2 oz.; lemon juice, 6 dashes; cream, 2 oz.; 1 egg.

2.—Break 1 egg in mixing glass, add 1 oz. Catawba syrup, 1½ oz. brandy syrup, 2 oz. plain cream. Shake well with ice and use fine stream. Serve in bell glass.

Quince Flip.—Quince syrup, 2 oz.; cream, 3 oz.; 1 egg; shaved ice.

Rose Cream.—Rose syrup, 12 dr.; cream, 4 oz.; white of 1 egg.

Rose Mint.—Rose syrup, 6 dr.; mint syrup, 6 dr.; cream, 3 oz.; white of 1 egg.

Sherbet.—Sherry syrup, 4 dr.; pineapple syrup, 4 dr. raspberry syrup, 4 dr.; cream, 2 oz.; 1 egg.

Sherry Flip.—Sherry syrup, 2 oz.; cream, 3 oz.; 1 egg. Shake, strain and add soda water. Mace on top.

Strawberry.—One egg in mixing glass, add 2 oz. of strawberry syrup, 2 oz. plain cream. Shake well with ice. Use fine stream and serve in bell glass.

Violet Cream.—Violet syrup, 12 dr.; cream, 4 oz.; white of 1 egg.

Milk or Cream

Syrup (desired flavor), 1 oz.; shaved ice, ½ tumblerful; rich milk, ½ tumblerful. Shake vigorously and fill tumbler with plain soda from fine stream.

Banana.—Banana syrup, 12 dr.; cream, 4 oz.; 1 egg.

Chocolate.—1.—Chocolate syrup, 3 oz.; ice cream, 2 tablespoonfuls; milk, enough to fill a soda tumbler. Put into shaker, mix well and serve with cracked ice and straws.

2.—Chocolate syrup, 2 oz.; sweet milk, sufficient. Fill a glass full of shaved ice, put in the syrup and add milk until the glass is almost full. Shake well and serve without straining. Put whipped cream on top and serve with straws.

Clam Juice.—Clam juice, 1½ fl.oz.; milk, 2 fl.oz.;

Eggs and Milk or Cream Drinks

soda water, 5 fl.oz. Add a pinch of salt and a little white pepper to each glass; shake well.

Coffee.—Large glass chipped ice, ¼ full; coffee syrup, 2 oz.; sweet cream, 2 oz. Shake thoroughly and draw on soda in the shaker. Put a spoonful of whipped cream in the glass and pour in the drink, using the fine soda stream.

Mineral Milk.—Draw 6 oz. plain carbonated water into 8-oz. tumbler; fill with plain sweet cream; stir and serve.

Mint.—Mint syrup, 1½ fl.oz.; angostura bitters, ½ fl.dr.; milk, 3 fl.oz. Carbonated water (coarse stream), enough to fill 8-oz. glass. Serve "solid."

Peach.—Peach syrup, 1 oz.; grape juice, ½ oz.; pineapple syrup, ½ oz.; shaved ice, ½ glass. Fill the glass with milk, shake well and serve with 2 straws.

Sherbet.—Shaved ice, ½ glass; strawberry syrup, 1 oz.; pineapple syrup, 1 oz.; vanilla syrup, 1 oz.; milk to nearly fill glass. Shake well, add soda water, fine stream, and pour from tumbler to shaker several times. Serve in a 12-oz. glass, with straws.

Strawberry.—Strawberry syrup, ½ oz.; vanilla syrup, ½ oz.; orange syrup, ½ oz.; brandy, 3 dashes; shaved ice, ¼ glass; milk, enough to fill glass. Top with whipped cream.

Chapter V.

FRAPPÉS

Making Frappés

FRAPPÉS are semi-frozen beverages, served in glasses or "ice cups," and are considered delicious drinks in the hot season. They are mainly composed of fruit juices, with an addition of sugar or syrup. They are also made of different kinds of punch, such as champagne, coffee, etc. In point of color they should correspond with the nature of fruit used. The freezing process should consist of the preparation being placed in a freezer or packer imbedded in broken salted ice, the vessel is twisted to the right and left alternately with the hand. As the composition becomes frozen up the sides of the can remove it with a palette knife by scraping it down into the composition and mix it with a spatula, remembering that frappé must be only half frozen, resembling snow, and just sufficiently liquid to admit of its being poured into glasses.

Blackberry

Juice of 1 lemon; blackberry syrup, ½ oz.; raspberry syrup, ½ oz. Fill a 14-oz. glass two-thirds full of shaved ice. Shake well; do not strain; ornament with fruit and use real straws.

Chocolate

Dissolve 1 lb. of chocolate (powdered) with 4 qt. of water, adding 2 lb. of sugar, seeing that the chocolate is

Frappés

fully dissolved; remove from the fire and strain. When cold, flavor with vanilla and freeze after the manner laid down for frappé.

Coffee

1.—Java coffee syrup, 1½ lb.; coffee, about 5 oz. of best Grind the coffee fresh every time you want to use it. Put 1 qt. of the mixture into the farina boiler; when very hot add the coffee, stir well, cover the boiler, let it draw for 10 minutes, stir again, take off the fire and set in a warm place to settle, then pour off the clear part. Cook rest of the cream, add the coffee and sugar, dissolve it, strain through fine muslin, cool and freeze. May also be served with whipped cream.

2.—To every quart of clear, good Mocha coffee add 1 lb. of sugar and freeze as above.

Lemon

Make an ordinary lemon water ice, rich in fruit flavor and good and sweet; then freeze.

Maple

Two oz. maple sugar, 3 oz. plain cream, large teaspoonful of ice cream; shake well with ice, use only fine stream and serve in bell glass.

Orange

1.—Orange syrup, 1 oz.; ice; then add in the following order: Powdered sugar, 1 tablespoonful; orange syrup, ½ oz.; lemon syrup, 2 dashes; raspberry syrup, 1 dash; acid-phosphate solution, ¼ oz. Fill the glass with soda water, stir well, strain into a mineral water glass and serve.

2.—Orange syrup, 1½ oz.; ice cream, 2 oz.; plain cream, 2 oz.; ice, ¼ glass. Shake, strain, toss and serve.

Pineapple

Peel and crush 2 pineapples; then make a boiling syrup of 2½ lb. sugar and 2 qt. of water and pour it over the

Beverages—Non-Alcoholic

pineapples. Let it stand until nearly cold, then add the juice of 5 lemons; strain, press the liquid from the pineapples; pour into freezer, add 4 egg whites and freeze. Then work in a good ¼ pt. of maraschino.

Tea

For tea frappé cover 3 tablespoonfuls of mixed tea with 2 qt. of boiling water. Let it stand about 10 minutes, then strain, sweeten to taste, cool and freeze to a mush.

Chapter VI.

GINGER ALES, BEERS, POP, ETC.

Ginger Ale

CARBONATED.—1.—To make the extract, proceed as follows: Bruised ginger, 128 parts; cardamom seed, 2 parts; oil lemon, ½ part; Cayenne pepper, 8 parts; alcohol dilute, 256 parts. Mix the aromatics, moisten with the alcohol, pack in a percolator and percolate until exhausted. Dissolve the oil of lemon in the percolate.

2.—To charge the fountains: Extract ginger ale, 6 dr.; acid solution, 6 dr.; syrup simplex, 5 pt.; sugar coloring (carmine), 2 dr.; water, 6 gal. Mix. Charge with carbonic-acid gas to 120 to 130 lb.

3.—The acid solution is made as follows: Citric acid, 3 oz.; water, 6 oz. Mix and make a solution.

Extract.—1.—Soluble essence of ginger, 1½ pt.; essence of lemon, soluble, 1½ oz.; essence of ginger oil, soluble, 1½ oz.; extract of vanilla, soluble, 1½ oz.; soluble essence rose oil, ¾ oz.; tincture cinnamon, soluble, 1½ dr.; artificial essence pineapple, ¾ dr.; essence capsicum, 3 dr.; mix.

2.—Tincture of ginger, 1 gal.; tincture of capsicum, 7½ oz.; extract of orange, 3 oz.; extract of lemon, ½ oz.; caramel, 5 oz.; water, 1½ gal.; sugar, 2 lb.; magnesium carbonate, 1 lb. Mix and allow to stand 12 hours. Shake occasionally and filter.

3.—Jamaica ginger, coarse powder, 4 oz.; mace powder, ½ oz.; Canada snakeroot, coarse powder, 60 gr.; oil of lemon, 1 fl.dr.; alcohol, 12 fl.oz.; water, 4 fl.oz.; mag-

Beverages—Non-Alcoholic

nesium carbonate or purified talcum, 1 av.oz. Mix the first four ingredients and make 16 fl.oz. of tincture with the alcohol and water by percolation. Dissolve the oil of lemon in a small quantity of alcohol, rub with magnesia or talcum, add gradually with constant trituration the tincture and filter. The extract may be fortified by adding 4 av.oz. of powdered grains of paradise to the ginger, etc., of the above before extraction with alcohol and water.

4.—Capsicum, coarse powder, 8 oz.; water, 6 pt.; essence of ginger, 8 fl.oz.; diluted alcohol, 7 fl.oz.; vanilla extract, 2 fl.oz.; oil of lemon, 20 drops; caramel, 1 fl.oz. Boil the capsicum with water for 3 hours, occasionally replacing the water lost by evaporation, filter, concentrate the filtrate on a hot-water bath to the consistency of a thin extract, add the remaining ingredients and filter.

5.—Jamaica ginger, ground, 12 oz.; lemon peel, fresh, cut fine, 2 oz.; capsicum, powder, 1 oz.; calcined magnesia, 1 oz.; alcohol and water, of each sufficient. Extract the mixed ginger and capsicum by percolation so as to obtain 16 fl.oz. of water, set the mixture aside for 24 hours, shaking vigorously from time to time, then filter and pass through the filter enough of a mixture of 2 volumes of alcohol and 1 of water to make the filtrate measure 32 fl.oz. In the latter macerate the lemon peel for 7 days and again filter.

6.—To be used in the proportion of 4 oz. of extract to 1 gal. of syrup; Jamaica ginger, in fine powder, 8 lb.; capsicum, in fine powder, 6 oz.; alcohol, a sufficient quantity. Mix the powders intimately, moisten them with a sufficient quantity of alcohol and set aside for 4 hours. Pack in a cylindrical percolator and percolate with alcohol until 10 pt. of percolate have resulted. Place the percolate in a bottle of the capacity of 16 pt. and add to it 2 fl.dr. of oleoresin of ginger; shake, add 2½ lb. of finely powdered pumice stone and agitate thoroughly at intervals of one-half hour for 12 hours. Then add 14 pints of water in quantities of 1 pt. at each addition, shaking briskly meanwhile. This part of the operation

Ginger Ales, Beers, Pop, Etc.

is most important. Set the mixture aside for 24 hours, agitating it strongly every hour or so during that period. Then take oil of lemon, 1½ fl.oz.; oil of rose (or geranium), 3 fl.dr.; oil of bergamot, 2 fl.dr.; oil of cinnamon, 3 fl.dr.; magnesium carbonate, 3 fl.oz. Rub the oils with the magnesia in a large mortar and add 9 oz. of the clear portion of the ginger mixture, to which has been previously added 2 oz. of alcohol, and continue trituration, rinsing out the mortar with the ginger mixture. Pass the ginger mixture through a double filter and add through the filter the mixture of oils and magnesia. Finally pass enough water through the filter to make the resulting product measure 24 pt., or 3 gal. If the operator should desire an extract of more or less pungency, he may obtain his desired effect by increasing or decreasing the quantity of powdered capsicum in the formula.

Ginger Beer

1.—Soluble essence of lemon, 1 oz., Jamaica ginger (bruised), 12 oz.; English honey, 12 oz.; lemon juice, 1 pt.; cane sugar, 9 lb.; distilled water, to make 9¼ gal.; white of an egg. Boil the ginger with 1½ gal. of water for half an hour, then add the sugar, honey and lemon juice, and make up with water to 9¼ gal. When cold, add the white of an egg and essence of lemon and stir well together. Set aside in a closed vessel for about 5 days and then bottle.

2.—Jamaica ginger, 2½ oz.; moist sugar, 3 lb.; cream tartar, 1 oz.; juice and peel of 2 lemons; brandy, ½ pt.; good ale yeast, ¼ pt.; water, 3½ gal. This will produce 4½ doz. bottles of excellent ginger beer, which will keep 12 months. Boil the ginger and sugar for 20 minutes in the water, slice the lemons and put them and the cream of tartar in a large pan; pour the boiling liquor over them and stir well; when milk is warm add the yeast; cover and let it remain 2 or 3 days, skimming frequently; strain through a cloth into a cask and add the brandy. Bung down very close; at the end of 2 weeks draw off and bottle, cork very tightly. If it does not work well, add a very little more yeast.

3.—Brown sugar, 2 lb.; boiling water, 2 gal.; cream of tartar, 1 oz.; bruised ginger root, 2 oz. Infuse the ginger in the boiling water, add your sugar and cream of tartar; when lukewarm strain; then add ½ pt. good yeast. Let it stand all night; then bottle; if you desire, you can add 1 lemon and the white of an egg to fine it.

4.—*English.*—Water, 3 gal.; pulverized ginger, 3 oz.; sugar, 4 lb.; cream tartar, 4 oz. Boil and when cold add 2 tablespoonfuls of yeast. Allow it to stand over night, then filter and bottle.

5.—*Fermented.*—For a good recipe for fermented ginger beer to put up in stone jugs, take best Jamaica ginger, ground, 1 lb.; tartaric acid, 6 oz.; gum arabic, 1 lb.; oil lemon, ½ oz.; sugar, 21 lb.; water, 21 gal.; yeast ½ pt. Stir the ginger, sugar and water very thoroughly together. Dissolve the gum in sufficient water to give it the consistency of cream; to this add the lemon oil and shake them well together. Add this mixture to the sugar solution. Now stir in the yeast. As soon as a brisk fermentation is established, strain through a jelly bag. Let it work for another day or two and then bottle. This will make 20 gal.; you can double or quadruple the proportions if you want to make a larger batch.

6.—*Powder.*—a.—Jamaica ginger, powdered, 1 oz.; sodium bicarbonate, 7 oz.; sugar, 1¾ lb.; oil of lemon, 1 fl.dr. Make into powders.

b.—Ginger, bruised, ½ oz.; cream of tartar, ¾ oz.; essence of lemon, 4 drops. Mix. Some sugar may be added if it be thought desirable to make the packet look bigger. For use this powder is to be added to 1 gal. of boiling water, in which dissolve 1 lb. of lump sugar, and when the mixture is nearly cool 2 or 3 tablespoonfuls of yeast are to be added. The mixture should be set aside to work for 4 days, when it may be strained and bottled.

Ginger Ales, Beers, Pop, Etc.

Gingerade

Dissolve 3 lb. granulated sugar in 2 gal. of water. Then add the well-beaten whites of 3 eggs and 2 oz. powdered ginger. It is well to moisten the ginger before adding it to the whole with just a little water. Now place over the fire in an enameled saucepan, bring slowly to the boiling point, skim and stand aside to settle. When cold, add the juice of 1 large lemon and ¼ oz. yeast, dissolved in 2 tablespoonfuls of warm water. Mix thoroughly, strain, fill the bottles, cork tightly and tie the corks, putting them at once in a cool place. Ready for use in 2 days.

Ginger Mint

Lemon syrup, 4 oz.; ginger syrup, 12 oz.; tincture capsicum, 2 dr.; tincture menth. vir., ½ dr. Mix, serve with shaved ice and straws. Decorate with mint leaves.

Ginger Pop

1.—Five lb. of cream of tartar; ginger, 8 oz.; sugar, 35 lb.; essence of lemon, 5 dr.; water, 30 gal.; yeast 2 qt.

2.—Take 5½ gal. water; ginger root (bruised), ¾ lb.; tartaric acid, ½ oz.; white sugar, 2¼ lb.; whites of 3 eggs, well beaten; 1 small teaspoonful lemon oil; 1 gill yeast. Boil the root for 30 minutes in 1 gal. water; strain and put the oil in while hot; mix. Make over night; in the morning skim and bottle.

3.—Five lb. of loaf sugar to 5 gal. of cold water, 4 lemons, 2 oz. white root ginger, 4 oz. cream tartar. Boil the sugar and ginger (previously pound the latter); when it has boiled 15 minutes strain it through a flannel cloth into a large crock, put in the cream tartar, slice also the lemon into it; let it stand until milk-warm, then add a teacup of yeast; let it stand a little, then bottle it tightly in stone bottles; in 3 days it will be fit for use.

4.—*Imperial.*—Cream of tartar, 3 oz.; ginger, 1 oz.;

Beverages—Non-Alcoholic

white sugar, 24 oz.; lemon juice, 1 oz.; boiling water, 1½ gal. When cool, strain and ferment with 1 oz. yeast. Bottle.

5.—*Royal Pop.*—To 3 gal. of water add ½ lb. cream tartar, ¾ oz. ginger, 3½ lb. white sugar, ½ dr. essence of lemon, ½ pt. yeast. The corks should be tied down.

Chapter VII.

GLACÉS

GLACÉS should be served in small, handsome punch glasses, with small spoons to match.

Claret

Lemon, 1 oz.; claret, 1 oz.; cream, 2 oz.; cracked ice, ½ glassful. Shake, strain, draw coarse stream into shaker, to fill a 12-oz. glass. Toss and serve with 2 straws stuck through a slice of lemon in glass.

Crushed Fruit

Crushed fruits served in the following manner make a delicious and refreshing drink: Crushed fruit, 12 dr.; juice of half a lemon; shaved ice. Put the ice into a small glass, add the fruit and lemon juice, stir well.

Pineapple

a.—Two spoonfuls crushed pineapple, ½ oz. pineapple syrup, shaved ice.

b.—Pineapple snow is a mixture of shaved or cracked ice, cream and pineapple syrup with or without carbonated water, the whole being topped off with shaved ice.

c.—Pineapple syrup, 1 oz.; powdered sugar, 1 teaspoonful; shaved ice, ½ glassful. Add some carbonated water, stir vigorously in a shaker, strain into an 8-oz. glass, fill the latter with the coarse stream of carbonated water, stir again and add a piece of pineapple or some crushed pineapple.

Chapter VIII.

GRAPE JUICE

Flavor and Quality

IN the making of unfermented grape juice a great deal of judgment can be displayed and many variations produced so as to suit almost any taste by the careful selection of the varieties of grapes from which it is made.

Equally as pronounced variations in color can be had, as, for instance, almost colorless, yellow, orange, light red, red and a deep purple.

Unfermented grape juice may be made from any grape; not only this, but unfermented juice is made from other fruits as well; for instance, apples, pears, cherries and berries of different kinds. The richer, sweeter and better in quality the fruit, the better will be our unfermented juice. If, on the other hand, the fruit is sour, green and insipid, the juice will be likewise.

Fermentation

Fermentation may be prevented in either of two ways.

1.—By chemical methods, which consist in the addition of germ poisons or antiseptics, which either kill the germs or prevent their growth. Of these the principal ones used are salicylic, sulphurous, boracic and benzoic acids, formalin, fluorides and saccharins. As these substances are generally regarded as adulterants and injurious, their use is not recommended.

2.—Mechanical means are sometimes employed. The germs are either removed by filtering or a centrifugal apparatus, or they are destroyed by heat, electricity, etc. Of these, heat has so far been found the most practical.

Practical tests so far made indicate that grape juice

Grape Juice

can be safely sterilized at from 165 to 176° F. At this temperature the flavor is hardly changed, while at a temperature much above 200° F. it is. This is an important point, as the flavor and quality of the product depend on it.

This information is intended for the farmer or the housewife only. Readers who desire to go into the manufacture of grape juice in a systematic manner for commercial purposes are referred to Bulletin 24, Bureau of Plant Industry, Department of Agriculture, on the same subject.

Home Manufacture

Use only clean, sound, well-ripened but not over-ripe grapes. If an ordinary cider mill is at hand, it may be used for crushing and pressing, or the grapes may be crushed and pressed with the hands. If a light-colored juice is desired, put the crushed grapes in a cleanly washed cloth sack and tie up. Then either hang up se-

Fig. 1.—Cloth Hand Press

curely and twist it or let two persons take hold, one on each end of the sack (Fig. 1) and twist until the greater part of the juice is expressed. Then gradually heat the juice in a double boiler or a large stone jar in a pan of hot water, so that the juice does not come in direct contact with the fire, at a temperature of 180 to 200° F.; never above 200° F. It is best to use a thermometer, but if there be none at hand heat the juice until it steams, but do not allow it to boil. Put it in a glass or enameled vessel to settle for 24 hours. Carefully drain the juice from the sediment and run it through several thicknesses

Beverages—Non-Alcoholic

of clean flannel, or a conic filter made from woolen cloth or felt may be used. This filter is fixed to a hoop of iron which can be suspended wherever necessary (Fig. 2).

Fig. 2.—Cloth or Felt Filter

After this fill into clean bottles. Do not fill entirely, but leave room for the liquid to expand when again heated. Fit a thin board over the bottom of an ordinary wash

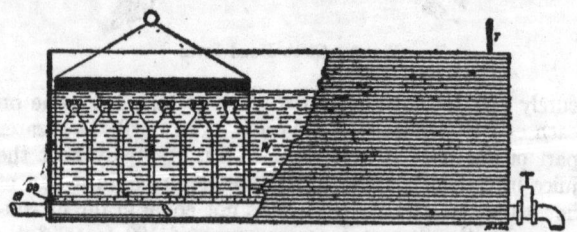

Fig. 3.—PASTEURIZER FOR JUICE IN BOTTLES
DB, double bottom. ST, steam pipe. W, water bath. T, thermometer.
(Bottle shows method of adjusting a cord holder of sheet metal.)

boiler (Fig. 3), set the filled bottles (ordinary glass fruit jars are just as good) in it, fill in with water around the

Grape Juice

bottles to within about an inch of the tops and gradually heat until it is about to simmer. Then take the bottles out and cork or seal immediately. It is a good idea to take the further precaution of sealing the corks over with sealing wax or paraffin to prevent mold germs from entering through the corks. Should it be desired to make a red juice, heat the crushed grapes to not above 200°

Fig. 4.—Drip Bag

F., strain through a clean cloth or drip bag, as shown in Fig. 4 (no pressure should be used), set away to cool and settle and proceed the same as with light-colored juice. Many people do not even go to the trouble of letting the juice settle after straining it, but reheat and seal it up immediately, simply setting the vessels away in a cool place in an upright position where they will be undisturbed. The juice is thus allowed to settle, and when wanted for use the clear juice is simply taken off the sediment. Any person familiar with the process of canning fruit can also preserve grape juice, for the principles involved are identical.

One of the leading defects so far found in unfermented juice is that much of it is not clear, a condition which very much detracts from its otherwise attractive appearance and due to two causes already alluded to. Either the final sterilization in bottles has been at a higher tempera-

Beverages—Non-Alcoholic

ture than the preceding one or the juice has not been properly filtered or has not been filtered at all. In other cases the juice has been sterilized at such a high temperature that it has a disagreeable, scorched taste. It should be remembered that attempts to sterilize at a temperature above 195° F. are dangerous, so far as the flavor of the finished product is concerned.

Another serious mistake is sometimes made by putting the juice into bottles so large that much of it becomes spoiled before it is used after the bottles are opened. Unfermented grape juice properly made and bottled will keep indefinitely, if it is not exposed to the atmosphere or mold germs; but when a bottle is once opened it should, like canned goods, be used as soon as possible, to keep it from spoiling.

Grape Juice Formulas

1.—The juice as it comes, being too sweet to drink should be prepared by the following formula and kept on ice ready to serve: Bottled grape juice, 2 pt.; water, 2 pt. A small amount of cracked ice should be added.

2.—Make a plain soda lemonade and only fill the glass within 1 inch of the top. Over this pour carefully ½ inch of the pure grape juice. This is a delicious drink.

3.—Put in the bottom of a wineglass 2 tablespoonfuls of grape juice; add to this the beaten white of 1 egg and a little chopped ice; sprinkle sugar over the top and serve. This is often served in sanitariums.

Bohemian Cream.—One pt. thick cream, 1 pt. grape-juice jelly; stir together; put in cups and set on ice. Serve with lady fingers.

Besides the recipes just given many more are enumerated, such as grape ice, grape lemonade, grape water ice, grape juice and egg, baked bananas, snow pudding, grape gelatine, junket and grape jelly, tutti-frutti jelly, grape float, grape jelly, grape juice plain, grape soda water and scores of others.

Cocktail.—Don't Care syrup, 1½ oz.; grape juice, 3 oz.; half 12-oz. glass of shaved ice and soda water to

Grape Juice

fill. Finish with maraschino cherries and serve with straws and spoon.   Ap.

Egg Phosphate.—Grape syrup, 1 oz.; egg, 1; phosphate, 3 dashes; 1 teaspoonful of ice. Shake and proceed in making an egg phosphate.

Grape Cup.—Grape juice, 1 pt.; English breakfast tea (concentrated), 1 oz.; prepared lime juice, 4 oz.; acid solution phosphate, ½ oz.; 1 pint water. Add a lump of ice and let stand until cold. Fill glass three-quarters full and fill with plain soda as it is served.

Lemonade.—Fill glass two-thirds full of fine ice; juice of 1 lemon; grape syrup, 1½ oz.; shake and fill with soda. Decorate with slice of lemon.

Malted Grape.—Make a malted syrup, using 12 oz. of extract of malt and 6 oz. of simple syrup. To serve, use 1¼ oz. of this syrup, ½ oz. of pure Concord grape juice and fill the glass with soda.

Nectar.—Take the juice of 2 lemons and 1 orange, 1 pt. of grape juice, 1 small cup of sugar and 1 pt. of water. Serve ice cold. If served from punch bowl, iced lemon and orange add to the appearance.

Pineapple.—Into a 12-oz. glass draw 1½ oz. of pineapple syrup and add 2 oz. of Concord grape juice, 1 oz. of sweet cream and a little finely shaved ice. Shake thoroughly and add enough carbonated water to fill the glass, using the fine stream mostly. Strain into a clean glass and serve.

Punch.—1.—Boil together 1 lb. of sugar and ½ pt. of water until it spins a thread; take from the fire and when cold add the juice of 6 lemons and 1 qt. of grape juice. Stand aside overnight. Serve with plain water, apollinaris or soda water.

2.—Into a 12-oz. glass, 2 oz. plain syrup, fill glass half full fine shaved ice, 3 oz. grape juice, fill glass with carbonated water, stir and top off with slice pineapple or orange.

3.—Fill glass two-thirds full of shaved ice; grape juice, 1 oz.; orange syrup, 1 oz.; lemon juice, 1 dash;

Beverages—Non-Alcoholic

Jamaica ginger, 1 dash. Fill with soda, mix and decorate with a slice of pineapple and cherry.

4.—Pineapple syrup, 1 oz.; pure grape juice, 1 oz.; lime juice, 3 dashes. Two-thirds glass of ice. Fill with soda and decorate with a slice of pineapple.

5.—Lemon syrup, 1 oz.; grape juice, 1 oz.; orange water ice, 1 scoop. Shake and fill glass with soda. Serve still and decorate with a slice of lemon and orange.

6.—Into a 12-oz. glass draw 1½ oz. of grape syrup, 1 oz. of grape juice. Add 3 dashes of lemon juice. Fill one-third full of orange water ice and balance with carbonated water. Mix and decorate.

7.—Into a 12-oz. glass draw 1½ oz. of orange syrup. Into this squeeze the juice of ½ lemon and add 1 oz. of grape juice. Fill one-third full of ice and balance with carbonated water. Mix and decorate.

Sherbet.—Orange syrup, 2 fl.oz.; grape juice, 2 fl.oz. Draw into a 12-oz. glass, half fill the latter with shaved ice, then fill it with plain water, stir with a spoon and serve with straws.

For 8 persons mix 1 pt. of grape juice (unfermented), juice of lemon and 1 heaping tablespoonful of gelatine, dissolved in boiling water; freeze quickly; add beaten white of 1 egg just before finish.

Syllabub.—Fresh cream, 1 qt.; whites of 4 eggs; grape juice, 1 glass; powdered sugar, 2 small cups; whip half the sugar with the cream, the balance with the eggs; mix well; add grape juice and pour over sweetened strawberries and pineapples or oranges and bananas. Serve cold.

Chapter IX.

ICE CREAM BEVERAGES

For Fountains

Banana

1.—Slice a banana in two. Place a spoonful of vanilla ice cream in the center and top off with maraschino cherries and pour cherry syrup over it.

2.—Into a 12-oz. glass draw 1 oz. of sweet cream and 1 oz. of vanilla syrup; into this slice half a banana; add a portion of ice cream; shake thoroughly, then fill the glass with soda, using the fine stream only. Pour without straining into a clean glass and top off with whipped cream. Serve with a spoon.

3.—Peel and split a banana, lay both halves together on the bottom of a large saucer. On the top of the banana put a cone-shaped measure of ice cream and over this pour a little crushed pineapple, a few powdered nuts, a spoonful of whipped cream. Top with a cherry.

4.—Split a banana lengthwise and cover with a portion of 3 kinds of ice cream and 1 water ice, so arranging the ice cream as to make the colors contrast nicely.

Cantaloupe

1.—Take ½ cantaloupe, cut off a piece of bottom so it will stand, add a No. 12 scoop of vanilla cream, and, if possible, watermelon ice. If this is impossible, substitute what water ice you may have on hand. Over this pour 1 ladle of crushed raspberries, top with nuts, whipped cream and a cherry and place mint leaves on the side.

2.—Cut a cantaloupe in halves, take out the seeds

and fill in with ice cream, grate nutmeg over it. Serve on thin china dish with soda spoon. The cantaloupe should be kept ready ice cold.

Celery Cocoa Cream

One oz. chocolate paste, 1 oz. cream, 4 dashes essence of celery. Stir while filling up with hot soda. Top off with whipped cream and serve with celery salt.

Cherry Cream

Spoonful ice cream in 8-oz. stem glass. Almost fill with shaved ice. Add 2 oz. cherry syrup, top with layer of ice cream and add a maraschino cherry.

Chocolate

Put the proper amount of chocolate syrup into the glass. Then run in enough carbonated water to half fill the glass. Next put in a lump of vanilla ice cream the size of an egg. Then draw on the fine stream of carbonated water and top off the whole with a tall, foaming billow of whipped cream.

Cream Puff

Break a fresh egg into a shaker, draw an ounce of orange syrup, add a good-sized spoonful of ice cream and shake very thoroughly. Then without straining fill the shaker with fine stream. Pour from shaker to glass, top with grated nutmeg and serve with a straw. Chocolate Cream Puff and Coffee Cream Puff may be made by using the syrups named instead of orange.

Creamade

Juice from ½ lime; orange syrup, 1 oz.; pineapple syrup, 1 oz.; cream, 2 oz.; ice cream, ½ oz. Shake, fill the glass with the fine stream and top with a slice of pineapple.

Ice Cream Beverages

Cucumber à la Surprise

Line the halves of a long cucumber mold with a good-colored (not over-colored) green gage or other green water ice and fill in with lemon ice cream. Close the mold and freeze in the usual manner. Serve plain on a white china dish. In the season 1 or 2 natural leaves may be used on the dish under the cucumber.

Fig Soufflé

Cut a large fig into quarters, mix with vanilla ice cream and serve in a stem ice cream glass.

Fruit

1.—Shaved ice, ½ tumbler; ice cream, 1 tablespoonful; pure milk, 1 oz.; extract of vanilla, 1 dash; crushed strawberry, 1 teaspoonful; crushed pineapple, 1 teaspoonful; crushed raspberry, 1 teaspoonful; Catawba syrup, 1½ oz. Shake well, then add plain soda. Ap.

2.—Crushed strawberries, ½ oz.; crushed peaches, ½ oz.; ice cream to fill small glass.

Ice Cream Shake

One egg, 1 oz. marshmallow syrup, small quantity of ice cream,

Maple

In a large shaking glass put 4 oz. ice cream, 2 oz. maple syrup and 1 oz. plain cream. Shake and when thoroughly shaken fill with fine stream.

Marshmallow

Orange flower water, 4 oz.; gum arabic, 12 dr.; extract vanilla, ½ oz.; syrup, q. s. 8 pt. Mix. Serve with ice cream.

Nut Bamboo Soufflé

Ladle ice cream on fancy plate; add 1½ oz. coffee syrup and shredded cocoanut mixed; dress with whipped cream, whole dates, seeded and fancy whole cherries.

Beverages—Non-Alcoholic

Orange

Shaved ice, ½ tumblerful; 1 egg; vanilla syrup, 1 oz.; orange syrup, 1 oz.; ice cream, 1 tablespoonful. Fill the glass nearly full of cream, shake well and add a little soda water.

Peach

1.—Two oz. raspberry syrup, 2 tablespoonfuls peach ice cream. Serve as ice-cream soda.

2.—Peel about 1 doz. ripe, yellow, good-flavored peaches; slice fine into a dish and cover with about as much sugar as you have of fruit. Mash together thoroughly until the sugar is dissolved, then add an equal amount of simple syrup. This mixture will not keep fresh for more than 2 days. Serve as ice-cream soda.

3.—Shaved ice, ½ tumblerful; ice cream, 1 tablespoonful; fresh cream, 1 oz.; extract of peach, 1 dash; crushed peach, 1 tablespoonful; peach syrup, 1 oz.; plain soda (fine stream), 1 tumblerful.

Pineapple

Pineapple syrup, 2 oz.; cream, 2 oz.; 1 egg; ice cream 1 large ladle. Cinnamon may be added if desired. Shake and serve with slice of pineapple.

Sandwiches

Take lady fingers, separate and spread ice cream, either vanilla, lemon or strawberry, between each slice; place together and serve on plate.

Chapter X.

LEMON, LIME, MINT, ETC.

TAKE a little cracked ice and squeeze the juice of 2 limes. Add powdered sugar q. s. and 1 egg. Shake well together and strain into a glass and fill up with carbonic water. Cover top with cracked ice and insert 2 or 3 stalks of mint. Add a touch of nutmeg and 1 or 2 strawberries, or try the following.

Juice of half an orange, juice of half a lemon, 2 tablespoonfuls pineapple juice, 2 tablespoonfuls powdered sugar, ½ glass crushed ice. Fill glass with water, shake well and serve with straws.

Lemon

1.—Peel off the yellow rinds from 1 doz. fresh lemons, taking care that none of the rind is detached, but the yellow zest—that portion in which the cells are placed containing the essential oil of the fruit. Put these rinds into an earthen vessel, pour over them 1 qt. of boiling water and set aside in a warm situation to infuse. Express the juice from 2 doz. lemons, strain it into a porcelain bowl and add 2 lb. of fine white sugar, 3 qt. water and the infusion from the peels. Stir all well together until the sugar is completely dissolved. Now sample and if required add more acid or more sugar; take care not to have it too watery; make it rich with plenty of fruit juice and sugar.

2.—To the juice of 6 lemons and the yellow rind of 2 lemons add ½ lb. of sugar and 1 qt. of water. Ice the

Beverages—Non-Alcoholic

lemonade. Water may be added according to taste afterward.

3.—Peel off the rind, cut the lemon in two and squeeze the juice into a glass, add 2 tablespoonfuls powdered sugar, chipped ice and water; shake well and strain into a thin glass in which a little shaved ice has been placed; decorate with fruits and serve with straws. Soda lemonade may be made by adding soda water in place of plain water.

4.—Strain the juice of 1 lemon into ½ pt. of cold water, sweeten to taste, then stir in ¼ teaspoonful carbonate of soda, and drink while the mixture is in an effervescing state.

Apollinaris.—Juice of 1 lemon; powdered sugar, 1 spoonful; cracked ice, ¼ glass. Shake, strain and fill with Apollinaris water, add 2 cherries and slice of lemon.

Artificial.—1.—Loaf sugar, 2 lb.; tartaric acid, ½ oz.; essence of lemon, 30 drops; essence of almonds, 20 drops. Dissolve the tartaric acid in 2 pt. hot water, add the sugar and lastly the lemon and almond; stir well, cover with a cloth and leave until cold; put 2 tablespoonfuls into a tumbler and fill up with cold water. When lemons are cheap it never pays to bother with a substitute. The addition of a very little bicarbonate of potash to each tumblerful just before drinking will give a wholesome effervescing drink.

2.—Succus Limonium Factitius.—Citric or tartaric acid 2¼ oz.; gum, ½ oz.; pieces of fresh lemon peel, ¾ oz.; loaf sugar, 2 oz.; boiling water, 1 qt.; macerate with occasional agitation till cold and strain. Excellent.

3.—Water, 1 pt.; sugar, 1 oz.; essence of lemon, 30 drops; pure acetic acid to acidulate. Inferior. Both are used to make lemonade.

Boiled Lemonade.—1.—The juice of 3 lemons, 5 tablespoonfuls of sugar and 1 cupful boiling water added to the lemons and sugar. Set aside to cool. When ready for use, put in lemonade glasses with cracked ice and dilute with water.

Lemon, Lime, Mint, Etc.

2.—Allow 3 lemons to each qt. of water and about ½ lb. of sugar. Have the lemons perfectly clean, cut 2 thin slices from the center of each and lay aside. Chip off some of the thin yellow rind from several of the lemons and squeeze out the juice, pressing hard enough to extract some of the flavor of the skin. Put the juice, the clipped rind and the sugar in a large bowl; then pour on the desired amount of boiling water. Let it stand until cold, put away in the ice chest and when ready to serve fill the glasses one-third full of cold water or chipped ice; add the lemon water and a slice of the cut lemon. A maraschino cherry may be added.

Claret.—One-third glass cracked ice, 1 lemon, 2 oz. claret syrup. Shake well and add a glassful of plain soda. Stir, strain and add 1 slice lemon. Serve with 2 straws.

Diabetic Lemonade.—Citric acid, 5 grams; glycerine, 20 to 30 grams; water, 1,000 c.c.

Egg.—1.—Break 1 egg into a glass, beat it slightly, then add 1 dessertspoonful of lemon-juice; sugar to taste. 1 tablespoonful of crushed ice and a little cold water. Shake well until sufficiently cooled, then strain into another glass, fill up with iced water, sprinkle a little nutmeg on the top and serve.

2.—Break 1 egg in mixing glass, use 1 or 2 lemons, simple syrup to taste. Shake well with ice. Use fine stream of soda and serve in bell glass with nutmeg or cinnamon.

3.—Beat the white of an egg light and add to plain lemonade.

4.—Pour a pint of boiling water over a cup of sugar, the juice of 4 lemons and the thin, yellow rind of 2; cool, then chill. Beat the yolks of 4 eggs until lemon-colored and thick, and then the whites until stiff. Mix them thoroughly; add the lemon water and a pint of fine chipped ice or ice-cold water and serve.

Fruit.—Crush 6 fine strawberries or raspberries well, add 1 teaspoonful of powdered sugar, small or otherwise according to taste, the juice of 1 lemon, a little cold water

Beverages—Non-Alcoholic

and strain into a tumbler. Add a little crushed ice, fill up with cold water and serve.

Lemon Squash.—This is made in the same manner as lemonade, only leaving in the crushed halves of the lemon.

Milk.—1.—Dissolve ¾ lb. loaf sugar in 1 pt. boiling water and mix with 1 gill lemon juice and 1 gill sherry; then add 3 gills cold milk. Stir the whole well together and then strain it.

2.—Take 4 lemons, pare the rind as thin as possible; squeeze them into 1 qt. water, add ½ lb. fine sugar; let it stand 2 or 3 hours and pass it through a jelly bag.

3.—Effervescing (without a machine).—Put into each bottle 2 dr. sugar, 2 drops essence of lemon, ½ dr. bicarbonate potash, and water to fill the bottle; then drop in 35 or 40 gr. of citric or tartaric acid in crystals and cork immediately, placing the bottles in a cool place or preferably in iced water.

4.—Sesquicarbonate of soda, 2 scruples; sugar, 2 dr.; essence of lemon, 4 drops; water, ½ pt.; lastly, 8 dr. tartaric acid, in crystals. Care must be taken to avoid accidents from the bursting of the bottles.

5.—Into a soda-water bottle nearly filled with water put 1 oz. sugar; essence of lemon (dropped on the sugar), 2 drops; bicarbonate of potash in crystals, 20 gr., and, lastly, 30 to 40 gr. of citric acid, also in crystals. Cork immediately.

Pineapple.—1.—Carefully boil 1 lb. of sugar in 1 qt. of water until it forms a thin syrup, removing all scum as it rises. Set it to cool. Meantime squeeze the juice of 4 lemons into a dish. Peel a large, ripe pineapple, remove the eyes and grate it into a large punch bowl. Add the lemon juice and stir it well through the pineapple. Then stir in the syrup. Let the mixture stand a couple of hours and then add 1 qt. of ice water. Put a big lump of ice in a punch bowl, strain the mixture through a fine sieve into the bowl, ornament the top with cut fruits and serve in glass cups.

Lemon, Lime, Mint, Etc.

2.—For pineapple lemonade use the juice of 4 small lemons, a can of shredded pineapple, a cupful of sugar and 4 cupfuls of water. Make a syrup of the sugar and water and cool it before adding the lemon juice.

Preservation of Lemon Juice.—Agitate a prolonged time with finest powdered talcum, filter, add sugar, boil and then fill hot into bottles and seal while still hot.

Powder.—1.—Take 1 oz. crystallized citric acid, rub it fine and mix thoroughly with 1 lb. dry pulverized white sugar. Put in a single drop of oil of lemon peel to flavor it and mix well; preserve in bottles for future use. In place of citric acid you may take tartaric acid.

2.—Tartaric acid, 1 oz.; powdered sugar 4 oz.; essence of lemon, fine, 1 dram. Mix these ingredients well together, spread them on a plate, stir and turn over repeatedly until thoroughly dry. Divide into 20 equal portions, wrap them carefully in separate papers and store for use in an air-tight tin. Each portion is sufficient for 1 glass of lemonade.

Seltzer.—Take the juice of 1 lemon with ½ glass of chipped ice, 1 oz. of lemon syrup made from the fruit and 1 teaspoonful powdered sugar. Draw on about 2 oz. of soda and stir well until the sugar is dissolved. Strain into a tall mineral glass and fill with soda, using the fine stream to stir. Serve while foaming. If you have no freshly made lemon syrup cut 2 or 3 slices of the lemon rind into the glass when mixing. The powdered sugar must be used to give "life" to the drink.

Lime

1.—Lime fruit syrup, ½ oz.; lemon syrup, ½ oz.; solution acid phosphate, 1 dram; shaved ice, 2 oz. Mix with soda, stir thoroughly, strain into 8-oz. glass, fill slowly with coarse stream and stir again.

2.—Pure lemon syrup, 1 oz.; lime juice, ½ oz. Pour over fine ice in mineral glass, fill up with soda and stir.

3.—Into a 13-oz. glass, tall and slender, draw 1½ oz.

Beverages—Non-Alcoholic

of grape juice, squeeze the juice of 1 lime and add 3 dashes of Angostura bitters, 2 dashes of phosphate and 1½ oz. of simple syrup. Fill the glass one-third full of fine ice and the balance with carbonated water. Mix and decorate.

Cordial.—Boric acid, ¼ oz.; citric acid, 2 oz.; sugar, 3 lb.; water, 2 pt. Dissolve by heat, When cold add lime juice, 30 oz.; tincture of lemon, 2 oz.; water to 1 gal. Mix and color with caramel.

Pepsin.—Pure pepsin, 260 gr.; distilled water, 3 oz.; glycerine, 3 oz.; alcohol, 1½ oz.; purified talcum, ½ oz.; lime juice enough to make 1 pt. Dissolve the pepsin in the water mixed with 8 fl.oz. of lime juice, add the glycerine and alcohol and then the remainder of the lime juice; incorporate the talcum and set aside for several days, agitating occasionally, and then filter, adding through the filter enough lime juice to make 1 pt. of finished product. To make a syrup of this add enough simple syrup to make 3 qt. and mix thoroughly.

Vichy.—Into an 8-oz. glass of vichy shake a few dashes of lime juice from your spirit bottle, or squeeze into it the fresh juice of half a lime.

Orange

1.—The juice of 15 oranges, the rind of 3 oranges, 2 qt. of water, ¾ lb. of loaf sugar, crushed ice. Remove the peel of 3 oranges as thinly as possible, add it and the sugar to 1 pt. of water, then simmer gently for 20 minutes. Strain the orange juice into a glass jug, and add the remaining 3 pt. of cold water. As soon as the syrup is quite cold strain it into the jug, add a handful of crushed ice and serve at once.

2.—Slice crosswise 4 oranges and 1 lemon; put them into an earthen jug with 4 oz. of lump sugar; pour upon these 1 qt. of boiling water and allow to stand covered for 1 hour. Decant and ice.

3.—Simple syrup, ½ fl.oz.; tincture of orange peel, ½

Lemon, Lime, Mint, Etc.

dr.; citric acid, 1 scruple; fill the bottle with aerated water.

4.—Lemon juice, 1 oz.; orange juice, 2 oz.; granulated sugar, 4 teaspoonfuls; shaved ice, ½ glass. Mix in some soda by stirring, strain into 12-oz. glass and fill with coarse stream of carbonated water.

Effervescing, or Aerated, or Sherbet.—a.—Mix 1 lb. of syrup of orange peel, 1 gal. water and 1 oz. citric acid, charge strongly with carbonic-acid gas with a machine.

b.—Syrup orange juice, ¾ oz.; aerated water, ½ pt.

c.—Mix 1 lb. syrup of orange peel, 1 gal. water, and 1 oz. citric acid and charge it strongly with carbonic-acid gas with a machine.

d.—Syrup of orange juice, ¾ fl.oz.; aerated water, ½ pt.

Raspberry

1.—Add to 1 qt. fresh ripe berries the juice of 1 lemon and 1 tart orange. Bruise with a wooden spoon, add 1 pt. of water and let it stand an hour; meanwhile boil ¾ lb. of sugar with 1 qt. of boiling water and let this become cold. Rub the fruit through a fine sieve; add to the syrup and serve with shaved ice in glasses or simply chilled. Currants may be used in the same way.

2.—Raspberry vinegar, 2 oz.; sugar, 1 tablespoonful. Fill 8-oz. glass with coarse stream.

Chapter XI.

MALT BEVERAGES

Cherry

MALT extract, 8 oz.; tincture celery seed, 2 dr.; orange syrup, 4 oz.; comp. tincture gentian, 1 dr.; lemon syrup, to make 2 pt. Mix and serve 1 oz. in an 8-oz. mineral glass, with or without phosphate.

Coca

1.—Fluid extract coca, 1 oz.; alcohol, 1 oz.; extract malt, to make 4 pt.

2.—Extract malt, 4 oz.; coca cordial, 1 oz.; cherry syrup, 10 oz. Mix. Trim with fresh cherry.

3.—Extract malt, 4 oz.; coca cordial, 1 oz.; syrupy phosphoric acid, ½ dr.; lemon syrup, 10 oz. Mix. Trim with sliced lemon.

4.—Draw 1 oz. of coca wine syrup into an 8-oz. glass, add 1 oz. of malt extract, a couple of dashes of phosphate and fill with soda. If desired, the phosphate may be omitted.

C—K—

1.—Malt extract, 8 oz.; vanilla extract, 1 dr.; orange syrup, 2 oz.; cinnamon syrup, 2 oz.; coca-kola, 2 oz.; simple syrup, 18 oz. This can be served with foam in 12-oz. glass or in 8-oz. glass.

2.—Extract of malt, 2 lb.; kola wine syrup, 3 pt.; coca wine syrup, 1 pt.; cinchona wine syrup, 1 pt; pure orange wine, 1 pt.; spirit of rose, ¼ fl.oz.; acid solution of phos-

Malt Beverages

phate, 8 fl.oz. The kola wine syrup is made by adding 2 pt. of kola wine to 3 pt. of simple syrup. The coca wine syrup is made by adding 2 pt. of coca wine to 3 pt. of simple syrup.

3.—Malt extract, 8 oz.; coca-kola syrup, 24 oz. Serve still in 8-oz. glass with or without phosphate. Coca-kola syrup for the above is composed as follows: Fluid extract of kola, 2 oz.; elixir of calisaya, 3 oz.; wine of coca, 6 oz.; extract of vanilla, 4 dr.; fruit acid, 1 oz.; syrup enough to make 1 gal.

Fruit

Malt extract, 12 oz.; raspberry syrup, 2 oz.; cinnamon syrup, 2 oz.; rose syrup, 2 oz.; orange flower water, 2 dr.; orange syrup, 12 oz. Serve with or without phosphate.

Iron Malt

Extract of malt, 8 oz.; elixir of beef, iron and wine, 8 oz.; pineapple syrup, 8 oz.; simple syrup, 1 pt. Mix and serve still in an 8-oz. mineral glass.

Kola

1.—Malt extract, 6 oz.; pineapple juice, 4 dr.; fluid extract kola, 2 dr.; extract vanilla, 2 dr.; fruit acid, 2 dr.; lemon syrup, 25 oz. May be served still or foamed, with or without phosphate.

2.—Make same as the cocoa malt, using any tonic syrup containing the fluid extract of kola nuts.

Malt Wine Cordial

Malt wine, 8 oz.; orange syrup, 24 oz. Serve solid in 8-oz. glass.

Chapter XII.

MALTED MILK AND MEAD

How to Prepare Malted Milk

THE following method is recommended by the editor of *Modern Medicine:* To a pint of milk add 1 tablespoonful of malt. The milk may be heated to a temperature of 60° F. After that it should be brought to a boiling point and boiled for 20 to 30 minutes. This will check the further action of the malt. Milk thus treated does not form large, hard curds in the stomach and agrees perfectly with many persons who cannot digest milk in its ordinary form. This method of peptonizing milk is much preferable to the old way, in which various preparations of pancreatin were employed; these animal substances not infrequently imparted a very unpleasant flavor and odor and sometimes poisonous substances. Owing to the present difficulty in buying malted milk the manufactured article is recommended.

1.—Put a tablespoonful in a shaker, fill half full with cold water, shake thoroughly, strain into a 12-oz. glass and fill with fine stream. Cracked ice may be used if desired.

2.—Malted milk, 1 tablespoonful; pepper and salt or sugar; water, 8 oz.

3.—Vanilla syrup, 2 teaspoonfuls; uncharged water or milk, 2 tablespoonfuls; cream, plain, 2 tablespoonfuls; cracked ice, sufficient; malted milk, 1 tablespoonful. Put in a shaker, shake thoroughly, strain and fill glass with plain soda, fine stream.

4.—Malted milk, 2 oz.; plain cream, 1 oz.; plain water, ice cold, to fill 10-oz. glass. Shake well and top off with

Malted Milk

whipped cream and grated nutmeg if desired, or serve plain. Cracked ice may be used, but the cold water makes a better, creamier drink.

Cocoa

Chocolate syrup, 1 oz.; plain cream, 1 oz.; shaved ice, sufficient; plain water, 2 oz.; malted milk, 2 tablespoonfuls. Put in a shaker, shake thoroughly, strain and fill glass with fine stream.

Coffee Syrup

Prepare a syrup of 8 oz. malted milk, 16 oz. sugar, 2½ oz. coffee extract, 24 oz. water. Dissolve malted milk and coffee in water. Strain, cool, add coffee extract and color with caramel.

Coffee Punch

Malted milk coffee syrup, 2 oz.; shaved ice, ½ glass; milk, ½ oz. Fill 12-oz. glass with soda and sprinkle on nutmeg.

Egg

1.—Vanilla syrup, 1 oz.; plain cream, 1 oz.; 1 egg; shaved ice, sufficient; plain water, 2 oz.; malted milk, 2 tablespoonfuls. Put in shaker, shake thoroughly, strain and fill glass with fine stream and sprinkle with nutmeg.

2.—Put 1 egg in mixing glass; vanilla syrup, 1 to 2 oz.; plain cream, 3 oz.; malted milk, 2½ teaspoonfuls. Shake well with ice. Use fine stream only and serve in bell glass.

3.—Coffee or chocolate syrup, 1½ oz.; 1 egg; sweet cream, 1 oz.; malted milk, 2 teaspoonfuls; shaved ice. Shake thoroughly and fill with soda, using fine stream mostly.

4.—Plain syrup, ½ oz.; sherry wine, 1 tablespoonful; 1 egg; cream, ½ oz.; sufficient ice; malted milk, 1 tablespoonful. Put in shaker, shake thoroughly, fill glass with heavy and fine stream; strain into 12-oz. thin glass.

5.—One egg; malted milk, 1 teaspoonful; clam bouillon, ½ oz.; hock syrup, 1 oz.; cracked ice, ¼ tumblerful. Shake well, strain and add 1 dash of liquid phosphate,

Beverages—Non-Alcoholic

filling with plain soda. Pour from shaker to tumbler and serve with nutmeg and straw.

Hot Malted Milk

Malted milk, 1 dessertspoonful; hot soda, 1 cupful. Season with pepper and salt.

Ice Cream

Vanilla syrup, 2 teaspoonfuls; uncharged water or milk, 4 oz. or 1/3 glass; ice cream, 2 tablespoonfuls; Horlick's malted milk, 1 tablespoonful. Put in a shaker, shake thoroughly, strain and fill glass with plain soda, fine stream.

Milk Orange

Orange syrup, 2 teaspoonfuls; uncharged water or milk, 4 oz. or 1/3 glass; cracked ice, sufficient; eggs, 1 or 2; Horlick's malted milk, 1 tablespoonful. Put in shaker, shake thoroughly, strain and fill glass with plain soda.

Syrup

Malted milk, 8 oz.; hot water, 8 oz.; simple syrup, 4 pt.

MEAD

Mead is an old-fashioned beverage, but a very pleasant one, if care is taken in making it. It is generally made overstrong, too much honey being used to the proportion of water.

1.—On 30 lb. honey (clarified) pour 13 gal. soft water, boiling hot. Clarify with the whites of eggs, well beaten; boil again, remove all scum as it rises, add 1 oz. of best hops and boil for 10 minutes, then pour the liquor into a tub to cool, spreading a slice of toast on both sides with yeast, and putting it into the tub when the liquor is nearly cold. The tub should stand in a warm room. When fermentation has thoroughly begun, pour the mixture into a cask, and as it works off, fill up the cask, keeping back some of the liquor for this purpose. Bung down closely when fermentation has ceased, leaving a peg hole, which can be

Mead

closed up in a few days. Let it remain a year in the cask before bottling off.

2.—Water, 10 gal.; strained honey, 2 gal.; burned white ginger, 3 oz. troy; lemons, sliced, 2. Mix all together and boil for half an hour, carefully skimming all the time. Five minutes after the boiling commences add 2 oz. troy of hops; when partially cold put it into a cask to work off. In about 3 weeks it will be fit to bottle.

3.—Cherry juice, 1 pt.; rose syrup, 4 oz.; cinnamon water syrup, 8 oz.; mead extract, 4 oz.; fruit acid, ½ oz. Mix thoroughly with 6 pt. of simple syrup.

4.—Mead extract, 8 oz.; Angostura bitters, 12 oz.; honey, ½ gal.; rock candy syrup, 1½ gal.; tartaric (or citric) acid, 1 oz.; water, 4 oz.

5.—Tonka beans, 2 dr.; mace, 2 dr.; cloves, 1 oz.; cinnamon, 1 oz.; ginger, 1 oz.; nutmeg, 1 oz.; pimento, ½ oz.; sassafras bark, 3 oz.; lemon gratings, 1 oz.; orange gratings, 1 oz. Bruise the drugs in a mortar or grind them very coarse and tie them loosely in a cheesecloth or muslin bag. Suspend them in 2 gal. of simple syrup and heat to 80° C. for a few hours, the longer the better, providing the temperature is not too high. The sassafras and pimento should be boiled in 2½ pt. of water until it has boiled down to about 1½ pt. Filter and add 2 pt. of honey and then mix with the other syrup. Add syrup enough to make 2½ gal. and filter through a felt filter bag.

6.—*Coloring Mead.*—Mead syrups may all be colored with caramel; when served they should look like a dark root beer.

7.—*Extract.*—Sarsaparilla, 2 lb.; lignum vitæ wood, 1 lb.; licorice root, 1 lb.; ginger root, 12 oz.; cinnamon bark, 12 oz.; coriander seed, 6 oz.; aniseed, 2 oz.; mace, 4 oz. Contuse or cut very finely and put up in 2 or 4 oz. packages.

8.—*Serving Mead.*—Into a 12-oz. glass draw 1½ to 2 oz. and fill within about an inch of the top with carbonated water. Mix by pouring and then foam by the use of a fine stream as in serving root beer.

Chapter XIII.

PHOSPHATES

PHOSPHATES for the soda fountain are a solution of acid phosphate with any of the fruit or flavored syrups, omitting the soda foam, as phosphates are served solid. To each gallon of flavored syrup 8 fl.oz. of acid phosphate is added.

Acid Phosphates

1.—Bone ash, 32 av.oz.; sulphuric acid, 24 av.oz.; water, sufficient to make 1 gal. Mix the bone ash with 2 pt. of water in a glass or earthenware or other container which is not acted upon by the acid; add the acid previously diluted with the remainder of the water and mix thoroughly. Set the mixture aside for 24 hours with occasional stirring, then transfer the same upon a strong muslin strainer and subject to pressure, avoiding contact with metals; add to the magma some water and let drain until 1 gal. of liquid has been obtained, then filter through paper.

2.—Phosphoric acid, 50 per cent., 64 parts; precipitated chalk, 12 parts; calcined magnesia, 1 part; potassium carbonate, 1 part; distilled water, 178 parts. Add the chalk to the acid gradually and then add the magnesia and stir well. Dissolve the potassium carbonate in 9 fl.oz. of the water, add the solution gradually to the acid liquor, admix the remainder of the water, set aside for 1 or 2 hours and filter.

3.—Phosphoric acid, 8 oz.; potassium phosphate, 80

Phosphates

gr.; magnesium phosphate, 160 gr.; sodium phosphate, 80 gr.; calcium phosphate, 240 gr.; water, to make 8 pt.

Apricot

Apricot syrup, 96 fl.oz.; peach syrup, 16 fl.oz.; orgeat syrup, 8 fl.oz.; solution acid phosphate, 8 fl.oz. Mix.

Calisaya

Elixir of calisaya, 16 fl.oz.; solution of acid phosphate, 8 fl.oz.; orange syrup, sufficient to make 1 gal. Mix.

Celery

1.—Celery essence (4 oz. to pint), 16 fl.oz.; solution acid phosphate, 8 fl.oz.; lemon syrup, sufficient to make 1 gal. Mix.

2.—Fluid extract of celery seed, 4 fl.oz.; solution acid phosphate, 8 fl.oz.; orange syrup, 32 fl.oz.; lemon syrup, sufficient to make 1 gal. Add the fluid extract of celery to the acid solution, let stand for several hours, pass through a wetted paper filter and mix with the syrups.

3.—Tincture celery seed, 1 oz.; pineapple juice, 8 oz.; juice of 1 lemon; simple syrup, q. s. 4 pt.

Cherry

1.—Solution of acid phosphate, 8 fl.oz.; cherry juice, red, 16 fl.oz.; raspberry juice, 8 fl.oz.; syrup, sufficient to make 1 gal. Mix.

2.—Solution of acid phosphate, 8 fl.oz.; wild cherry syrup, 32 fl.oz.; orange syrup, sufficient to make 1 gal. Mix.

3.—Wild Cherry.—a.—Solution of acid phosphate, 8 fl.oz.; cherry juice, any black, 8 fl.oz.; syrup of wild cherry U. S. P., 16 fl.oz.; oil of bitter almond, 10 drops; syrup, sufficient to make 1 gal. Mix.

b.—Essence bitter almond, 10 drops; acid phosphate, 12 oz.; fruit acid, 1 oz.; simple syrup, 3 qt.; caramel coloring, 1 dr.; cochineal coloring, ¼ dr.

Beverages—Non-Alcoholic

c.—Oil bitter almond, 6 drops; acid phosphate, 2½ oz.; caramel, 6 dr.; rock candy syrup, enough to make 2 pt. Dissolve the oil of bitter almond in ¼ oz. of alcohol and mix with the other ingredients.

Chocolate

Chocolate syrup, 1 oz., and cracked ice; add a little solution acid phosphate and fill with plain soda.

Coca

Fluid extract of coca, 1 fl.oz.; solution of acid phosphate, 8 fl.oz.; vanilla syrup, sufficient to make 1 gal. Add the fluid extract of coca to the acid solution, let stand for several hours, pass through a wetted paper filter and mix with syrup.

Cranberry

Cranberry syrup, 1 fl.oz.; solution acid phosphate, a teaspoonful plain soda, 7 oz. Mix and serve.

Egg

1.—Draw into a thin 9-oz. tumbler 2 oz. of Maltese (red) orange syrup and add an egg, a few squirts of acid phosphate and a small piece of ice; shake well, fill shaker with soda water—using the large stream only—and strain.

2.—Syrup lemon, ½ oz.; 1 fresh egg; solution acid phosphate, 1 dr. Serve the phosphate from an essence bottle.

Frozen Phosphate

Fill 8 or 9-oz. glass with finely shaved ice, add 3 dashes of solution of acid phosphate and nearly cover the ice with the desired syrup; serve with a spoon.

Fruit

1.—Solution of acid phosphate, 8 fl.oz.; cherry syrup 16 fl.oz.; pineapple syrup, 16 fl.oz.; raspberry syrup, 16

Phosphates

fl.oz.; strawberry syrup, 16 fl.oz.; orange syrup, 16 fl.oz.; lemon syrup, sufficient to make 1 gal. Mix.

2.—Into a mineral water (7 or 8 oz.) glass draw 1 to 1½ oz. of the specified fruit syrup, add 1 dr. dilute phosphoric acid or phosphate solution; in another glass draw plain carbonic-acid water and pour into the first tumbler or glass to fill it, avoiding foam. This is preferable to making a long line of varying fruit phosphate syrups.

Grape

1.—Solution of acid phosphate, 8 fl.oz.; grape juice, 16 fl.oz.; raspberry syrup, sufficient to make 1 gal.

2.—Grape juice, 1 oz.; orange syrup, 2 oz.; acid phosphate, 20 drops. Serve in a mineral glass.

Ginger

1.—Solut. ess. ginger, 2 oz.; solut. ess. lemon, ½ oz.; solut. acid phosphate, 8 oz.; syrup, 8 pt.

2.—Solution of acid phosphate, 8 fl.oz.; tincture of ginger, 4 fl.oz.; lemon syrup, sufficient to make 1 gal. Add the tincture of ginger to the acid solution, let stand for several hours and pass through a wetted paper filter and mix with the lemon syrup.

Kola

1.—Solution of acid phosphate, 8 fl.oz.; fluid extract of kola, 4 fl.oz.; vanilla syrup, sufficient to make 1 gal. Add the fluid extract of kola to the acid solution, let stand several hours, pass through a wetted paper filter and mix with the vanilla syrup.

2.—Fluid extract of kola, 1 oz.; soluble essence of lemon, ½ oz.; compound tinc. of vanilla, 6 dr.; acid solution of phosphate, 2 oz.; rock candy syrup, to 32 oz.

Lemon

1.—Lemon syrup, 7 pt.; pineapple syrup, 1 pt.; solut. acid phosphate, 8 fl.oz.

Beverages—Non-Alcoholic

2.—Solution of acid phosphate, 8 fl.oz.; lemon syrup, sufficient to make 1 gal. Mix.

3.—Ext. lemon, 1 fl.oz.; tinc. celery seed, 2 fl.oz.; pineapple juice, 8 fl.oz.; acid phosphate, 6 fl.oz.; syrup, to make 8 pt.

Mint

Spirit of spearmint, 2 fl.dr.; solution of acid phosphate, 2 fl.dr.; simple syrup, enough to make 32 fl.oz. The syrup may be colored a pale green by adding a tincture made by macerating spinach in alcohol.

Orange

1.—Solution of acid phosphate, 8 fl.oz.; orange syrup, sufficient to make 1 gal. Mix. Blood orange phosphate syrup may be prepared in the same manner by using blood orange syrup.

2.—Essence of orange (1-8), 1 to 4 fl.dr.; solution acid phosphate, 12 oz.; solution citric acid (50%), 1 oz.; caramel coloring, 1 dr.; cochineal coloring, 15 m. The quantities given are sufficient to flavor 1 gal. of syrup.

3.—Blood Orange.—Raspberry juice, 6 oz.; extract orange, 1½ oz.; fruit orange, ¾ oz.; syrup, 1 gal.; red coloring, enough. The addition of raspberry juice improves the orange flavor. The acid phosphate (1 dr.) is added when the drink is served.

4.—Cider.—A so-called orange cider phosphate may be made by adding to each gallon of finished product from the following formula about 4 oz. of dilute phosphoric acid or an equal quantity of solution of acid phosphates of the National Formulary.

Express the juice from sweet oranges, add water equal to the volume of juice obtained and macerate the expressed oranges with the juice and water for about 12 hours. For each gal. of juice add 1 lb. of granulated sugar, grape sugar or glucose, put the whole into a suitable vessel, covering to exclude the dust, place in a warm location until fermentation is completed, draw off the clear

Phosphates

liquid and preserve in well-stoppered stout bottles in a cool place.

Pepsin

1.—Essence of pepsin, 8 oz.; tincture of celery seed, 1 oz.; lemon syrup, enough to make 4 pt.

2.—Solution of pepsin, N. F., 8 oz.; raspberry syrup, 16 oz.; solution of acid phosphate, 4 oz.; syrup, enough to make 4 pt. Lime juice, orange, grape and other phosphates are similarly made.

Pineapple

1.—Take a large glass with the fruit and shaved ice about half full, add a little phosphate and draw on soda, stirring with the fine stream. It may be served as it is with straws or strain into a thin mineral glass.

2.—Solution of acid phosphate, 8 fl.oz.; orange syrup, 16 fl.oz.; vanilla syrup, 8 fl.oz.; pineapple syrup, sufficient to make 1 gal. Mix.

Raspberry

1.—Raspberry syrup, 1 gal.; solut. acid phosphate, 8 oz.; solut. ess. rose, ¼ oz.

Strawberry

1.—Strawberry syrup, 7 pt.; vanilla syrup, 8 oz.; pineapple syrup, 8 oz.; solut. acid phosphate, 8 oz.

2.—Solution of acid phosphate, 8 fl.oz.; pineapple syrup, 16 fl.oz.; strawberry syrup, sufficient to make 1 gal. Mix.

3.—Wild Strawberry.—a.—Strawberry syrup (from juice), 6 pt.; lemon syrup, 1 pt.; infusion wild cherry (fresh), 1 pt.; tartaric acid, 2½ dr. Dissolve the acid in the infusion and add, with the lemon syrup, to the syrup of strawberry. Serve without foam in thin mineral glasses.

b.—Strawberry syrup, 6 pt.; lemon syrup, 1 pt.; fresh infusion wild cherry, 1 pt.; tartaric acid, 2½ dr.

Beverages—Non-Alcoholic

Dissolve the acid in the infusion and add with the lemon syrup of strawberry. Serve without foam in thin mineral glasses.

Tangerine

Tangerine syrup, 7 pt.; pineapple syrup, 8 fl.oz.; muscatel wine, 8 fl.oz.; solut. acid phosphate, 8 fl.oz.

Chapter XIV.

PUNCHES

INTO a 12-oz. glass draw 1½ oz. of simple syrup. Into this squeeze the juice of 1 lemon and 1 orange. Fill 1-3 full of lemon ice and balance with carbonated water.

2.—Into a 12-oz. glass draw 1½ oz. of tonic syrup and break into it an egg. Add the juice of a small orange, an ounce of grape juice and a little fine shaved ice. Shake thoroughly and fill with carbonated water, the same as when making an egg phosphate. Strain into a clean glass and serve.

3.—Into a 14-oz. glass draw 2 oz. of pineapple syrup, 1 oz. of grape juice and ½ oz. of claret wine. Into this squeeze the juice of ½ of an orange and fill 1-3 full of fine ice. Fill with soda and mix with spoon, decorate with slice of an orange and 2 cherries on picks. Serve with straws.

4.—Into a 12-oz. glass draw ½ oz. of raspberry syrup, 1 oz. of lemon syrup and 1 oz. of claret wine (the wine can be replaced by grape juice). Into this squeeze the juice of ½ a lemon, fill glass 1-3 full of fine ice and the balance with carbonated water. Mix by stirring, decorate with a slice of lemon and serve with straws.

5.—Yolk of 1 egg; grape juice, 1 oz.; lemon juice, 2 dr.; powdered sugar, 2 teaspoonfuls. Mix well together: add the hot water, top off with whipped cream and serve with nutmeg and cinnamon.

6.—Into a 12-oz. glass draw ¾ oz. of raspberry, ¾ oz. of orange syrup and 1 oz. of grape juice. Into this squeeze the juice of ½ a lemon and fill 1-3 full of ice, then fill with soda water and mix. Into this put 2 cherries and 2 pineapple cubes on toothpicks. Serve with straws.

Cider

Chip the thin yellow rind from a lemon, bruise it slightly and add a cup of sherry wine. Let it stand an hour. Squeeze the juice of 1 lemon and 2 oranges over 1½ cups of granulated sugar, add a quart of cider that has a slight "nip," then pour over the lemon rind and sherry. Turn into a freezer and freeze same as water ice. Serve in glasses and over each pour a teaspoonful of brandy.

Claret

Claret syrup, ½ oz.; orange, 1 slice; lemon, 1 slice; shaved ice, ¼ glass. Fill 12-oz. glass with coarse stream, stir, decorate with fruit and serve with straws.

Coffee

Malted milk coffee syrup, 2 oz.; shaved ice, 2-3 glass; milk, 4 oz. Fill with plain soda, stir rapidly, serve spices to please.

Fruit

1.—The Pure Fruit Punches, without the addition of any kind of liquor, are made the same as any water ice, only keep the composition at 15° instead of 20°, and freeze only about half, in order to have the punch in a semiliquid state. You may add 2 to 3 whites of eggs for every 12 quarts of water ice.

2.—Into a 14-oz. glass draw 1 oz. of pineapple syrup, ½ oz. of raspberry syrup and ½ oz. of lemon syrup. Into this squeeze the juice of ½ a small grapefruit. Fill the glass 1-3 full of orange ice and the balance with carbonated water, mix and decorate with a slice of orange.

3.—In 3 pt. of water dissolve 1 lb. of sugar. Run through a felt filter bag and add ½ pt. of orange juice, ½ pt. of lemon juice, 4 oz. of either strawberry or raspberry con-

Punches

centrated syrup. Place in a punch bowl and ice. Add ½ pt. of fresh cut pineapple cubes and ¼ pt. of preserved fruits.

4.—Strawberry syrup, 2½ pt.; orange syrup, 2½ pt.; pineapple syrup, 2½ pt.; lemon juice, ½ pt. Mix well and strain. To 1½ oz. of this syrup add ¼ tumblerful of shaved ice, 3 strawberries, 1 slice of pineapple, 1 slice of orange and sufficient carbonated water to fill the glass.

5.—Strawberry syrup, orange syrup, pineapple syrup, raspberry syrup, of each 1 pt.; grape juice, 4 pt. Serve in mineral glass same as any syrup.

6.—Lemon syrup, 1 pt.; strawberry syrup, 1 pt.; orange syrup, 1 pt.; acid phosphate, ½ oz.; 1 sliced orange. Serve 1½ oz. in mineral water, add shaved ice. Fill glass with solid soda, top with maraschino cherries and serve with a straw.

7.—Into a 14-oz. glass draw ¾ oz. each of strawberry, orange and raspberry syrup. Into this squeeze the juice of ½ lemon. Fill 1-3 full of fine ice, add a spoonful of fruit salad and fill with carbonated water and mix.

8.—Lemons, 1 doz.; oranges, ½ doz.; grated pineapple, 1-3; sugar to taste; strain through sieve; add water enough to make 1 gal. Garnish with strawberries, raspberries or maraschino cherries.

Grape

1.—Grape juice, 2 oz.; sweet cream, 2 oz.; ice cream, 1 spoonful; bitters, 3 dashes. Shake thoroughly, strain, pour back into shaker and add soda to fill glass. Throw as for mixing egg drinks. Nutmeg may be added if desired.

2.—In an 8-oz. stem glass place 1 oz. of orange syrup, add ½ oz. of grape juice, a slice of lemon and cracked ice. Fill with soda and serve.

Mint

Put into a punch bowl 1 cup of granulated sugar and the juice of 6 lemons. Peel 3 lemons and slice them very thin. When the sugar has dissolved add the sliced lemon,

Beverages—Non-Alcoholic

1 doz. sprays of mint and an abundance of crushed ice. Now stir in 3 bottles of imported ginger ale and enough green vegetable coloring matter to make the punch of the desired green shade.

Orange

Grate the yellow rind from 2 oranges and add 1 lb. of white sugar and 1 pt. of water. Stir together until the sugar is entirely dissolved and boil 5 minutes after it comes to a boil. When cold add the juice of 1 lemon and the juice of 4 oranges. Pour over cracked ice and add about 1 qt. of clear water.

Pineapple

1.—Cut a peeled pineapple into small pieces and cover with a cup of sugar; stand until syrup is drawn out; then strain, squeezing hard, and set in ice. Serve in tiny glasses of crushed ice, adding a dash of maraschino to each glass as you pour in the pineapple syrup.

2.—To the juice of 6 lemons and 6 oranges add sugar to taste, with sliced pineapple and a few bits of lemon peel, 2 qt. of water and chopped ice to cool.

Pistachio

1.—Pistachio syrup, 1½ oz.; cream, 1 oz.; Jamaica rum, 3 dashes; crushed ice. Fill with soda, shake well, grate a little nutmeg on the top.

2.—Pistachio syrup, ½ oz.; lime juice syrup, ½ oz.; raspberry syrup, ½ oz.; ice cream, 3 oz.; ice, ½ glass. Shake, strain, toss and serve.

Raspberry

1.—Raspberry syrup, 1½ oz.; juice of ½ lemon; blackberry brandy, ½ oz. Fill 10-oz. glass half full shaved ice and fill with soda, adding small piece of lemon peel. Straws.

2.—Raspberry wine (unfermented), 2 oz.; lemon juice, 1 dash, drawn in 8-oz. mineral glass half full of shaved ice. Fill glass with plain soda, squeeze piece of lemon or orange rind into the punch and serve with cut straws.

Punches

Strawberry

Crush 1 qt. of ripe strawberries with ½ pt. of raspberries and strain the juice through a hair sieve. Make a syrup with 2 large cupfuls of sugar and 1½ cups of water. Mix with the juice and syrup a large glass of sweet port wine and keep on ice for several hours. Serve in small glasses with macaroons or lady fingers.

Tutti Frutti Punch

Boil for 5 minutes 1 qt. of water and 1 lb. of sugar. Add grated rinds of 2 lemons and 4 oranges and continue boiling for 5 minutes. Strain and add 1 qt. cold water. Extract the juice from the lemons and oranges, strain and mix with 1 lb. of seeded Malaga grapes, 2 sliced tangerine oranges, 4 slices pineapple, contents of 1 pt. bottle of maraschino cherries. Serve from a punch bowl in which a cube of ice has been placed.

Chapter XV.

SUNDAES

LADLE of ice cream; circle center with 6 peppermint wafers on toothpicks, lay on top cube of pineapple, small piece of sliced orange and a whole cherry.

2.—Ginger cordial syrup, mix with ginger fruit, pour over vanilla ice cream, sprinkle with cinnamon. Serve in sundae cup and top off with maraschino cherries.

3.—Place 5 macaroons around edge of saucer. Place a cone of vanilla ice cream (measured out with a 10-to-the-quart ice disher) in the center of the saucer. Over the ice cream pour ½ ladleful of pineapple fruit and 1 oz. of maple syrup. Top off with a small measure of maple sugar.

4.—In a 9-oz. stem glass place vanilla cream, 1 scoop; strawberry cream, 1 scoop; crushed pineapple, 1 oz.; crushed raspberries, 1 oz. Place a lady finger at each side in top of glass. Top with whipped cream and a cherry.

Cherry

Turn a measure of ice cream in a saucer champagne glass, pour over this several maraschino cherries and 1 oz. of cherry phosphate syrup. Serve with a spoon. Can be improved by adding a little whipped cream.

Chocolate

Strawberry syrup, 10 oz.; vanilla syrup, 10 oz.; raspberry syrup, 8 oz.; chocolate syrup, 4 oz. Pour a ladle of this sauce over plain ice cream.

Sundaes

Chop Suey for Sundaes

1.—Seeded raisins, ½ lb.; shredded cocoanut, 2 oz.; green cherries, 4 oz.; red cherries, 4 oz.; sliced pineapple, 4 oz.; dates, 4 oz. Chop and mix; add maple and cherry syrup, equal parts, to thin enough to serve; 2 oz. port wine and 2 oz. sherry wine add to the flavor.

2.—Half lb. of figs chopped into small pieces, ½ lb. of seeded dates cup up, 1 lb. of English walnuts broken, but not too fine. Add syrup enough to make 2 qt., color dark red. Fill a sundae glass 2-3 full of ice cream, pour over it a large ladle of chop suey, a little whipped cream and a cherry on top.

Dates Stuffed

Use soufflé dish; put 5 stuffed dates around ice cream; flavor with maraschino juice; top with whipped cream and cherries.

Nut Sundae

1.—Ice cream; sliced orange, cut in diamond-shaped pieces; sliced pineapple, cut in triangular shape; English walnuts; maraschino cherries. The nuts and fruit are to be arranged artistically and no syrup used.

2.—In a saucer place a No. 8 cone of vanilla ice cream. Around the ice cream place a ring of marshmallows, above this a ring of 6 walnut halves. Add 2 red and 2 green or white cherries and over all pour 1 oz. of grape juice. Serve N. wafers.

3.—Small spoonful ice cream in sundae cup, then pour over some grated walnuts, then some more ice cream, then top off with sliced bananas and whipped cream.

4.—Ladle of ice cream; top with usual amount of fruits mixed, raspberries, sliced peaches and claret syrup; a teaspoonful of nut sundae; dress with whipped cream if desired, fancy whole cherries and cubed pineapple.

5.—Chop 1 lb. of mixed nuts and add 10 oz. of crushed strawberry and 10 oz. of crushed pineapple sauce. Pour over plain ice cream.

6.—Into a sundae cup turn a cone-shaped measure of

ice cream, over this pour a ladleful of walnut bisque, or walnut flakes, made according to directions on package, or sprinkle broken nuts over the top of the cream and pour on it an ounce of maple syrup. This can also be served topped with whipped cream and a cherry.

Pineapple

The use of pineapple in larger pieces, rather than the fine crushed, is recommended, as it makes a better appearance, and it is nicer to eat with ice cream. The pineapple as it comes from the jars should be diluted with 2 parts of plain syrup in bowl on counter. Turn a cone-shaped measure of ice cream into sundae glass. Over this pour a ladleful of the fruit from the bowl and serve with a spoon.

Strawberry

For this purpose it is better to use the whole fruit rather than the crushed strawberry. The whole strawberries as they come from the jars should be diluted with 2 parts plain syrup in bowl on counter. Turn a cone-shaped measure of ice cream into a sundae glass, over this pour a ladleful of fruit from the bowl and serve with a spoon.

Tutti Frutti

Mix the following in a porcelain container: Crushed pineapple, ½ pt.; crushed strawberry, ½ pt.; crushed cherries, ½ pt.; crushed peach, ½ pt.; crushed blackberry, ½ pt.; prune juice, ½ pt.; and a sufficient amount of simple syrup to give it the desired working consistency. Serve same as all sundaes.

Watermelon

Take a long glass dish and lay on it a neat slice of the heart of a ripe watermelon, avoiding the seeds. On one end of the dish put a small ladleful of pineapple water ice, at the other end place a similar quantity of orange water ice. Pour over all a little strawberry syrup and put a maraschino cherry on the water ice at each end of the dish.

Chapter XVI.

HOT BEVERAGES

Beef

ADD 1 oz. of sweet cream to a cup of beef bouillon and top with whipped cream and you have a delicious drink.

2.—About 5 gr. crystal pepsin, ½ oz. boiling water. Dissolve, then add 1 teaspoonful beef bouillon, 1 cupful hot soda. Serve with pepper and salt.

3.—First make an extract by taking 6 oz. extract of beef, 16 oz. hot water, 5 dr. tincture of black pepper. Dissolve the beef extract in the hot water and add the tincture of black pepper. To make the tincture of black pepper take 2 oz. of whole black pepper, crush it, add 10 oz. alcohol. Steep and filter. To dispense, take 1 oz. of the beef extract, dash of cream, dash of salt and dash of celery salt. Fill up with hot water, stirring with spoon while filling.

4.—Beef jelly, 8 oz.; hot water, 1 pt.; extract of celery, 1 dr.; caramel, 1 dr. Dissolve the beef jelly in the hot water and add the celery and caramel. Use a shaker top in the bottle, as there is likely to be a sediment which necessitates shaking. In a 6 or 7-oz. cup place about 2 teaspoonfuls of this extract, draw on a sufficiency of hot water, add salt to suit the taste and stir with a spoon.

Calisaya Tonic

Fluid extract cinchona, 1 oz.; lemon syrup, 1 oz.; lemon juice, 1 oz.; hot water, 7 oz.

Beverages—Non-Alcoholic

Checkerberry

Draw ½ oz. of wintergreen spray and 1 oz. of red orange syrup into a mug and fill with hot water. Top with whipped cream. It may also be served by using 1 oz. wintergreen syrup and omitting the orange, but the first is to be preferred. The two syrups may be kept mixed and ready for dispensing.

Chicken Cream

Two oz. of concentrated chicken and ½ oz. of sweet cream. Stir while adding hot water, after seasoning with a little spice.

Chocolate

1.—Soluble powdered extract of chocolate, about 1 teaspoonful; hot soda, sufficient quantity to dissolve. Stir well and add loaf sugar, 4 cubes; prepared milk, 1 dessertspoonful; hot soda, 1 cupful; whipped cream, 1 tablespoonful.

2.—Chocolate syrup, 2 oz.; sweet cream, ½ oz.; fill with hot water, 6 oz. Serve with whipped cream. It is essential that the best grade of chocolate, such as Phillips', be used, and the flavor plenty strong to have the drink good.

3.—Add to 1 lb. of cocoa an equal amount of pulverized sugar; put a heaping teaspoonful of this powder in a mug and make into paste with a little water, then fill with hot soda, stirring briskly. Finish with ice cream or whipped cream.

4.—Chocolate syrup, 1 to 1½ oz.; 1 egg; cream, ½ oz.; hot water, enough to fill an 8-oz. mug. Prepare as with hot egg checkerberry.

5.—One egg; chocolate syrup, 1¼ oz.; sweet cream, 1 teaspoonful. Shake well, strain and add 1 cupful hot soda and 1 tablespoonful whipped cream.

6.—Place a full ½ oz. of cream chocolate in cup and fill with hot water, or, better, with hot milk and hot water mixed. Top with a spoonful of whipped cream.

Hot Beverages

7.—To be served from a hot soda apparatus having large cans; 2 qt. water, 2 lb. sugar, 1 qt. milk, 1 lb. powdered chocolate or 1 qt. cream chocolate. Put water into can over slow fire, let it come almost to a boil, add chocolate, milk and sugar, simmer for 5 minutes, pour into urn and keep it hot. Draw this chocolate into cup, add more sugar if desired and top with whipped cream.

Syrups.—1.—Chocolate, 8 oz.; granulated sugar, 4 oz.; boiling water, 28 oz.; chocolate syrup, enough to make 1 gal. Select a rich brand of chocolate. Grate or scrape fine and triturate with the sugar; then in a large warm mortar form a paste by trituration, gradually adding 18 oz. of boiling water; transfer to a porcelain vessel, heat slowly, stirring well; gradually add the remainder of the water, bring to a boil and boil for 5 or 6 minutes, stirring constantly; stir for some time after removing from the fire, then bring to a boil again and boil for 1 minute. By this means separation of cocoa butter is prevented, and the mixture does not require straining, but simple skimming. Add the syrup and the mixture may be flavored with vanilla extract or other flavors. Care must be exercised to make a smooth paste in the beginning and to avoid scorching at the last. A quantity of the chocolate may be kept on hand in a grated or scraped form, mixed with the proper amount of sugar. In serving use 1½ oz. of the syrup, add an ounce of cream, fill the mug with hot water, top with whipped cream and serve with crackers and a spoon.

2.—Good soluble cocoa, 3½ oz.; water, 2 pt.; granulated sugar, 40 oz.; vanilla extract, 4 dr. Heat the water to boiling, stir in the cocoa. gradually added; add the sugar; when latter is dissolved, strain and add the extract. Serve like the preceding.

3.—Powdered chocolate, 4 oz.; starch, ½ oz.; water, 2½ pt.; sugar, 2½ lb.; vanilla extract, 2 dr. Mix the chocolate and starch by trituration, mix intimately with part of the water, pour on the remainder of the water in

Beverages—Non-Alcoholic

a boiling condition, stir well and heat to boiling until the starch is cooked, stirring constantly; add the sugar, stir until dissolved, add the vanilla extract. Serve like preceding.

4.—Powdered cocoa, 3 lb.; water, ½ gal.; cream, 2 pt.; tincture of vanilla, 5 oz.; salt, 1 teaspoonful; simple syrup, enough to make 1 gal.

5.—Take 1½ lb. good sweet chocolate; grate fine; add 1 gal. milk while stirring; then beat a few minutes with egg beater to make it light and serve with whipped cream. This should be made in porcelain-lined urn of even temperature and stir occasionally.

6.—Chocolate, 1 lb.; sugar, 6 oz.; boiling water, q. s. to make 1 gal. Grate or scrape the chocolate fine and triturate it with 2 oz. of the sugar (this may be done preliminarily, and in larger quantities, if necessary), then in a large warmed mortar form a paste under the pestle by the gradual addition of boiling water up to 40 fl.oz. Transfer to a porcelain dish, slowly heat, and stirring in well, gradually add the remaining 4 oz. of sugar and 20 oz. of boiling water and bring the whole to the boiling point for 5 or 6 minutes, then remove and stir until ebullition ceases; return to fire and boil for 1 minute. By this means the cocoa butter will not separate, and the product will not need straining, but skimming only. The attention is devoted to obtaining a smooth paste at the first step and in not overheating at the last.

7.—Chocolate, 3 cakes; gelatine 1 small package; sugar, 9 lb.; hot water, 8 pt. Boil for 5 minutes and strain.

8.—Make the syrup by taking 4 oz. of light soluble cocoa; granulated sugar, 2 lb.; boiling hot water, 1 qt.; vanilla extract, 1 oz. Dissolve the cocoa in the hot water by stirring, then add the sugar and dissolve. Strain and when cold add the vanilla extract. To dispense, take 2 oz. of cocoa syrup and 1 oz. of cream. Turn on the hot water stream and stir while filling. Top with whipped cream.

Hot Beverages

Clams

Clam juice, like beef tea, must always be served hot. It spoils very readily and must be kept on ice.

Clam juice may be served in the proportion of ½ to 1 oz. to an 8-oz. mug, filling the latter with hot water and serving with a spoon; also giving the patron celery salt, salt and pepper cellars and soda crackers. The clam juice is served more acceptably by adding an ounce of milk, better yet by using half water and half milk and still better by using all hot milk. A small amount of butter causes a marked improvement.

1.—Extract clam bouillon, about 2 tablespoonfuls; prepared milk, about 1 dessertspoonful; extract aromatic soup herbs, about 5 drops; extract celery and pepper about 5 drops; hot soda, sufficient to fill cup.

2.—Blend. Use 1 oz. clam bouillon, ½ oz. tomato catsup or bouillon; fill cup with boiling water; season with salt, pepper and celery salt. A dash of sherry wine in clam bouillon makes a very fine clam punch.

3.—Extract clam bouillon, 2 tablespoonfuls; prepared milk, 1 dessertspoonful; extract aromatic herbs, 5 drops; extract white pepper, 5 drops; hot water, 1 cupful.

4.—Clam juice, ¼ oz.; beef extract, ¼ oz.; cream, 1 oz.; essence of celery, 4 dashes. Stir while adding hot water. Serve with spices.

5.—Clam juice, 2 oz.; lemon juice, 3 dashes; pepper and salt; water, 6 oz.

6.—Powdered Jamaica ginger, 1 teaspoonful; cream, 1 oz.; clam juice, 1 oz.; butter, 1 teaspoonful. Fill with hot water and season with celery salt.

7.—Clam juice, 1 oz.; tomato catsup, ¼ oz.; butter, ¼ oz.; dash of cream. Add hot water, stirring well, and serve with spices.

8.—Clam juice, 1 oz.; cream, ½ oz. Fill with hot soda, serve pepper and salt and celery salt.

9.—Clam juice, 2 dr.; beef extract, 1 dr.; cream, 1 oz.; essence of celery, 5 drops; hot water, to make 8 oz.

10.—Clam juice, ¼ oz.; beef extract, ¼ oz.; cream,

Beverages—Non-Alcoholic

1 oz.; essence of celery, 4 dashes. Stir while adding hot soda. Serve with spices.

Coffee Extract

1.—Select a good brand of coffee. It should be freshly ground each time you prepare your extract.

Moisten 1 lb. of fine ground, but not powdered, coffee with 4 oz. of cold water. Pack in a glass percolator. Add 1 pt. of boiling water, cover lightly and let stand for 1 hour; draw the cork and add sufficient boiling water to percolate 1 pt. Heat to the boiling point and allow it to pass through the coffee a couple of times. The strength should now be exhausted and you should have a pint of good coffee extract.

2.—Moisten 10 oz. of Mocha and Java or other good coffee with a little water. Pack in a glass percolator. Add 1 oz. of good French brandy with sufficient boiling water to percolate 30 oz. Cover tightly and let macerate for about an hour; then percolate.

3.—Moisten 20 oz. of good freshly roasted and ground coffee in a mixture of 2 oz. of glycerine and 4 oz. of cold water. Pack in a glass percolator. Add 2 oz. of glycerine and let stand for half an hour. Then add 14 oz. of boiling water and macerate for an hour. Then percolate until about a pint of good strong extract is obtained.

Some formulas call for dilute alcohol as a menstruum, but the above is preferable for hot soda purposes, since alcoholic extracts of coffee do not retain either the flavor or the aroma that the others do.

Burnt Coffee.—Allow 3 teaspoonfuls of good coffee to each ½ pt. of water. Sweeten it rather more than ordinarily, and strain it into small cups. Pour a little brandy into each over a spoon, set fire to it, and when the spirit is partly consumed the flame should be blown out, and the coffee drunk immediately.

Roasting Coffee (a French recipe).—Add, before roasting, to every 3 lb. of coffee a piece of butter the size of a nut and a dessertspoonful of powdered sugar. It is then

Hot Beverages

roasted in the usual manner, and a tin in a slack oven, or a frying pan over the fire, will serve, with care. A rotating coffee roaster is of course much better. The addition of the butter and sugar develops the flavor and aroma of the berry; the butter employed must, of course, be of the very best quality and must be used only in very small quantities.

Serving.—1.—In using from ¼ to 1 oz. of extract, depending upon the strength of the extract and how strong a cup of coffee you desire, coffee may be served black or with half-hot milk or with a little sweet cream, allowing the customer to sweeten to taste.

2.—One egg; extract of Mocha, 1 dessertspoonful; sweet cream, 1 teaspoonful; syrup, 1 oz. Shake well, strain and add 1 cupful hot soda and 1 teaspoonful whipped cream.

Egg

1.—Break fresh egg into mixing glass and shake well without ice. Pour into bouillon cup ½ oz. of beef tea extract. Draw hot water to fill cup and serve with 2 Graham crackers.

2.—One-half to 1 oz. liquid extract of beef, 1 egg, salt and pepper to season, hot water to fill an 8-oz. mug. Stir the extract, egg and seasoning together with a spoon to get well mixed; add the water, stirring briskly meanwhile. Then strain and serve. Or shake the egg and extract in a shaker, add the water and mix by pouring back and forth several times from shaker to mug.

3.—One egg, 1 oz. beef tea extract, ½ spoonful dairy butter. Add several ounces hot soda and stir until the butter is dissolved. Fill up with hot soda.

4.—One egg, ½ oz. lime juice, 1 oz. lemon syrup, hot water enough to fill an 8-oz. glass. Prepare like hot egg checkerberry.

5.—Into a 10-oz. glass squeeze the juice of ½ of an orange add 2 teaspoonfuls of powdered sugar and 1 egg. Shake thoroughly, strain into a clean glass and fill with hot water as directed.

Beverages—Non-Alcoholic

6.—One oz. orangeade, 1 egg, ½ oz. cream, hot water to fill cup. Mix syrup, egg and cream in egg shaker; mix well and add the hot water.

7.—One egg; lemon juice, about 3 teaspoonfuls; soluble extract lemon, about 10 drops; confectioner's sugar, 3 large teaspoonfuls; prepared spice, small quantity; extract cognac, about 15 drops. Place these ingredients in a combination shaker and thoroughly shake; then strain through julep strainer into hot soda cup; to this add 2 large tablespoonfuls of whipped cream. Draw hot water into side of cup and stir bottom only.

8.—Break a fresh egg into a tumbler; add 3 dashes solution of acid phosphate, 1½ oz. of orange syrup, and shake thoroughly; then add hot water slowly into the shaker, stirring briskly meanwhile. Strain carefully into mug and serve. Checkerberry may be used instead of orange syrup.

Ginger

1.—Loaf sugar, 4 cubes; soluble extract ginger ale, 10 drops; soluble extract lemon, 10 drops; fruit acid, 10 drops; 1 cupful hot soda.

2.—Use 1 oz. ginger punch to a cup and fill with hot water, adding small piece crystallized ginger.

Grape

1.—Grape juice, 1 oz.; lemon syrup, ½ oz.; few drops sherry; hot water.

2.—Grape juice, hot, is preferred by many and is very beneficial. It may be taken before meals and often in the place of a regular meal. Heat in porcelain, agate or glass—never in tin—using one-third water if desired.

Kola

Take 1 oz. kola punch in 8-oz. cup and draw 6 oz. hot water into another mug; pour a little alcohol over the hot water and ignite. Mix by pouring from one cup to the other a few times.

Hot Beverages

Lemonade

One of the original drinks so often made but served poorly is hot lemonade. There are numerous ways of preparing hot lemonade—and if you are as particular about making it good as you certainly are about your hot chocolate, there is no good reason why it will not profit you for your trouble. To make it from the juice of ½ a lemon: 1 teaspoonful powdered sugar; twist a small portion of lemon peel over the cup so as to get a flavor of the lemon; then fill cup with hot water and stir.

Lime

1.—Lime juice, ½ oz.; lemon or ginger syrup, 1 oz.; hot water to fill. Lime juice with lemon or plain syrup or with sugar and hot water may be dispensed as "hot limeade."

2.—Lime juice, 1 oz.; strawberry juice, ½ oz.; sugar, 1 spoonful. Fill up with hot water, stirring well.

Malted Milk

1.—Malted milk, 1 tablespoonful; pepper and salt or sugar; water, 8 oz.

2.—Malted milk (in powder), 2 spoonfuls; cream, 3 spoonfuls. Mix to a paste, fill with soda, serve celery salt.

3.—Two tablespoonfuls of malted milk, hot water to fill. While adding the water stir the mixture with a spoon so as to make it smooth. Season with salt and pepper, or with celery salt, and serve with soda crackers. Some dispensers add a couple teaspoonfuls of cream.

Egg.—Into a mixing glass draw 1½ oz. of chocolate syrup; into this break an egg and add 1 oz. of sweet cream and 2 teaspoonfuls of malted milk. Shake thoroughly and strain into a clean 10-oz. glass and fill with hot water.

Chocolate.—Pour 1 oz. of hot chocolate syrup into a mug and 2 teaspoonfuls of malted milk; reduce to a

Beverages—Non-Alcoholic

smooth paste and fill with hot milk or hot water and a little cream. Top with whipped cream if desired. This can be prepared by pouring finished cocoa over the powdered milk, but it is not the best way and it does not mix as well. Where powdered cocoa is used mix the two powders together dry, before adding your hot water. It is a good plan, if you use this method, to have the two already mixed for use. Use 1 part cocoa to 4 parts of malted milk and mix thoroughly.

Coffee.—Pour ½ oz. of coffee extract into a cup in which you have previously prepared a plain malted milk without salt. If you use finished coffee then put the powder in the mug and fill with hot coffee instead of hot water and add a little sweet cream, topping with whipped cream if you desire.

Mock Turtle Bouillon

Make an extract of mock turtle by taking 2 oz. extract of beef, 2 oz. concentrated chicken, 8 oz. of clam juice, 3 pt. of hot water, 1 oz. tincture black pepper, 3 dr. essence of celery, 1 dr. essence of orange peel. Mix and dissolve thoroughly. To dispense, take 2 oz. of the mock turtle extract and ½ oz. sweet cream. Stir while adding hot soda. Serve spices.

Orange

Orange syrup, 1½ oz.; hot water to fill. Make the syrup stronger than for cold soda.

Oyster Broth

To 1 oz. oyster juice add a teaspoonful of cream, a little butter and season to taste.

Phosphate

Cherry.—Prepare a syrup with 12 oz. of cherry juice, 1½ lb. of sugar and 6 oz. water. Dissolve the sugar in the juice and water. In serving put 1½ oz. of the

Hot Beverages

mixture in the mug and add 1 dr. of acid phosphate solution, filling the mug with hot water. If desired, the phosphate may be kept mixed with the syrup.

Pepsin.—Liquid pepsin, 1 teaspoonful; liquid phosphate, 2 dashes; lemon syrup, 1 oz.; hot water, 1 cupful.

Pistachio

Pistachio or almond syrup, 1 oz.; cream syrup, 1 oz.; cream, ½ oz.; rum or bitters, a dash. Fill with hot soda, stirring well. Serve cinnamon.

Raspberryade

Raspberry vinegar syrup, ½ oz.; raspberry juice, ½ oz.; lime juice, ½ oz. Add hot water, stirring well.

Sundaes

Cherry.—Over pineapple ice cream pour a ladleful of hot cherry syrup.

Chocolate.—Rich hot chocolate syrup poured over a ladleful of plain or nut ice cream is very delicious. A few chopped nuts may be sprinkled over the top.

Chocolate Sauce.—Chocolate or cocoa, 1½ lb.; granulated sugar, 6 lb.; water (distilled or pure), 3 pt.; extract vanilla, 1½ oz.; brandy, 2 oz.; extract almond, ½ oz. Dissolve cocoa and sugar in water, strain while hot through cheesecloth; add vanilla and brandy. Keep in a chafing dish or water bath, not too hot a fire, as it solidifies or gets too thick; add a little water. Serve hot over ice cream in sundae cup.

Maple.—Pour a ladleful of hot maple syrup over vanilla ice cream, sprinkle ground hickory nuts over top. Serve with N. wafers.

Mint.—Over a ladleful of vanilla ice cream pour a heavy hot menthe syrup and place 3 crème de menthe cherries on top.

Strawberry.—Over a service of vanilla ice cream a ladleful of hot crushed strawberry. Do not let the strawberry reach a boiling degree, as it destroys the flavor.

Beverages—Non-Alcoholic

Tea

1.—*How to Prepare Tea.*—a.—In the best restaurants of the Chinese quarter in San Francisco tea is never made in a teapot, but each cup is brewed separately. The cup itself is different; it is a small bowl covered with a strainer and a lid. A tiny bundle of long tea leaves is placed in the strainer and the boiling water is poured over it. This first infusion is invariably thrown away as being unfit to drink. This procedure has caused the leaves to swell, and when next the boiling water is poured on it filters through slowly and is allowed to steep for a few moments. When the strainer is removed the golden liquid that remains in the bowl ready for drinking, without milk or sugar, is as different from the tea ordinarily served as champagne is from ginger pop.

b.—In order to make good tea it is necessary that the water should be quite boiling, but it must on no account be water that has boiled for some time or been previously boiled, cooled and then reboiled. It is a good plan to empty the kettle and refill it with fresh cold water, and make the tea the moment it reaches boiling point. Soft water makes the best tea, and boiling softens the water, but after it has boiled for some time it again becomes hard. When water is very hard a tiny pinch of carbonate of soda may be put into the teapot with the tea, but it must be used very sparingly, otherwise it may impart a very unpleasant taste to the beverage. Tea is better made in an earthen than a metal pot. One good teaspoonful of tea will be found sufficient for two small cups, if made with boiling water and allowed to stand 3 or 4 minutes; longer than this it should never be allowed to stand. The delicate flavor of the tea may be preserved and injurious effects avoided by pouring the tea, after it has stood 3 or 4 minutes, into a clean teapot which has been previously heated.

2.—By a new process the delicate aroma and flavor of the bloom-tip orange Pekoe blend has been retained. To

Hot Beverages

serve—Add a dessertspoonful and fill with boiling water, add lump of sugar and whipped cream.

3.—Tea extract, 2 dr.; sugar, 2 teaspoonfuls, or rock candy syrup, 1 oz.; add cream if desired. Fill mug with hot soda and syrup.

4.—Loaf sugar, 4 cubes; extract Oolong tea, 1 dessertspoonful; prepared milk, 1 dessertspoonful; hot soda, 1 cupful; whipped cream, 1 tablespoonful. Hot water may be used instead of the hot soda.

Tomato

1.—Usual amount of tomato extract, spoonful malted milk, little cream, hot water.

2.—Take ½ to 1 teaspoonful of beef extract, or about 1 oz. of good liquid beef extract and ½ oz. of tomato catsup, with enough hot water to fill an 8-oz. mug. Season to taste. Another tomato beef bouillon is made by taking ½ oz. of beef extract, ¼ oz. of tomato catsup and ½ oz. of cream. Stir while filling with hot water and serve with spices.

3.—Pour 2 oz. of tomato soup into a cup, add ½ oz. of sweet cream, fill with boiling water and season with salt, pepper and celery salt.

4.—Beef extract, ½ oz.; tomato bouillon extract, 1 oz. Fill cup with hot milk and serve with Graham wafers, salt and pepper.

9

Chapter XVII.

BEVERAGES FOR THE SICK

Arrowroot

ARROWROOT, 1 dessertspoonful; castor sugar, 1 teaspoonful; milk or water, ½ pt. Mix the arrowroot smoothly with a little cold milk, boil the remainder and pour it on, stirring briskly meanwhile. Return to the stewpan and boil for 5 minutes, stirring all the time. Add the sugar and serve. If preferred, an equal quantity of water may be substituted for the milk.

Barley Water

1.—Barley, 2 tablespoonfuls; water, 2 qt.; sugar, 1 tablespoonful. Wash the barley well; put the barley and water into a saucepan and bring it to a boil; then boil very slowly for 2 hours, strain it, add sugar and let it cool. Barley water is very cooling and nourishing. The barley may afterward be used for a pudding or put into soup.

2.—One tablespoonful of patent barley (flour), a pinch of salt, a little cold water, ½ pt. of boiling water (or milk), sugar or port to taste. Mix the barley well with cold water until a smooth paste, about the thickness of cream, is formed; then add ½ pt. of boiling water (or milk, which is preferable); put into an enameled saucepan, add sugar or wine to taste, simmer for 10 minutes, stirring all the time with a silver or wooden spoon.

Beverages for the Sick

Bran Tea

Bran, 2 tablespoonfuls; honey, 1 tablespoonful; gum arabic, 1/4 oz.; water, 1 pt. Boil the bran in the water for 20 minutes. Add the gum arabic and honey, stir from time to time until dissolved and strain through muslin. A useful remedy for hoarseness and sore throat.

Lemonade Preparation

For the production of lemonade preparations for the sick the *Pharmaceutische Rundschau* gives the following recipes:

1.—Strawberry Lemonade; Citric acid, 6; water, 100; sugar, 450; strawberry syrup, 600; cherry syrup, 300; claret, 450; aromatic tincture, 15 drops.

2.—Lemonade Powder: Sodium bicarbonate, 65; tartaric acid, 60; sugar, 125; lemon oil, 21 drops.

3.—Lemonade Juice: Sugar syrup, 200; tartaric acid, 15; distilled water, 100; lemon oil, 3; tincture of vanilla, 6 drops.

4.—Lemonade Lozenges: Tartaric acid, 10; sugar, 30; gum arabic, 2; powdered starch, 0.5; lemon oil, 6 drops; tincture of vanilla, 25 drops, and sufficient diluted spirit of wine so that 30 lozenges can be made with it.

Linseed Tea

Whole linseed, 1 oz.; licorice, 1/2 oz.; sugar candy, 1/2 oz.; the juice of 1/2 lemon; the finely cut rind of 1/4 lemon; 1 pt. cold water. Wash and drain the linseed and simmer it with the water, licorice and lemon rind for about half an hour. Add the sugar candy, and when dissolved strain and stir in the lemon juice.

Oatmeal

Fine oatmeal, 1 tablespoonful; water, 1 pt., or milk and water mixed; sugar to taste; a pinch of salt. Mix the oatmeal with a little cold water, boil the remainder, pour in the blended oatmeal and stir until boiling. Simmer gently for half an hour, stirring frequently. Strain, add

Beverages—Non-Alcoholic

a pinch of salt and sweeten to taste. Nutmeg, ginger, butter or cream is frequently added when the gruel is intended as a remedy for a cold.

Rice Water

1. (Dr. Pavy).—Wash well 1 oz. of Carolina rice with cold water. Then macerate for 3 hours in 1 qt. of water kept at tepid heat, and afterward boil slowly for 1 hour and strain. May be flavored with lemon peel, cloves or other spice. This preparation is useful in dysentery, diarrhea, etc.

2.—Take of rice 2 oz., let it be well washed and add to it 2 qt. water. Boil it for 1½ hours and then add sugar and nutmeg as much as may be required. To be taken *ad libitum*. Rice, when boiled for a considerable time, assumes a gelatinous form, and, mixed with milk, is a very excellent diet for children. It possesses, in some measure, a constipating property which may be increased by boiling the milk.

Sago

Fine sago, 1 dessertspoonful; castor sugar, 1 dessertspoonful; boiling water, ½ pt.; port wine, 1 glass. Let the water be quite boiling in a stewpan, then sprinkle in the sago and boil gently until it is quite clear, stirring from time to time. Add the sugar and wine and serve.

Toast Water

Toast 1 crust of bread very brown and hard, but do not burn it, or it will impart a disagreeable flavor to the water. Put it into a jug, pour over it 1 pt. of cold water; let it soak for 1 hour, then strain and use.

Chapter XVIII.

CIDERS

How to Make Good Cider and to Keep It

IN localities where the apple crop is abundant the preparation of cider for market is a profitable industry when intelligently undertaken, and there are few beverages more palatable and less harmful than cider when properly prepared. Unfortunately there are few farmers who really know how to make good cider or how to care for and keep it when made.

In the first place, apples not perfectly sound and well ripened are not fit for making cider. The russet is one of the best of apples for this purpose, but other and more commonly available varieties need not be slighted.

To prevent bruising the fruit intended for the cider press should always be hand-picked. After sweating each apple should be wiped dry, examined, and any damaged or decayed fruit thrown out and used for making vinegar cider.

In the grinding or pulping operation the seed is often crushed and is apt to taint the juice, so that despite the loss and extra time required it is always better to core the apples before grinding them, as the cider will not only taste and look better, but keep better. A cheap and handy coring machine is shown in Fig. 1. In this the coring tube, which may be of tin, free from iron rust, projects through a common bench or table, and is surrounded by an ordinary furniture spring, P, which supports a piece of wood, A. This has a hole in the center of it, over and partly into

Beverages—Non-Alcoholic

which the apple is placed. The lever, D, on which the piece of wood, B, similar to A, but having an aperture only large enough to admit the coring tube, is loosely hung by side pins, is held in position by the spring, S. The operation of the machine will be readily understood by referring to Fig. 2, in which it is shown in section.

All ironwork about the mill or press (rings, rivets, etc.) should be tinned or coated with good asphaltum varnish,

Coring Machine and Filter
CIDER MAKING

as the color and sometimes taste of the cider are apt to be affected by contact with the rusty metal.

In pressing the pomace many of the best cider makers prefer to use haircloth in place of straw between the layers, as it is more cleanly and does not affect the taste of or add anything to the expressed juice.

As the cider runs from the press it should be filtered

Ciders

through a hair sieve into a clean wooden vessel capable of holding as much juice as can be extracted in one day.

Under favorable conditions the fine pomace will rise to the surface in about 24 hours—sometimes less—and in a short time grow very thick. Then it should be watched, and, when white bubbles begin to appear at the surface, the liquid should be drawn off slowly from a faucet placed about 3 inches from the bottom of the tank, so as not to disturb the lees The liquid drawn off should be received in clean, sweet casks and must be watched. As soon as white bubbles of gas appear at the bunghole, it must be drawn off (racked) into clean casks as before, and this racking repeated as often as necessary until the first fermentation is completely at an end. Then the casks should be filled up with cider in every respect like that already contained in it and bunged up tight. Many cider makers add a gobletful of pure olive oil to the cider before finally putting in the bung and storing.

If it is desired to keep cider perfectly sweet—and this is rarely the case—it should be filtered on coming from the press and then sulphured by the addition of about ¼ oz. of calcium sulphite (sulphite of lime) per gallon of cider and should be kept in small, tight, full barrels. The addition of a little sugar—say, ¼ lb. per gal.—improves the keeping qualities of tart cider.

An easily constructed cider filter is shown in Fig. 3 and consists in a barrel provided with a tap near the bottom. The lower part is filled with dry wood chips covered with a piece of flannel. Over this a layer of clean rye straw is packed down, and then the barrel is filled with clean quartz sand, not too fine.

When the first fermentation of cider has been checked and the liquid barreled it should be allowed to stand until it acquires the proper flavor.

Much of the excellency of cider depends upon the temperature at which the fermentation is conducted. The casks containing the juice should be kept in a cellar, if possible, where the temperature does not exceed 50° F. When left

Beverages—Non-Alcoholic

exposed to the air, or kept in a warm place, much of the sugar is converted into vinegar and the liquor becomes hard and rough. On the contrary, when the fermentation is conducted at a low temperature, nearly the whole of the sugar is converted into alcohol and remains in the liquid instead of undergoing acetification. The change from alcohol to vinegar (acetous fermentation) goes on most rapidly at a temperature of about 95° F. and at a lower temperature the action becomes slower, until at 46° F. no such change takes place. Independently of the difference in quality of fruit used, the respect of temperature is one of the chief causes of the superiority of the cider made by one person over that made by another in the same neighborhood.

The more malic acid and less sugar present, the less the tendency to acetous fermentation; hence it often happens that tart apples produce the best cider. But cider made from such apples can never equal in quality that prepared at a low temperature from fruit rich in sugar, which, if properly cared for, will keep good 20 years.

When the first fermentation has subsided, and the liquor has developed the desired flavor in storage, it is drawn off into other barrels which have been thoroughly cleansed and sulphured, either by burning in the bunghole a clean rag dipped in sulphur or, what is better, by thoroughly rinsing the inside with a solution of bisulphite of calcium prepared by dissolving about ¼ lb. of the sulphite in 1 gal. of water.

The isinglass—6 oz. or more (in solution) to the barrel—should be stirred in as soon as transferred, and then a sufficient quantity of preserving powder of bisulphite of lime (not sulphate or sulphide), previously dissolved in a little of the cider, to entirely check fermentation. The quantity of this substance required rarely exceeds ¼ oz. to the gallon of cider. A large excess must be avoided as it is apt to injuriously affect the taste.

Some makers sweeten their cider by additions, before fining, of sugar or glucose, the quantity of the former

Ciders

varying from ¾ lb. to 1½ lb., while as a substitute about 3 times this quantity of glucose is required. Sweetened cider, when properly cared for, develops by aging a flavor and sparkle resembling some champagnes. Such ciders are best bottled when fined.

Artificial

The following, when properly prepared, makes a passable substitute for cider and a very pleasant drink:

Catechu, powdered, 3 parts; alum, powdered, 5 parts; honey, 640 parts; water, 12,800 parts; yeast, 32 parts.

Dissolve the catechu, alum and honey in the water, add the yeast and put in some warm place to ferment. Fermentation should be carried on in the manner and under the precautions so frequently described in a drug paper (*i. e.*, the container should be filled to the square opening, made by sawing out 5 or 6 inches of the center of a stave, and the spume skimmed off daily as it arises). In cooler weather from 2 weeks to 18 days will be required for thorough fermentation. In warmer weather from 12 to 13 days will be sufficient. When fermentation is complete add the following solution:

Oil of bitter almond, 1 part; oil of cloves, 1 part; caramel, 32 parts; alcohol, 192 parts.

The alcohol may be replaced by twice its volume of any good Bourbon whisky. A much cheaper but correspondingly poor substitute for the above may be made as follows:

1.—Twenty-five gal. of soft water, 2 lb. tartaric acid, 25 lb. brown sugar and 1 pt. of yeast are allowed to stand in a warm place, in a clean cask with the bung out, for 24 hours. Then bung up the cask, after adding 3 gal. of whisky, and let stand for 48 hours, after which the liquor is ready for use.

2.—Tartaric acid, 2 parts; common brown sugar ("New Orleans"), 25 parts; rain water, 200 parts; yeast 1 part. Put into a clean keg or cask, with the bung out, and let stand in a warm place 24 hours. Add 25 parts of rectified al-

Beverages—Non-Alcoholic

cohol, bung tightly and let stand 48 hours, when it will be ready for use. The above is improved by adding to each gallon of spirit from 1 to 2 fl.dr. of apple essence (obtainable from dealers in bar supplies, or probably from any wholesaler). This gives it the apple aroma and flavor.

3.—Artificial Cider.—Filtered water, 20 gal.; moist sugar, 12 lb.; tartaric acid, ½ lb.; rectified alcohol, 3 pt.; elder and melilot flowers, of each 4 oz.

When the fermentation is finished, it should be placed in a cool cellar and left to repose for 10 days, then fined with isinglass and bottle; the bottles should be kept lying down.

Bottling Cider

To have good bottled cider, it is necessary first that care should be taken in its manufacture. Apples picked by hand and perfectly ripe and sound are essential to the best quality. They should lie some time after picking. They should then be sorted, their surface wiped dry, and all the rotten fruit rejected. The cider may then be made in the usual manner by grinding and pressing. The cider should then be stored in a cool place to mature. After 3 or 4 months it should be racked off carefully, and then fined by adding to each hogshead 1 lb. of isinglass finings. In 2 weeks from the time that the finings are added it should be again racked off, and if found sufficiently clear and sparkling it is ready for bottling; if not, it should be again fined and allowed to stand 2 weeks. Before bottling, the bung should be left out of the casks for 10 or 12 hours to permit the escape of carbonic-acid gas. The cider may then be placed in bottles and the corks loosely placed in. The bottles should then be allowed to stand 24 hours. The corks may then be driven in and wired down. If the corks are driven in and wired when the cider is first put into the bottles there will be great danger of breaking the bottles by the accumulating pressure of the gas. All additions of flavoring materials are a decided damage to cider made from a fine quality of fruit, though they may im-

Ciders

prove juice of a poor quality. If the directions here given be strictly followed, a delicious cider will be produced.

Canning Cider

Cider may be preserved sweet for years by putting it up in air-tight cans, after the manner of preserving fruit. The liquor should be first settled and racked off from the dregs, but fermentation should not be allowed to commence before canning.

Champagne Cider

The following are some of the beverages found in the market under the name of "champagne cider" and are made:

1.—Cider (pure apple), 3 bbl.; glucose syrup (A), 4 gal.; wine spirit, 4 gal.

The glucose is added to the cider, and after 12 days' storage in a cool place the liquid is clarified with ½ gal. of fresh skimmed milk and 8 oz. of dissolved isinglass. The spirit is then added and the liquor bottled on the fourth day afterward.

2.—Pale vinous cider, 1 hhd.; wine spirit, 3 gal.; glucose, about 30 lb.

The liquid is stored in casks in a cool place for about 1 month, when it is fined down with 2 qt. of skimmed milk and bottled. Much of this and similar preparations are doubtless sold for genuine champagne.

3.—Pineapple cider, 20 gal.; wine spirit, 1 gal.; sugar, 6 lb.

Fine with 1 gal. of skimmed milk after 2 weeks' storage in wood and bottle.

4.—Another Formula.—Good pale vinous cider, 1 hhd.; proof spirit, 3 gal.; honey or sugar, 14 lb. Mix well, and let them remain together in a moderately cool place for 1 month, then add orange flower water, 3 pt., and in a few days fine it down with skimmed milk, ½ gal. A similar article, bottled in champagne bottles, silvered and labeled, is said to be sometimes sold for champagne.

5.—Another Formula.—To every 8 gal. of sweet, still

Beverages—Non-Alcoholic

cider add 2 pt. of strained honey, or, in its absence, 2 lb. of sugar. Stir well, bung the cask and let stand for 8 days. Add 5 fl.oz. of skimmed milk or 1-3 oz. of dissolved isinglass and immediately thereafter 2¾ pt. of diluted alcohol. Let stand for 4 days, bunging up the cask tightly.

6.—Good pale cider, 100 gal.; alcohol, 3 gal.; sugar or honey, 24 lb. Mix them. If sugar be employed, dissolve it in a part of the cider and add the solution to the remainder. Let the mixture stand during 2 weeks in a moderately cool place, taking care that fermentation does not begin. Finally take out a few gallons, mix them intimately with a few gallons of skimmed milk and incorporate the mixture thoroughly with the contents of the cask. After clarification bottle the clear liquid and secure the corks. Keep the bottles on their sides or standing top down in a moderately cool place.

Cheap Cider

Mix well together 10 gal. cold water, 7½ lb. brown sugar, ¼ lb. tartaric acid, add the juice expressed from 2 or 3 lb. dried sour apples, boiled.

Working Formula for Cherry and Pineapple Cider or Wine

A general working formula for making fruit wines is about as follows: Ripe selected fruit, 2 parts; granulated sugar, 1 part; water, 1½ parts; alcohol, pure (cologne spirit), sufficient.

The fruit, perfectly ripe and sound, free from decayed parts and extraneous matter, is crushed and placed in an earthen or wooden open vessel or tub, the water added and well beaten together, then allowed to stand for 48 hours, with occasional stirring, after which, by means of a press or a coarsely meshed cloth strainer, the liquid portion is separated from the mass or pulp. To the expressed liquid is added the sugar, and, when dissolved, place in a container of such capacity as nearly to fill the same. An old wine, brandy or whisky package, when free from mustiness, is preferable to a new one or one that has never been used, as these frequently impart an objectionable woody taste to the finished product. However, when such wine or liquor packages are not obtainable, the new containers should be first filled with water, allowed to soak for a day or two, then emptied and well sulphured by burning sulphur in the same. The expressed juice is then placed in the barrel and allowed to ferment, the rapidity of the fermentation depending largely upon the maintenance of the proper temperature (which is from 78 to 80° F.) and, if favorable, 4 or 5 days will suffice. It is then racked off into a clean barrel, filling nearly up to the bunghole, leaving the same open and from day to day adding small portions of the alcohol, so that 1 gal. of the spirit is used to 50 gal. of finished product. When the last of the spirit has been added, drive in the bung and allow to mature, and when it has become clear and bright it may be drawn off in bottles.

In making cherry wine some of the seeds should be crushed, as they aid in imparting the delicacy of taste and flavor of the fruit.

To Clear Cider

Ground horseradish, 4 pt.; nearly 1 lb. of thick gray filtering paper to the barrel; shake or stir until the paper has separated into small shreds. Let it stand 24 hours, then draw off the cider by means of a siphon or stopcock.

To Improve Cider

Cider, 1 hhd.; rum, weak flavored, 2 gal.; alum, dissolved, 1 lb.; honey or coarse sugar, 15 lb.; sugar coloring, q. s.; bitter almonds, ½ lb.; cloves, ½ lb.; mix, and after 3 or 4 days fine down with isinglass. For champagne cider omit the coloring and fine with 2 qt. milk; this will render it very pale.

Orange Cider (Orange Wine)

Many of the preparations sold under this name are not really orange ciders, but are varying mixtures of uncertain composition, possibly flavored with orange. The following are made by the use of oranges:

Beverages—Non-Alcoholic

1.—Sugar, 8 av.lb.; water, 2¾ gal.; oranges, 15. Dissolve the sugar in the water by the aid of a gentle heat, express the oranges, add the juice and rinds to the syrup, put the mixture into a cask, keep the whole in a warm place for 3 or 4 days, stirring frequently, then close the cask, set aside in a cool cellar and draw off the clear liquid.

2.—Express the juice from sweet oranges, add water equal to the volume of juice obtained and macerate the expressed oranges with the juice and water for about 12 hours. For each gal. of juice add 1 lb. of granulated sugar, grape sugar or glucose; put the whole into a suitable vessel, covering to exclude the dust, place in a warm location until fermentation is completed, draw off the clear liquid and preserve in well-stoppered stout bottles in a cool place.

3.—Orange wine suitable for "soda" purposes may be prepared by mixing 3 fl.oz. of orange essence with 13 fl.oz. of sweet Catawba or other mild wine. Some syrup may be added to this if desired.

How to Preserve Cider

A pure, sweet cider is only obtainable from clean, sound fruit, and the fruit should therefore be carefully examined and wiped before grinding.

In the press, use haircloth or gunny in place of straw. As the cider runs from the press, let it pass through a hair sieve into a large open vessel that will hold as much juice as can be expressed in one day. In one day, or sometimes less, the pomace will rise to the top and in a short time grow very thick. When little white bubbles break through it, draw off the liquid through a very small spigot placed about 3 in. from the bottom, so that the lees may be left behind. The cider must be drawn off into very clean, sweet casks, preferably fresh liquor casks, and closely watched. The moment the white bubbles, before mentioned, are perceived rising at the bunghole, rack it again. It is usually necessary to repeat this three times. Then fill up the cask with cider in every respect

Ciders

like that originally contained in it, add a tumbler of warm, sweet oil, and bung up tight. For very fine cider it is customary to add at this stage of the process about ½ lb. of glucose (starch sugar) or a smaller portion of white sugar. The cask should then be allowed to remain in a cool place until the cider has acquired the desired flavor. In the meantime clean barrels for its reception should be prepared as follows: Some clean strips of rags are dipped in melted sulphur, lighted and burned in the bunghole and the bung laid loosely on the end of the rag so as to retain the sulphur vapor within the barrel. Then tie up ½ lb. of mustard seed in a coarse muslin bag and put it in the barrel, fill the barrel with cider, add about ¼ lb. of isinglass or fine gelatine dissolved in hot water.

This is the old-fashioned way, and will keep cider in the same condition as when it went into the barrel, if kept in a cool place, for a year.

Professional cider makers are now using calcium sulphite (sulphite of lime) instead of mustard and sulphur vapor. It is much more convenient and effectual. To use it, it is simply requisite to add ⅛ to ¼ oz. of the sulphite to each gallon of cider in the cask, first mixing the powder in about a quart of the cider, then pouring it back into the cask and giving the latter a thorough shaking or rolling. After standing bunged several days to allow the sulphite to exert its full action it may be bottled off.

The sulphite of lime (which should not be mistaken for the sulphate of lime) is a commercial article, cost moderate if bought by the barrel. It will preserve the sweetness of the cider perfectly, but unless care is taken not to add too much of it, it will impart a slight sulphurous taste to the cider. The bottles and corks used should be perfectly clean, and the corks wired down.

A little cinnamon, wintergreen or sassafras, etc., is often added to sweet cider in the bottle, together with a dram or so of bicarbonate of soda at the moment of driving the stopper. This helps to neutralize the acids and renders

Beverages—Non-Alcoholic

the liquid effervescent when unstoppered, but if used in excess it may prejudicially affect the taste.

To Keep Cider

1.—Place in each barrel immediately on making, mustard, 4 oz.; salt, 1 oz; ground chalk, 1 oz. Shake well.
2.—Mustard seed, 1 oz.; allspice, 1 oz · olive oil, ¼ pt.; alcohol, ½ pt.

Cider Preservative, Bismuth as a

L. Defour and Daniel find that the addition of 10 grams of bismuth subnitrate to each hectoliter of cider prevents, or materially retards, the hardening of the beverage on exposure to air during use from casks; not only so, but the presence of the bismuth salt renders alcoholic fermentation more complete.

To Keep Cider Sweet

When the cider has reached the flavor required add 1 to 2 tumblerfuls of grated horseradish to each barrel of cider.

Quince Cider

Take a quantity of ripe quinces, cut into quarters, and with the pips, etc., removed. Boil these in a copper with double their weight of water; when boiled to perfect softness pour the must into a vat. To this add, for every 50 pt. of must, 2 lb. of sugar and ½ lb. of yeast, diluted in a sufficiency of hot water. Mix the whole well together and allow to ferment. Then strain and bottle.

Raisin Cider

This is made in a similar way to raisin wine, but without employing sugar, and with only 2 lb. of raisins to the gallon, or even more, of water. It is usually fit for bottling in 10 days and in a week longer is ready for use.

Ciders

Sparkling Cider

Sparkling cider is a brilliant, refreshing and very agreeable beverage, which will keep for a long time, and, by some connoisseurs, is preferred to champagne. Pure ciders are very rich in sugar, and they often yield a great deal of alcohol which quickly flies to the head of the consumer, as grape champagne does. Those who require a good, healthful, refreshing drink should always use the milder ciders.

In making Normandy cider, which is the most sparkling, the cider is allowed to stand for 3, 4, 5 or 6 weeks, during which fermentation proceeds. The time varies according to the nature of the apples and also to the temperature of the store. When it is very warm the first fermentation is usually completed in 7 days. Before bottling, the liquid must be fined, and this is best performed with catechu dissolved in cold cider; 60 grains catechu per hectoliter of cider is sufficient. This is well rummaged up in the vats with a stick and then the cider is left to settle for a few days. The cider at this stage is still sweet, and it is a point of considerable nicety not to carry the first fermentation too far. Very strong bottles should obviously be employed, such, for example, as champagne bottles, and the corks should be wired down. The bottles should not be quite filled, so as to allow more freedom for the carbonic-acid gas which forms.

When the bottles have been filled, corked and wired down, they should be placed in a good cellar, which should be dry, or else the cider will taste of the cork. The bottles should not be laid for 4 or 5 weeks, or breakage will ensue. When they are being laid they should be placed on laths of wood or on dry sand; they should never be stowed on cold or damp floors.

Some makers of Normandy "champagne" have recourse to various dodges in order to increase the "gasiness" of their wares, especially if these latter are of poor quality; but these can generally be recognized. A fine bouquet is given to the best ciders by pouring into each

Beverages—Non-Alcoholic

bottle, before filling it with cider, a small liquor glass of good cognac, but some bottlers content themselves with adding a little cider brandy to the liquor about a week before bottling off. Should the cider be relatively poor in sugar, or should it have been fermented too far, then about 10 to 12 grams of powdered loaf sugar are added to each little bottle, or else a measure of sugar candy syrup, before pouring in the cider.

Chapter XIX.

WINES AND WINE MAKING

THE grapes are not removed from the vine until they are quite ripe. As the maturation not only of different varieties, but of the same kind, is dependent upon the season, no stated period can be fixed for the commencement of the vintage. The grapes are ready to be gathered when the white kind becomes of a brownish yellow color and the red or blue very dark purple or nearly black. Shears, pruning knives or scissors are used for the removal of the fruit from the vine.

In making the finer wines, previous to being pressed, the bunches are carefully examined, and any unripe or damaged grapes are picked off and used to make inferior wine, or in the gathering the unripe specimens are left on the branch to ripen. The blue and dark varieties, when intended for the best wines, are, with few exceptions, removed from the stalks before being pressed; the white grapes are pressed with the stalks.

Except with those grapes which produce wines that are likely to become viscous or ropy, the stalks are not left for any length of time in contact with the grape juice or must. There are various modes of separating the grapes from the stalks. One method consists in the employment of a wooden fork or trident ½ yd. or more in length. By turning this round in a wooden pail filled with the fruit the grapes become detached from the stalks, which are thus brought to the surface and removed.

In another contrivance the separation is effected by inclosing the bunches in cages made of parallel wires.

Beverages—Alcoholic

Inside the cage there is a stirrer. When this is turned by an external handle the grapes alone drop through the wires, leaving the stalks in the cage. Sometimes the separation is accomplished by means of hurdles, which are so manipulated that the fruit only shall pass through the meshes.

Previous to their being pressed the grapes have to undergo the preliminary process of bruising or crushing. This is sometimes done by their being trodden under the naked feet of men on a large wooden stage or platform; at other times the mean wear heavy boots, while in some cases the grapes are placed in a vat and bruised with a kind of wooden pestle. Sometimes they are crushed between wooden grooved rollers. Of all these processes, the first, although the least cleanly, possesses the advantage of not crushing the pips or stalks, and is thus free from the risk of imparting an unpleasant flavor to the wine.

There is considerable divergence in the statements of different writers as to the yield of must or juice from ripe grapes. Payen says it amounts to from 94 to 96% of the total weight of the grape. Dupré and Thudichum obtained from three samples of grapes, respectively, 78.75%, 76.75% and 72.25%. Wagner averages it from about 60 or 70%.

When a white wine is required, the bruised grape, whether of the white or red variety, is at once pressed, except when, as happens with some kinds of fruit, it is kept to allow of the development of the bouquet. The mode of procedure is different when a red wine is to be prepared. The crushed grapes must then be kept in a tub or vat, loosely covered over, until an examination of a small quantity of the juice shows it has acquired the necessary color. For it to do this sometimes takes from 3 to 4 days to a month.

During this period alcohol has been formed in the pulp, and this, with the tartaric acid of the fruit, has dissolved out of the coloring principle of the grape. Great care is necessary at this stage to prevent the too long exposure of the crushed and fermenting fruit to the air.

Wine presses are of various patterns.

In many wine-making establishments iron presses have supplanted wooden ones, over which they possess the advantages of greater cleanliness and non-absorption of the must. The wine press in general use in the Gironde consists of a tall, round basket, made of perpendicular laths. The fruit is placed in this basket, and upon the fruit a wooden block, to which a screw is attached; a nut works upon the screw from above downward and presses the wooden block upon the fruit, the liquid from which is forced out through the laths and collected.

In the manufacture of champagne and some red wines, very powerful presses are employed, but these possess the objection of pressing the fixed oil from the pips and an unpleasantly tasting juice from the stalks, and thereby damaging the product. In some establishments centrifugal machines have been used, not only with the result of yielding a better wine, but of effecting a considerable gain in time and labor.

The must, being received into proper receptacles, next undergoes the vinous fermentation. In the case of white wines the must is kept separate from that subsequently procured by submitting the husks, pips and stalks to additional pressure, and is sold as the first or superior wine.

But with red wines the husks (and in some cases the marc) are thrown into the fermenting vat, by which means the wine acquires an additional amount of coloring matter. In this case, when the completed wine is drawn off, the husks are again pressed, and the wine so obtained added to the first instalment. As the tannic acid is derived from the skins and seeds of the grape, wines prepared in this manner usually contain a considerable amount of this substance.

The fermentation is conducted in different countries at different temperatures, and, of course, with different results. When must is fermented at 15 to 20° C. (59 to 68° F.) it yields a wine strong in alcohol, but wanting in bouquet; while if the fermentation be carried on at 5 to 15°

Beverages—Alcoholic

C. (41 to 59° F.) the product will be a wine rich in bouquet, but poor in alcohol.

The wines of Spain, the south of France, Austria and Hungary are produced at the higher temperature, and those of Germany, for the most part, at the lower one. The fermentation is carried on in large wooden vats. In some places vats of sandstone or brick are used for this purpose. The fermentation of white wines, such as those of the Rhine and Gironde, is effected in new and perfectly clean casks or hogsheads, the bungholes of which are left open to allow the escape of the carbonic acid. Opinions differ as to whether air should be admitted or not during fermentation. The process is undoubtedly quickened if the must be aerated. The aeration is sometimes performed by a bellows fitted with rose nozzle. During the operation of blowing in the must is to be kept at a low temperature to prevent the volatilization of the bouquet. When the opposite method is followed various devices are in use for excluding the air, or at any rate an excess of it. In some cases the vat, being provided with a suitable lid, has a hole or is arranged with a tube for the escape of the carbonic acid. Koles and Bamberger accomplish the same end, without letting in the external air, by means of a glass tube bent twice at right angles; one limb of the tube passes through the bunghole into the vessel of water. In another contrivance the lid of the vat is fitted with a valve, which, opening only outward, allows of the exit of the carbonic acid.

Red wines are fermented in large and, in most cases, open vats, fitted in the inside with perforated shelves, which, being below the surface of the liquid, prevent the husks rising to the top and setting up acetous fermentation. After the completion of the fermentation of Burgundy wines, in some places it was formerly the filthy custom for men to enter the vat and by their vigorous movements to mix the contents.

It is satisfactory to learn that this particularly objectionable practice is getting very much into disuse.

Wines and Wine Making

The length of time necessary for the completion of the fermentation varies with the locality, the temperature of the apartment and with the quality of the wine required. In France, for the ordinary descriptions of wine, it generally takes from 3 days to 1 week, and in Germany from 1 to 2 weeks. With the finer kinds of wine it occupies 4, 5 or 6 weeks. The progress of the fermentation may be estimated from the specific gravity of the liquid, since as the fermentation proceeds and the sugar is undergoing conversion into alcohol, the wine of course becomes more attenuated and its specific gravity diminishes. It has been calculated that ½% of the alcohol present in the wine escapes during fermentation, as well as a considerable quantity of carbonic acid. An apparatus has been invented for collecting these products by causing them to pass into water by means of a hydraulic bung.

When the fermentation is over the wine is run into casks, any sediment, such as lees or yeast, being left behind in the fermenting vessel. It is most important that the casks used for this purpose should be absolutely clean. Before a cask is used a second time it should be thoroughly sulphured.

Those wines which contain a large amount of alcohol are sometimes allowed to remain in the fermenting vat until they have cleared, but weak wines are immediately drawn off into the cask to prevent the setting in of the acetous fermentation. The casks must be filled to the bungholes. A second or minor fermentation takes place in the wine when in the cask, during which tartar or bitartrate of potash is deposited on the sides of the cask and yeast at the bottom. This second fermentation should be allowed to go on at a low temperature, 5 to 10° C. (41 to 50° F.), and at a slow rate. In some cases it is made to extend to 3 or 6 months.

When the second fermentation is over the casks are filled to the bunghole and securely closed, or the wine is at once drawn into fresh casks to be stored. In these it remains closely bunged up until more tartar is deposited, after which is may be racked off into bottles or casks. When wine is to be stored for any length of time it is necessary to repeat the racking off frequently. Racking is performed by means of a siphon inserted in the bunghole or by a cock suitably fixed in the cask. If the racked wine is not perfectly clear, it is fined by the addition of isinglass, previously softened by soaking in a small quantity of wine. After the addition of the isinglass the cask is then filled to the bunghole, closed and remains undisturbed for about 6 weeks, and if, at the end of that time, it is not perfectly bright it is made to undergo a second racking. In wine-making countries blood and solution of glue are sometimes used for fining red wines which contain much tannin. Milk is also occasionally employed for the same purpose. The racking should be performed in cool weather and preferably in the early spring.

The manufacture of champagne differs in its details from that of the so-called still wine. The best wine is made from a black grape of very fine quality, known as the *Noirien*, or *Pineau*, and grown in the champagne district. None but the best selected grapes are used; all those that are rotten, unripe or in any way unsound being rejected. The grapes are gathered when they have attained their greatest size. The vintage commences early in October. To prevent the juice being colored by the skin of the grape, the fruit is submitted to pressure as quickly as possible after being gathered. Very powerful machines are employed for this purpose, since the champagne grape, unlike other varieties, is not previously crushed. Great care is taken to apply the pressure evenly and to conduct the operation with all expedition, for if this exceeds 2 hours the must will be colored. The grapes are sometimes pressed 4 times. In good seasons the must obtained from the different pressings is mixed together. In middling ones the first yield is kept for making the best wines, nor is the fourth mixed with the other two. The light-colored must is first conveyed into a large vat, where it remains for 6, 12 or 18 hours, according to the temperature.

At the end of this time certain vegetable matters that would damage the taste of the ensuing wine, as well as render it liable to a second fermentation, become deposited. Directly the must has cleared it is run into small barrels of 200 liters capacity, in which it undergoes fermentation. Sometimes the clearing of the juice is accomplished by filtration; at others, when the weather is warm and fermentation sets in so rapidly as not to allow the impurities to subside, it is run into casks filled with the fumes from burning sulphur. By this means the excessive fermentative action is arrested and sufficient time is given for the dregs to settle. The juice having been made clear by either of the above methods is drawn into barrels, which are arranged in rows in the cellars. The barrels are filled to the bung, the froth, which is formed during the fermentation flowing out at the bungholes. In some wine-making establishments the barrels are tightly bunged up, there being previously added to the contents 1% of brandy. The casks are opened at the end of December and the wine fined by means of isinglass, this operation being conducted at the lowest possible temperature. If, at the end of a fortnight, it has not become bright, it is left for another fortnight, and then, if not clear, it undergoes a second fining. The fining process must be used with caution; when overdone it diminishes and frequently stops the activity of the subsequent fermentation. To obviate this the wine should be judiciously exposed to the air and a minute quantity of yeast added to each hogshead before it is bottled.

When the wine has cleared, before being bottled, cane sugar is added to it, since the quantity of undecomposed natural sugar in the wine is not sufficient to furnish the requisite amount of carbonic-acid gas, the ingredient to which champagne owes its effervescent properties.

Champagne bottles constitute a very considerable item in the trade expenses of the wine maker. He pays the glass manufacturer liberally for them, and some wine makers give orders for as many as from 50,000 to 205,000 at a time.

The bottles as they arrive are examined by an experienced person, and those which contain flaws of any kind, or are not perfectly new, symmetrical and strong, are rejected. These average about 10%. The bottles are required to be as nearly as possible of uniform weight and thickness. The inside of each bottle is scrubbed by means of a revolving hair brush and clean water. After being drained, the bottles are rinsed with 90% alcohol and closed with an old but clean cork. They are thus ready, when required, for filling. The wine maker also expends a large amount of money in the purchase of corks, which must be of the best and soundest description. It has been found to be very false economy to use inferior kinds. The wine being drawn into bottles to a height of 2 or 3 inches from the top of the neck, the bottles have next to be corked, the cork being secured in the bottle by a small iron band, called an *agrafe*. All these operations have to be performed deftly and rapidly by experienced workmen. With what speed they are accomplished may be imagined from the fact that an *atelier* of 5 workmen, who divide the labor, will bottle and cork from 1,200 to 1,500 bottles daily, 2 bottles passing through all hands in 1 minute. The corking, etc., finished, the bottles are next placed on their sides and stacked in cellars or caves, each stack being supported by thin laths.

As the summer approaches, the wine begins to show signs of fermentation, which increases with the hot weather. When the fermentation reaches such a stage as to cause the wine to occupy the previously unfilled space in the neck of the bottle, a large number of bottles begin to burst, as well as to leak; and in some years as much as 30% of the wine is lost from these causes. Two courses, each of which requires to be promptly adopted, are open to the wine maker under these circumstances. Either he must remove the wine to a cooler cellar or uncork the bottles. Sometimes, if the breakage, or *casse*, as it is termed, has not exceeded 7 or 8% by the time August is reached, he takes the chance of further loss and lets the wine remain, for with the fall in temperature, which usually occurs in September and October, the energetic action of the wine ceases and the breakage also.

The leaky and broken bottles are then removed from the sound ones, which are restacked and left until a yeasty substance has discontinued depositing upon their lower sides. The bottles are kept in this condition until required for sale. Before, however, they are in a fit state for the purchaser, the yeasty matter has to be removed and the wine to be liqueured. The yeast is got rid of as follows: The bottles are placed necks downward, on perforated shelves arranged in rows. A workman then seizes a bottle, and holding it in the inverted position, by a dexterous movement discharges the yeast from the side and brings it down upon the cork. This operation, which extends over some weeks, has to be repeated from time to time, until the supernatant wine is quite clear. The bottles are then very cautiously removed from the cellars to the corking and tying-down rooms, when they come into the hands of a workman called a disgorger. The disgorger, holding the bottle still neck downward, proceeds to liberate the cork by slipping off the *agrafe*, and when the cork is 3 parts out he quickly inverts the bottle. The cork is then forcibly ejected with a loud report by the froth which carries with it the greater part of the yeast and other solid matters, what remains of these being got rid of by the workman working his finger round the neck of the bottle, whereby they are detached and forced out by the still rising froth. The workman then places his thumb over the mouth of the bottle, which is afterward temporarily closed with an old cork.

The liqueur, which is next to be added, is of very varied composition, as almost every champagne maker has his favorite and special preparation.

The best liqueurs are made of some choice wine, mixed

Beverages—Alcoholic

with the purest cane sugar. The inferior kinds consist of a mixture of 90% alcohol, sugar and some flavoring material. A certain measured quantity of the liqueur is added to each bottle of wine. The bottle is then corked, wired, tied down and washed and the cork covered with tinfoil and labeled. It is then ready for sale and export. It sometimes happens that after the previous round of operations has been gone through the champagne becomes turbid and a minor second fermentation sets in. In this case it is made to undergo a repetition of the processes already described. It is a desideratum with every champagne maker that when the bottle is opened for its contents to be drunk, the removal of the cork should be accompanied with a full, deep and distinct report. When, instead of this, the report is short and sharp and resembles a popping noise, this is owing to the space beween the liquid and the cork, filled with the gas, being too small. When the gas escapes with a hissing noise, it is because the cork fits the neck of the bottle unequally or has not been driven in in a perfectly straight direction. The good name of any maker would be seriously liable to comport itself in this manner. He therefore spares no expense in providing himself with the very best and soundest corks. The best way to prevent the escape of the gas from the bottle is always to keep the bottles lying on their sides.

All effervescing wines are manufactured in a similar manner to champagne.

Since the alcohol in the wine is derived from the sugar contained in the must, it would seem that the sweetest and ripest grapes should yield the strongest product. When the decomposition of the sugar has been complete, this will be the result; but it frequently happens that, owing to an insufficiency in the must of the protein compounds which nourish the yeast cells (the *torula cerevisiæ*), by the agency of which the fermentation is accomplished, the whole of the sugar is not converted into alcohol, in which case a sweet wine will be produced, or the sweetness may be due to the alcohol formed stopping the fermen-

Wines and Wine Making

tation before all the sugar had been decomposed or to an excess of glycerine. If, on the other hand, the grape juice is rich in albuminous matter, but poor in sugar, the consequent wine will be what is termed a dry one. Such are the red wines of France and the Rhine.

TABLE SHOWING THE QUANTITY OF ALCOHOL IN WINE

Names, etc.	Alcohol of 0.7937 per cent by weight.	Proof spirit per cent by volume.
Port:		
Weakest	14.97	31.31
Mean of 7 samples	16.20	34.91
Strongest	17.10	37.27
White	14.97	31.31
Sherry:		
Weakest	13.98	30.84
Mean of 13 wines, excluding those very long kept in cask	15.37	33.59
Strongest	16.17	35.12
Mean of 9 wines long kept in cask in the East Indies	14.72	31.30
Madre da Xeres	16.90	37.06
Madeira:		
Long kept in cask in the East Indies—strongest	16.90	37.06
Long kept in cask in the East Indies—weakest	14.09	30.86
Teneriffe (long in cask at Calcutta)	13.84	30.21
Cercial	15.45	33.65
Lisbon (dry)	16.14	34.71
Shiraz	12.95	28.30
Amontillado	12.63	27.60
Claret	7.72	16.95
Château-Latour	7.78	17.06
Rosan	7.61	16.74
Ordinary Claret (Vin Ordinaire)	8.99	18.96
Rivesaltes	9.31	22.35
Malmsley	12.86	28.17
Rüdesheimer, first quality	8.40	18.44
Rüdesheimer, inferior	6.90	15.19
Hambacher, superior quality	7.35	16.15

According to Wagner, red French wines contain 9 to 14% by volume of alcohol; Burgundy, 9, 10 and 11%; Bordeaux, 10, 11 and 12%. Other French wines contain 8 to 10%; the wines of the Palatinate, 7 to 9.5%; Hungarian wines, 9 to 11%. Champagne contains 9 to 12%; Xeres, 17%; Madeira, 17 to 23.7%.

In addition to ethylic alcohol and water, which, as shown in the previous table, vary largely in the proportions in which they are present in different kinds of wine, most wines contain the following substances: Propylic, butylic, caprylic and caproic alcohols; acetic and enanthic ether; grape sugar (dextrose and levulose); glycerine; gums; pectin; coloring and fatty substances; protein bodies; carbonic acid, ordinary and levo-tartaric and racemic acids; citric acid; malic acid; tannic acid; acetic acid; lactic acid; succinic acid; organic and inorganic salts.

Of these the propylic and butylic, caprylic and caproic alcohols, the ethers, the glycerine, the carbonic, acetic, lactic and succinic acids are produced during fermentation, the remaining substances being original constituents of the grape juice, which also contains bitartrate of potash, but this being insoluble in weak spirit is thrown down or deposited as the conversion of sugar into alcohol proceeds. In its crude condition it is known as argol and is the source of cream of tartar and tartaric acid. As a result of its formation in the grape a considerable amount of the free acid is removed from the fruit. This is why wine made from grapes is so much superior and keeps so much better than that manufactured from fruits that abound instead in citric and malic acids. These latter require the addition of large quantities of sugar to disguise their acidity, a proceeding which frequently gives rise in them to a second fermentation and often to the consequent formation of acetic acid. The acetic ether in wine is produced by the mutual reaction of acetic acid and ethylic alcohol. Neubauer, dissenting from Dupré and Thudichum, says the enanthic ether is the constituent to which wines owe their bouquet. He regards this ether as a combination of various substances of which caprylic and caproic acid ethers are the most important. Their formation is believed to take place partly during and partly after fermentation. The rest of the non-volatile constituents, such as the sugar, the gum, the protein bodies, coloring matter, inorganic salts, etc., which remain behind when a wine is evaporated to dryness, constitute, with a certain quantity of substance the composition of which has not been defined, the extractive matter.

Wines and Wine Making

The amount of extractive matter in wines varies as greatly as from 1 to 20%. This difference occurs even in wines of a similar character and from the same district. Thus in Rhine wines it ranges from 10.6 to 4.2%, in the Palatinate wines from 10.7 to 1.9%, in Bohemian wines the mean is 2.26%, in the wines of Austria 2.64%, and in those of Hungary 2.62%. It is highest in sweet wines. In many adulterated wines, as the extractive matter is either very small or sometimes altogether absent, it has been proposed to employ the estimation of its amount in a wine as a test of its genuineness or the reverse.

Light wines owe their color, varying from pale yellow to brown, possibly to oxidized extractive matter or to the cask. The color of red wine is due to the action of its free tartaric acid on a blue substance residing in the skin of the grape. This body, which is known to wine makers as wine blue, and which bears a great resemblance to litmus, in turning red when acted upon by acids, was named *œnocyan* or *ocenocyamin* by Mulder or Maumené. It is insoluble in water, alcohol, ether, olive oil and oil of turpentine, but is dissolved by alcohol containing small quantities of tartaric or acetic acid. Glycerine was found to be a normal constituent of wine by Pasteur in 1859. As the wine matures the glycerine disappears. In Austrian wines Pohl found 2.6% of glycerine. In some wines it reaches 3%, but in most it seldom exceeds 1%. In old wines it exists only in very small quantity.

Imitation Wines

1.—From ripe saccharine fruits.—Take of the fruit, 4 to 6 lb.; clear soft water, 1 gal.; sugar, 3 to 5 lb.; cream of tartar (dissolved in boiling water), 1¼ oz.; brandy, 2 to 3%; flavoring as required. If the full proportions of fruit and sugar are used, the product will be good without the brandy, but better with it (if you have it on hand); 1½ lb. raisins may be substituted for each pound of sugar.

In the above manner are made the following wines:

Beverages—Alcoholic

Gooseberry wine, currant wine (red, white or black), mixed fruit wine (currants and gooseberries or black, red and white currants; ripe black heart cherries and raspberries, equal parts), a good family wine; cherry wine, colepress wine (from apples and mulberries, equal parts), elder wine, strawberry wine, raspberry wine, mulberry wine, whortleberry or bilberry wine; blackberry wine, damson wine, morella wine, apricot wine, apple wine, grape wine, etc.

2.—From dry saccharine fruit (such as raisins).—Take of the dried fruit, 4½ to 7½ lb.; clear soft water, 1 gal.; cream of tartar (dissolved), 1 oz.; brandy, 1½ to 4% (if you have it). Should the dried fruit employed be at all deficient in saccharine matter, 2 to 3 lb. of it may be omitted, and half that quantity of sugar or two-thirds of raisins added. In the above manner are made date wine, fig wine, raisin wine, etc.

3.—From acidulous, astringent or scarcely ripe fruits or those which are deficient in saccharine matter.—Take of the picked fruit 2½ to 3½ lb.; sugar, 3½ to 5½ lb.; cream of tartar (dissolved), ½ oz.; water, 1 gal.; brandy, 2 to 6% (if you have it).

In the above manner are made gooseberry wine, bullace wine, damson wine.

4.—From footstalks, leaves, cuttings, etc.—By infusing them in water, in the proportion of 3 to 6 lb. to the gal., or q. s. to give a proper flavor, or to form a good saccharine liquid, and adding 2½ to 4 lb. of sugar to each gallon of strained liquor; 1½ lb. of raisins may be substituted for each pound of sugar.

In the above manner are made grape wine (from the pressed cake of grapes), English grape wine, rhubarb wine (from garden rhubarb), celery wine, etc.

5.—From saccharine roots and stems of plants.—Take of the bruised, rasped or sliced vegetable 4 to 6 lb.; boiling water, 1 gal.; infuse until cold, press out the liquid and to each gal. add of sugar 3 to 4 lb.; cream of tartar, 1 oz.; brandy 2 to 5% (if you have it). For some roots and stems

Wines and Wine Making

the water must not be very hot, as they are thus rendered troublesome to press.

In the above manner are made beet-root wine, parsnip wine, turnip wine, etc.

6.—From flowers, spices, aromatics, etc.—These are prepared by infusing a sufficient quantity of the bruised ingredient for a few days in any simple wine (as that from sugar, honey, raisins, etc.), after the active fermentation is complete, or, at all events, a few weeks before racking them.

In the above manner are made clary wine (muscatel) (from flowers, 1 qt. to the gallon); cowslip wine (from flowers, 2 qt. to the gallon); elder flower wine (flowers of white-berried elder, ¾ pt.; and lemon juice, 3 fl.oz. to the gallon); ginger wine (1¼ oz. ginger to the gallon); orange wine (1 doz. sliced oranges per gallon); lemon wine (juice of 12 and rinds of 6 lemons to the gallon); spruce wine (¼ oz. of essence of spruce per gallon); juniper wine (berries, ¾ pt. per gallon); peach wine (4 or 5 sliced and the stones broken, to the gallon); apricot wine (as peach wine, but with more fruit); quince wine (12 to the gallon); rose clove gillyflower, carnation, lavender, violet, primrose and other flower wines (distilled water from the flowers, 1½ pt., or flowers 1 pt. to the gallon); mixed fruit wine; pineapple wine; cider wine; elder wine; birch wine (from the sap, at the end of February or beginning of March); sycamore wine (from the sap); malt wine (from strong wort); and the wines of any of the saccharine juices of ripe fruit.

7.—From saccharine matter.—Take of sugar 3 to 4 lb.; cream of tartar, ½ oz.; water, 1 gal.; honey, 1 lb.; brandy, 2 to 4%. A handful of grape leaves or cutting, bruised, or 1 pt. of good malt wort or mild ale may be substituted for the honey. Chiefly used as the basis for other wines, as it has little flavor of its own.

In all the preceding formulæ lump sugar is intended when the wines are required very pale, and good granulated sugar when this is not the case. Some of the preceding wines are improved by substituting good cider, perry or pale ale or malt wort for a whole or a portion of the water. Good porter may also be advantageously used in this way for some of the deep-colored red wines. When expense is no object, and very strong wines are wanted, the expressed juices of the ripe fruits with the addition of 3 or 4 lb. of sugar per gal., may be substituted for the fruit in substance and the water.

Management of Wines.

The remarks arranged under this heading are more particularly intended for the use of the maker, the dealer, and the private individual, as those which precede it are for the wine maker.

Age.—The sparkling wines are in their prime in from 18 to 30 months after the vintage. Thin wines of inferior growths should be drank within 12 to 15 months and be preserved in a very cool cellar. Sound, well-fermented, full-bodied still wines are improved by age, with reasonable limits, provided they be well preserved from the air and stored in a cool place having a pretty uniform temperature.

Acid Taste of Wines, To Remove.—Neutralize the excess of acid by powdered chalk.

Ages of Different Wines When at Their Prime.—The age named below for each wine will be found to be that at which it possesses its fullest flavor and when it will be best to drink it: Port, 20 years; Madeira, 10 years; Sherry, 10 years; Red Madeira, 6 years; Madeira-Malmsey, 5 years; Callavella, 4 years; Malaga, 3 years; Muscatel, 3 years; Red Hermitage, 20 years; White Hermitage, 20 years; Roussillon, 20 years; Rivesaltes, 20 years; Banyuls, 20 years; Collioure, 15 years; Salces, 10 years; La Palme, 10 years; Sigean, 8 years; Carcassonne, 8 years; Beziers, 8 years; Lunel, 8 years; Champagne, 6 years; Montpellier, 5 years; Frontignan, 5 years.

Alcoholizing.—Alcohol is frequently added to weak or vapid wines to increase their strength or to promote their preservation. In Portugal one-third of alcohol is commonly added to port before shipping it to England, as without this addition it generally passes into the acetous fermentation during the voyage. A little alcohol is also usually added to sherry before it leaves Spain. The addition of alcohol to wine injures its proper flavor, and hence it is chiefly made to port, sherry and other wines whose flavor is so strong as not to be easily injured. Even when alcohol is added to wines of the latter description they require to be kept for some time to recover their natural flavor.

Bottling.—The secret of bottling wine with success consists in the exercise of care and cleanliness. The bottles should be sound, clean and dry, and free from the least mustiness or other odor. The corks should be of the best quality, and immediately before being placed in the bottles should be compressed by means of a cork squeezer, or of one of the numerous machines made for this purpose. For superior or very delicate wines the corks are sometimes prepared by placing them in a copper or tub, covering them with weights to keep them down, and then pouring over them boiling water, holding a little pearlash in solution. In this liquid they are allowed to remain for 24 hours, when they are well stirred about in the liquid, drained and reimmersed for a second 24 hours, in hot water, after which they are well washed and soaked in several successive portions of clean and warm rain water, drained, dried out of contact with dust, put into paper bags and hung up in a dry place for use. Many wine merchants, however, disapprove of this course and merely dip the corks in clean cold water before inserting them in the bottles. The wine should be clear and brilliant, and if it be not so, it must undergo the process of fining before being bottled. The bottles, corks and wine being ready, the utmost cleanliness and care should be exercised during the process. Great caution should also be observed to avoid shaking the cask, so as not to disturb the bottoms. The remaining portion that cannot be drawn off clear should be passed through the wine bag, and, when bottled, should be set apart as inferior to the rest, or the lees are collected in a cask kept for the purpose, and the clear wine resulting from their subsidence is used for filling up casks about to be fined. The coopers, to prevent breakage and loss, place each bottle, before corking it, in a small bucket or boot having a bottom made of soft cork or leather, which is strapped on the knee of the bottler. The bottlers seldom break a bottle, though they flog in the corks very hard. The bucket or boot is now very largely supplanted by a corking machine, an apparatus which first submits the cork to great pressure and then immediately afterward drives it firmly into the neck of the bottle, in which, owing to its subsequent expansion, it fits very closely and perfectly. When the process of bottling is complete the bottles of wine are stored in a cool cellar on their sides, but on no account in an upright position. Sometimes they are placed in damp straw or in sweet, dry sawdust or sand.

Cellaring.—A wine cellar should be dry at bottom and either covered with good hard gravel or be paved with flags or concrete. Its gratings or windows should preferably open toward the north, and it should be sunk sufficiently below the surface to insure an equable temperature. It should also be sufficiently removed from any public thoroughfare so as not to suffer vibration from the passing of vehicles. Should it not be in a position to maintain a regular temperature, arrangements should be made to apply artificial heat in winter and proper ventilation in summer. The temperature should range from 55 to 65° F. For Burgundies the former temperature is the more suitable; for ports, sherries and strong wines the latter temperature.

Clarification of Wines.—If the wine is not clear and bright after racking it is necessary to clarify it. There are many causes which interfere with the proper brightness of wine, such as changes of temperature, in careless racking and others. Some wines clear themselves, so that clarification need not be resorted to. A great many

Wines and Wine Making

different substances have been employed in clarification. Many of the so-called clarifying powders are nothing but dried blood albumin. Isinglass, gelatine or fish glue is one of the best agents for clarification. It is dissolved in water until little more fluid than molasses. Gelatine prepared from bone is also used and may be obtained in sheets or in small pieces and sometimes in tablets. It is one of the best agents that can be used in clarifying and is especially valuable for clarifying white wine. After wine has been clarified with the gelatine it should be racked after standing a short time. Blood albumin affords a cheap and efficient means of clarifying the wine in large quantities. A gallon of blood beaten up with a gallon of the same kind of wine which it is desired to clarify will clarify 200 gallons of wine. Great care should be taken to have the blood fresh, as otherwise it is sure to injure, if not entirely destroy, the wine. It is especially successful in clarifying new wine. In case the wine loses a portion of its color it can be readily restored by an addition of the usual coloring matters.

Milk is used to some extent in place of the blood, but it is not as reliable. If the wine is of great value, the whites of eggs afford the best means of clarifying it, and should be used in all cases where expense is not an object. No pains should be spared to see that the eggs are entirely fresh, as otherwise the wines would be destroyed. The whites of the eggs are particularly efficient for white wine. The proper proportion is 1 egg per 10 gal. They should be beaten up with a small portion of wine with an eggbeater before adding to the wine. Gum arabic is also use, but is not as good as the white of egg or blood. Salt, alcohol and tannin and many other substitutes have been used with varying success. The ones already mentioned will give the best satisfaction.

Yellow White Wines.—The yellow color of white wines frequently stands in the way of their ready sale. It is removed by the blood albumin receipt given under clarification above. The receipt given under clarification of wines can be used to bring white wine which has turned yellow back to its normal color.

Earthy Flavor of Wines.—This defect in wines is apt to interfere seriously with their sale, as the taste is particularly disagreeable. It may be the result of several causes. The vineyards may not be properly cared for or in low, wet land. The treatment of wines which have earthy flavor requires much judgment and experience. Wines should be promptly clarified by the means already given and frequently racked. The white of egg receipt given under clarification is the best one to use for this defect. The addition of a small quantity of tannin dissolved in alcohol will also help to correct this defect.

Greenness.—This defect gives a very sour, unpleasant taste to the wine, owing to the malic and tartaric acids, which are in excess. There is no ordinary defect of wine which is more noticeable and more disagreeable than greenness. As its name implies, it is frequently caused by the use of unripe grapes. The treatment of the wine must be varied according to the taste. One of the various methods is to add from 1 to 3 qt. of old brandy to every 100 gal. of wine. Potassium tartrate affords a cheap and easy method of neutralizing the tartaric acid, forming potassium bitartrate, which may be afterward removed when the wine is right. The amount of potassium tartrate which may be used varies with the sourness of the wine, but 18 oz. per 100 gal. would be considered an average amount. Various other substitutes have been tried, but none is as successful as potassium tartrate.

Coloring Matters.—Various matters are largely employed to artificially heighten the colors of wines. The different spurious coloring matters can be detected by using a solution of lead acetate, and the precipitants formed give a good test by which the various colors can be determined.

1.—Malva flowers or hollyhock produce, when steeped in spirits for 24 hours, or even when boiled with water, a very beautiful purple.

Wines and Wine Making

2.—The pokeberry (the dark berries from the plant growing all over the United States) has a very dark red color.

3.—Whortleberry, huckleberry, elderberry, blackberry and mulberry.

4.—Cochineal gives a fine red color by boiling finely ground cochineal with cream of tartar.

5.—Brazil wood, sanders wood and logwood. These woods are boiled in water and the decoctions yield shades of color from red to blue.

6.—Orchil produces a beautiful purple.

7.—Red beets and carrots produce likewise a good color.

8.—Indigo solution, neutralized by potash, produces a fine blue.

9.—Annatto and extract of safflower produce a beautiful yellow.

10.—Red cabbage produces a beautiful bluish red.

11.—Turmeric is the most common color for yellow, as the spirit extracts all color immediately, as also quercitron bark.

12.—Garacine (extract of madder) produces various shades of red.

13.—Tincture of saffron (Spanish saffron) for yellow.

14.—Blue vitriol, or solution of indigo, produces blue.

15.—Burnt sugar produces a fine and permanent brown color for wines. It is best to boil down common sugar or loaf sugar nearly to dryness. It is then dissolved in hot water sufficient to make the consistency of syrup, and for the purpose of neutralizing it and making it a more permanent color, add to each gal. of sugar color about 1 oz. liquid ammonia.

16.—Green color for absinthe is prepared from a solution of extract of indigo and tumeric, dissolved in spirits.

17.—Violet is obtained by a solution of extract of logwood and alum.

18.—Alkanet root produces a fine blue red by macerating in alcohol.

Beverages—Alcoholic

19.—Barwood acquires a dark wine red color by digesting in alcohol.

20.—Brazil wood by being macerated in alcohol or by boiling for ½ hour, produces a deep red.

Spurious Coloring Matter.—The following coloring matters give, with lead acetate, the following precipitates: Pure red wine gives bluish gray, red poppy gives dirty gray, elderberry gives dirty green, bilberry gives grayish green, privetberry gives green, dwarf elderberry gives bluish gray to violet in the fresh berries and fine green in the fermented extract, mallow flower gives dark green, logwood gives feeble dark blue, Brazil wood gives wine red.

The following colors, when present, give the following precipitates with alum and ammonium carbonate: Pure red wine gives dirty green, red poppy gives slate gray, elderberry gives bluish gray, bilberry gives bright violet, privetberry gives bright green, dwarf elderberry gives bright violet, mallow flower gives bluish violet, logwood gives dark violet, Brazil wood gives carmine red.

Decanting.—In decanting wine care must be taken not to shake or disturb the crust when moving it about or drawing the cork, particularly of port wine. Never decant wine without a wine strainer, with some clean fine cambric in it, to prevent the crust and bits of cork going into the decanter. In decanting port wine do not drain it too close, as there are generally two-thirds of a wine-glassful of thick dregs in each bottle which ought to be rejected. In white wine there is not much deposit, but it should nevertheless be poured off very slowly, the bottle being raised gradually.

Detannation of Wines.—1.—The *Formulary* recommends the following method for removing the tannin or astringent matter from sherry wine: Sherry, 7 pt.; white of egg, 1 fl.oz.; alcohol, 1 pt. Beat the white of egg to a froth and mix it with wine; heat to about 170° F., or until the albumen is coagulated. Then cool, add the alcohol and after standing a few hours filter clear through paper.

This wine is a much better menstruum and preservative medicine for organic substances than sherry itself.

2.—Gelatine, 1 oz.; distilled water, 10 oz.; sherry wine, 7 gal. Dissolve the gelatine in the water by heating, add the solution to the wine, stir well and allow it to remain 6 hours, then filter. Before using the wine in wine of coca, cinchona or beef, wine and iron, to bring it up to the strength of stronger wine as recommended in the Pharmacopeia, add 6 oz. alcohol to each gallon. Red or white wine may be detannated after the above formula.

Detartarization.—Rhenish wines, even of the best growths, and in the finest condition, besides their tartar, contain a certain quantity of free tartaric acid, on the presence of which many of their distinctive properties depend. The excess of tartar is gradually deposited during the first years of the vatting, the sides of the vessels becoming more and more encrusted with it, but owing to the continual addition of new wine and other causes the liquid often gains such an excess of free tartaric acid as to acquire the faculty of redissolving the deposited tartar, which thus again disappears after a certain period. The taste and flavor of the wine are thus excited, but the excess of acid makes the wine less agreeable and probably less wholesome.

Under these circumstances the best corrective is pure neutral tartrate of potash. When this salt, in concentrated solution, is added to an acid wine the free acid combines with the neutral salt and separates from the liquid under the form of the sparingly soluble bitartrate of potash. If to 100 parts of a wine which contains 1 part of free tartaric acid we add 1½ parts of neutral tartrate of potash there will separate on repose at 70 to 75° F. 2 parts of crystallized tartar, and the wine will then contain only ½ part of tartar dissolved, in which there is only 0.2 part of the original free acid, 0.8 of the original free acid having been withdrawn from the wine. This method is particularly applicable to recent must and to wines which contain little, if any, free acetic acid. When this

Beverages—Alcoholic

last is present so much acetate of potash is formed as occasionally to vitiate the taste of the liquid.

Fermentation.—Chemists divide fermentation into 5 kinds, viz.:

1.—Saccharine fermentation, by which starch and gum are converted into sugar.

2.—Alcoholic or vinous fermentation, by which sugar is converted into alcohol.

3.—Viscous or mucilaginous fermentation, which converts sugar into slime or mucilage instead of alcohol.

4.—Acetous fermentation, by which alcohol is converted into vinegar.

5.—Putrid fermentation or putrefaction, which is exhibited in its most marked form in the putrefaction of animal substances.

Preventing Fermentation.—1.—According to the *Technologiste*, common resin prevents the formation of acetic acid in fermented liquids without having any disturbing effect on the process of alcoholic fermentation. The peculiar effect of the hop may be due, it is suggested, to its resinous matter rather than to its oils. Resin is added to sweet wines in Greece.

2.—Sodium silicate has been discovered to exert a very decided chemical action in checking alcoholic fermentation, in this respect being somewhat similar to borax, although much more energetic. A small quantity of the silicate will entirely arrest the fermentation of wine and also of milk.

Second fermentation, *La-pousse.*—Inordinate fermentation, either primary of secondary, in wine or any other fermented liquid, may be readily checked by sulphuration, or by the addition of sulphur, mustard seed, or sulphite of lime. The last must, however, be used with discretion.

Stopping fermentation.—Bottle the liquor and immerse a number of the bottles, with the mouths only projecting, in a large vessel of water. Loosen the stoppers and heat the water until of a uniform temperature of 180° F., then remove the bottles, stopper and seal them tightly and place in an inverted position.

Filtration of Bottled Wines.—Filter siphon, with siphon-shaped bent glass tube which in the short leg, at about the height of the bottle, has an egg-shaped enlargement that is filled with clean cotton wadding. According to the greater or lesser length of the long leg, the suction of the apparatus will be more or less vigorous, while at the same time the wadding will retain the particles causing turbidity. For repeated use the wadding is cleansed by boiling out in water and drying.

Fining.—1.—There are various modes of fining wine. Eggs, isinglass (true fish gelatine), gelatine and gum arabic are all used for the purpose. Whichever of these articles is used, the process is always the same. Supposing eggs (the cheapest) to be used: Draw a gal. or so of the wine and mix 1 qt. of it with the whites of 4 eggs by stirring it with a whisk; afterward, when thoroughly mixed pour it back into the cask through the bunghole and stir up the whole cask in a rotary direction with a clean split stick inserted through the bunghole. Having stirred it sufficiently, pour in the remainder of the wine drawn off until the cask is full. Then stir again, skimming off the bubbles that rise to the surface. When thoroughly mixed, by stirring close the bunghole and leave it to stand for 3 or 4 days. This quantity of clarified wine will fine 13 doz. of port or sherry. The other clearing ingredients are applied in the same manner, the material being cut into small pieces and dissolved in the quart of wine and the cask stirred in the same manner.

White wines are usually fined by isinglass. The quantity of isinglass varies with the quality and condition of the wine, and is regulated by the experience of the cellarman. Stout wines require a larger amount than thin ones. Even with stout ones it ought not to exceed ½ oz. to the hogshead. The Rhenish wines do not require more than ¼ oz., and the hocks still less. The choicest Russian (fish) isinglass only should be employed. It should be dissolved in cold water and thinned with wine. Red wines are generally fined with the whites of eggs in the proportion of 15 to 20 to the pipe. Sometimes, but rarely, hartshorn shavings or pale sweet glue is substituted for isinglass.

2.—Isinglass (gelatine). 1 lb.; stale beer, cider or vinegar, 3 or 4 pt. Mix and macerate until the former becomes gelatinous, then reduce it to a proper consistency with weak, mild beer, cider or any other liquid that the finings are intended for. A pint or more is the usual dose for a barrel of beer or porter and a quart for a hogshead of wine.

3.—Red Wines.—The operation is carried on in the same manner. To lighten up a wine add 6 eggs and a handful of salt, use the whites, yolks and shells.

4.—White Wines.—To fine 30 gal. white wine the whites of 3 eggs will be required with the addition of ½ an egg shell reduced to powder and a tablespoonful of salt. Beat up all together with a little of the wine and then pour gradually into the wine, stirring constantly.

Flatness.—This is removed by the addition of a little new brisk wine of the same kind or by sousing in 2 or 3 lb. of honey, or by adding 5 or 6 lb. of bruised sultana raisins and 3 or 4 qt. of good brandy per hogshead. By this treatment the wine will usually be recovered in about a fortnight, except in very cold weather. The process may be expedited if a tablespoonful or two of yeast be added and the cask removed to a warmer situation.

To Lay Down Wine.—Having carefully counted the bottles, they are stored away in their respective bins, a layer of sand or sawdust being placed under the first tier and another over it; a second tier is laid over this, protected by a lath, the head of the second being laid to the bottom of the first. Over this another bed of sawdust is laid, not too thick, then another lath, and so on till the bin is filled. Wine so laid in will be ready for use according to its quality and age. Port wine, old in the wood, will be ready to drink in 5 or 6 months, but if it is a fruity wine it will improve every year. Sherry, if of good quality, will be fit to drink as soon as the sickness (as its first condition after bottling is called) ceases, and will also improve, but the cellar must be kept at a perfectly steady temperature, neither too hot nor too cold, but about 55 or 60°, and absolutely free from draughts of cold air.

Insipidity.—See *Flatness.*

Maturation.—The natural maturation, or ripening of wine and beer by age, depends upon the slow conversion of the sugar which escaped decomposition in the gyle tun or fermenting vessel into alcohol. This conversion proceeds most perfectly in vessels which entirely exclude the air, as in the case of wine in bottles, as when air is present and the temperature sufficiently high it is accompanied by slow acetification. This is the case with wine in casks, the porosity of the wood allowing the very gradual permeation of the air. Hence the superiority of bottled over draught wine or that which has matured in wood. Good wine, or well-fermented beer, is vastly improved by age when properly preserved, but inferior liquor or even superior liquor, when preserved in improper vessels or situations, becomes acidulous from the conversion of its alcohol into vinegar. Tartness or acidity is consequently very generally, though wrongly, regarded by the ignorant as a sign of age in liquor. The peculiar change by which fermented liquors become mature or ripe by age is termed the insensible fermentation. It is the alcoholic fermentation impeded by the presence of the already formed spirit in the liquor and by the lowness of the temperature.

Mold or fungus is very frequently produced by keeping the wine in too warm a cellar, or in a cask not filled to the bunghole, or else in one from which the bung has been left out. As it forms mostly on weak wines its presence may be referred to a deficiency of alcohol.

The best method for its removal is either burning sulphur in a partially filled cask or drawing off the wine into a fresh cask in which sulphur has been previously burnt.

Beverages—Alcoholic

It is advisable that wines so treated should be drunk as soon as possible.

Wine sometimes has an unpleasant musty taste, which it has acquired from being put into a dirty cask or into one that has been unused for some time. This bad flavor, which is known as caskiness, may generally be removed by vigorously agitating the wine for sone time with a little sweet oil or almond oil. The cause of the bad taste is the presence of an essential oil, which the fixed oil combines with and carries to the surface, whence it may be skimmed off, or the wine lying under it may be drawn off. A little coarsely powdered and freshly burnt charcoal, or some slices of bread toasted until they become black, or a little bruised mustard seed sometimes effects the removal of the objectionable taste.

Mellowing Wines.—Cover the orifices of the vessel containing it with bladder closely fastened, instead of the usual materials, and an aqueous exhalation will pass through the bladder, leaving some fine crystallizations on the surface of the wine, which, when skimmed off, leaves the wine in a highly improved state of flavor. Remnants of wine covered in this manner, whether in bottles or in casks, will not turn mouldy as when stopped in the usual way, but will be improved instead of being deteriorated.

Ripening.—To promote the maturation or ripening of wine various plans are adopted by the growers and dealers. One of the safest ways of hastening this, especially for strong wines, is not to rack them until they have stood 15 or 18 months upon the lees, or, whether crude or racked, keeping them at a temperature ranging between 55 and 65° F. in a cellar free from draughts and not too dry. Full or heavy sherries or ports, when bottled and treated in this manner, ripen very quickly in a temperate situation.

Racking.—Racking should be performed in cool weather and preferably early in the spring. A clean siphon, well managed, answers better for this purpose than a cock or faucet. The bottoms, or thick portion, may be strained through a wine bag and added to some other inferior wine.

Wines and Wine Making

Ropiness, Viscidity.—This arises from the wine containing too little tannin or astringent matter to precipitate the gluten, albumen or other azotized substance, occasioning the malady. Such wine cannot be clarified in the ordinary way because it is incapable of causing the coagulation or precipitation of the finings. The remedy is to supply the principle in which it is deficient. M. François, of Nantes, prescribes for this purpose the bruised berries of the mountain ash in the proportion of 1 lb. to the barrel. A little catechu, kino, or, better still, rhatany, or the bruised footstalks of the grape, may also be conveniently and advantageously used in the same way. For pale white wines, which are the ones chiefly attacked by the malady, nothing equals a little pure tannin or tannic acid dissolved in proof spirit.

Sparkling, Creaming and Briskness.—These properties are conveyed to wine by racking it into closed vessels before the fermentation is complete and while there still remains a considerable portion of undecomposed sugar. Wine which has lost its briskness may be restored by adding to each bottle a few grains of white lump sugar or sugar candy. The bottles are afterward inverted, by which means any sediment that forms falls into the necks, when the corks are partially withdrawn and the sediment is immediately expelled by the elastic force of the compressed carbonic acid. If the wine remains muddy a little solution of sugar and finings is added and the bottles are again placed in a vertical position, and, after two or three months, the sediment is discharged as before.

To Sweeten Wine.—In 30 gal. of wine infuse a handful of the flowers of clary; then add 1 lb. of mustard seed, dry ground, put it into a bag and sink it to the bottom of the cask.

Tartaric Acid in Wine, Detection of Free.—Professor Claus evaporates to a syrup and agitates with ether. If free tartaric acid is present the ether leaves on evaporation a crystalline deposit which, if dissolved in water, gives, on the addition of an alcoholic solution of potassic acetate, a precipitate of tartar. The author proves the solubility of tartaric acid in ether, which is denied in most text books.

Sour Wine, To Restore.—Take calcined gypsum, in powder, 1 oz.; cream of tartar, in powder, 2 oz. Mix them in a pint or more of brandy (if you have it); pour it into the cask; put in also a few sticks of cinnamon and then stir the wine without disturbing the lees. Bung up the cask next day.

Sourness in Wine, to Correct a Bad Taste and Sourness.—Put in a bag the root of horseradish cut in bits. Let it down in the wine and leave it there 2 days; take this out and put in another, repeating the same till the wine is perfectly restored.

Formulas for Wines

Apple Wine.—1.—Finest cider, 60 gal.; brown sugar, ½ cwt.; bitter almonds, ¼ oz. Mix the cider and sugar and ferment; then rack the mixture and put into the cask the almonds, with 16 or 18 cloves and 3 or 4 pieces of bruised ginger. When fine bottle it and keep it in a cool place. The addition of a small piece of lump sugar to each bottle will make the cork fly out, as from champagne; but do not add this unless you have a very cold cellar to keep it in.

2.—Sugar, 40 lb.; cider, 15 gal. The cider must be pure and made only from really ripe, sound apples (this is important). If the wine is to be quite sweet, add another 10 lb. of sugar and put all into the cider, letting it stand till dissolved. Put the liquor into a cask, but leave it unfilled to the extent of 2 gal. Put the cask into a cool position, with the bung out for 48 hours. After this bung it up, but let there be a small vent somewhere—in the bung would do—until the fermentation is over. Then bung up securely and the wine will be ready for consumption in 12 months. There is no racking required in the manufacture of this wine. To remain in the cask 12 months. Make this in January or February.

3.—Put 5 gal. of good cider into a cask it will about ¾ fill, add 10 lb. of loaf sugar and stir occasionally with a piece of wood or cane until the sugar is quite dissolved. At the end of 48 hours put in the bung and place a small vent peg near the top of the cask. Allow the cask to remain for 12 months in a cool, dry place, when the wine will be ready for use.

Apricot Wine.—1.—Ripe apricots, 12 lb.; loaf sugar, 6 oz. to each qt. liquor. Wipe the apricots, cut them in pieces and let them boil in 2 gal. water. After boiling let them simmer till the liquor is strongly impregnated with the flavor of the fruit. Strain through a hair sieve and put 6 oz. lump sugar to every quart liquor. Boil again, skim very carefully and as soon as no more scum appears put it into an earthen pan. Bottle next day if it is quite clear and put 1 lump of sugar into each bottle. It should be fine wine in 6 months. Two hours to boil. Make this in August or September.

2.—Sound but not overripe apricots, 12 lb.; loaf sugar, 1 lb.; white wine, 1 pt.; water, 3 gal.; compressed yeast, 1 tablespoonful, or good brewer's yeast, 1 tablespoonful. Remove the stones of the fruit, take out the kernels and cut each apricot into 6 or 8 pieces. Put them into a preserving pan with the water, sugar and about half the kernels and simmer very gently for 1 hour. Turn the whole into an earthenware vessel, let it remain undisturbed until cool, then stir in the yeast. If compressed yeast is used it must previously be mixed smoothly with a little warm water. Cover the vessel with a cloth, let it remain undisturbed for 3 days, then strain the liquid into a clean, dry cask, add the white wine and bung lightly. At the end of 6 months draw off the wine into bottles, cork them closely, store in a cool, dry place for about 12 months and the wine will be then ready for use.

3.—Firm, ripe apricots, 12 lb.; loaf sugar; water, 2 gal. Prepare the fruit as directed in the preceding recipe, put it into a preserving pan with 2 gal. of cold water and half the kernels and boil gently for about 1 hour. Strain, return to the pan; to each quart of liquid add 6 oz. of loaf sugar, bring to the boil and remove the scum as it rises. Let the

Beverages—Alcoholic

whole simmer gently for 10 minutes, then turn into an earthenware vessel. Allow it to remain covered until the following day, pour into dry bottles, to each one add a lump of sugar and cork closely. Store in a cool, dry place for about 6 months, when the wine should be ready for use.

Blackberry Wine.—To 1 gal. of mashed blackberries add a quart of boiling water; let it stand for 24 hours, or nearly as long, then strain through a coarse bag or towel, adding 3 qt. of water and 2 lb. of brown sugar to each gallon of the mixture, making equal parts of water and juice; mix well, then put in demijohns, stone jugs or a tight, clean keg; close partially and put in a cool place; if in a warm place or left entirely open it will sour; if stopped entirely tight it will burst the vessel—but cork left loosely in; let it stand until fermentation ceases, which will be about October; then bottle, and this makes excellent wine and a fine medicinal drink for summer affections.

2.—The following is said to be an excellent receipt for the manufacture of superior wine from blackberries: Measure your blackberries and bruise them; to every gallon add 1 qt. of boiling water; let the mixture stand 24 hours, stirring occasionally; then strain off the liquor into a cask; to every gallon add 2 lb. of sugar; cork tight and let stand about 1 year, and you will have wine fit for use without any further straining or boiling. This wine is very highly recommended for household use.

Catawba Champagne.—Catawba, 20 gal.; cognac brandy, 1 qt. (if you have it); champagne syrup, 2 gal.

Champagne, Imitation.—1.—Prepared cider, 25 gal.; citric acid, 5 dr.; simple syrup, 1¼ pt.; water, 1¼ gal.; spirits (10 under proof), 2½ gal.; tartaric acid, 1¼ oz. Let this stand 12 days, then fine and bottle, if it is frothing and sparkling; if not, add more acid and fine again. Add to each bottle about 2 teaspoonfuls of syrup, made by dissolving ½ lb. rock candy in 1 pt. white wine.

2.—Cider, pale, 1 hhd.; spirit, 3 gal.; honey or sugar, 20 lb. Mix and allow to remain 2 weeks; then fine with skimmed milk, ½ gal. This will be very pale.

3.—**Gooseberry.**—Ferment together 5 gal. white gooseberries, mashed, with 4½ gal. water. Add 6 lb. sugar, 4½ lb. honey, 1 oz. finely powdered cream of tartar, 1 oz. dry orange and lemon peel and ½ gal. white brandy. This will produce 9 gal. Before the brandy is added the mixture must be strained and put into a cask.

Cherry Wine.—Take of cold water 10 gal.; cherries, 10 gal.; ferment. Mix raw sugar, 30 lb.; red tartar, in fine powder, 3 oz.; add brandy, 2 or 3 qt. This will make 18 gal. Two days after the cherries have been in the vat we should take out about 3 qt. of the cherry stones, break them and the kernels and return them into the vat again.

Cherry Wine, Black.—1.—Small black cherries, 24 lb.; sugar, 2 lb. to each gallon of liquor. Bruise the cherries, but leave the stones whole, stir well, and let the mixture stand 24 hours. Then strain through a sieve, add the sugar, mix again and stand another 24 hours. Pour away the clear liquor into a cask and when fermentation has ceased bung it closely. Bottle in 6 months' time. It will keep from 12 to 18 months. Time—To remain in the cask 6 months. Make this in July or August.

2.—Place 12 lb. of cherries, preferably small black ones, on a large dish and bruise them well with a large wooden spoon. Allow them to remain until the following day, then drain them well on a hair sieve and measure the juice into an earthenware vessel. To each quart of juice add ½ lb. of sugar, cover the vessel, let it stand for 24 hours and strain the liquor into a clean, dry cask. Bung closely, but provide the upper part of the cask with a vent plug; let it remain undisturbed for about 6 months, then drain off into bottles. Cork closely, store in a cool, dry place and use as required.

3.—Choose cherries as ripe as possible, without being overripe. They are mashed up or comminuted in some manner and the mass freed from pits is carefully measured. On account of a jelly-like substance in the juice, which makes it hard to handle, a little water is now added to the crushed mass and it is set aside for 24 hours. At the end of this time press off the mass, and to every quart of it add enough water, including that added at first, to make 2 qt. for every quart of cherries, first, however, dissolving in the said water, by the aid of heat, 2 lb. of refined sugar, and ½ dr. (30 gr.) of tartaric acid. Put the mixture in a clean keg or barrel, add a little brewer's yeast and let it ferment at a temperature of 70 to 75° F. for from 4 to 6 weeks. Draw the wine off, at the end of fermentation, into a clean container and let stand for 6 to 8 weeks (best in a temperature as near that at which it fermented) to ripen. It is now ready for bottling off. The bottles should be well stoppered and kept in a cool cellar.

Coca Wine.—This was originally a French preparation. Its strength is about 1 in 30 and the dose a wineglass. Coca wine is, roughly speaking, about one-sixth of the strength of the official liquid extract (*Extractum Cocae Liquidum*, B. P., or *Extractum Erythroxyli Fluidum* U. S.). To obtain the liquid extract, coca leaves are exhausted by percolation (which differs from either decoction or infusion) with proof spirit. At the termination of the process the strength should be adjusted so that 1 oz. = 1 of leaves. The process of percolation is as follows: The leaves are placed in a vessel very like an elongated funnel, closed at its base by a porous diaphragm. This funnel fits into a receiver, and a small tube passes up its outer side and enters it near the top, forming a means of communication between the two. Spirit is now poured on the leaves and the percolator closed. As the percolate filters slowly through into the reservoir the displaced air passes up the tube and so maintains an equilibrium in both vessels. The virtue of the coca leaves lies principally in the presence of the alkaloid cocaine. This, in the dried leaves, is supposed to exist as an inert salt, similar to many of the cinchona alkaloids in bark.

Cowslip Wine.—1.—To every gallon of water allow 3 lb. of lump sugar, the rind of 2 lemons, the juice of 1, the rind and juice of 1 orange, 1 gal. of cowslip pips. To

Wines and Wine Making

every 4½ gal. of wine allow 1 bottle of brandy. Boil the sugar and water together for ½ hour, carefully removing all the scum as it rises. Pour this boiling liquor on the orange and lemon rinds, and the juice, which should be strained; when milk-warm add the cowslip pips or flowers, picked from the stalks and seeds; and to 9 gal. of wine 3 tablespoonfuls of good fresh brewer's yeast. Let it ferment 3 or 4 days, then put all together in a cask with the brandy and let it remain for 2 months, when bottle it off for use. To be boiled ½ hour; to ferment 3 or 4 days; to remain in the cask 2 months. Make this in April or May.

2.—Four qt. of cowslip flowers, 4 qt. of water, 3 lb. of loaf sugar, the finely grated rind and juice of 1 orange and 1 lemon, 2 tablespoonfuls of brewer's yeast, or ¼ oz. of compressed yeast moistened with water. Boil the sugar and water together for ½ hour, skimming when necessary, and pour, quite boiling, over the rinds and strained juice of the orange and lemon. Let it cool, then stir in the yeast and cowslip flowers, cover with a cloth, and allow it to remain undisturbed for 48 hours. Turn the whole into a clean dry cask, add the brandy, bung closely, let it remain thus for 8 weeks, then draw it off into bottles. Cork securely, store in a cool, dry place for 3 or 4 weeks, and it will then be ready for use.

Currant Wine.—Squeeze the currants through a coarse bag; have equal parts of water and juice or 1-3 water, as taste may direct, and add 3 lb. of loaf sugar to each gallon of the mixture; mix well and bottle in stone jugs or demijohns; treat same way as blackberry wine—partially cork and keep in a cool place. Some keep a bottle of the mixture to fill up the vessels as they effervesce, but it is not always necessary. Bottle in October, when fermentation ceases; this make a beautiful and delicious wine and improves with age.

Red.—Ripe red currants. To each gallon of fruit allow 1½ gal. of cold water and 5 lb. either loaf sugar or good preserving sugar and ½ pt. of good brandy (if you

Beverages—Alcoholic

have it). Remove the stalks from the currants, put them into an earthenware bowl, bruise them well with a wooden spoon and drain off the juice. Put the juice aside, add the water to the berries, let it stand for 2 or 3 hours, stirring occasionally meanwhile. At the end of this time strain the liquid from the berries into the juice, add ¾ of the sugar, stir occasionally until dissolved, then pour the whole into a cask, filling it 3 parts full. Bung closely, but place a vent peg near the top of the cask and let the cask remain for 1 month where a uniform temperature of about 65° F. can be maintained. Dissolve the remainder of the sugar in the smallest possible quantity of warm water, mix it well with the contents of the cask, replace the bung and allow the cask to remain undisturbed for 6 weeks longer. Now drain off the wine into a clean, dry cask, add the brandy, let the cask stand for about 6 months in a dry, warm place, then bottle and cork tightly. The wine may be used at once, but will be better if kept for 12 months at least.

Red Currant and Raspberry Wine.—Red currant juice, 5 gal.; raspberry juice, 1 pt.; water, 10 gal.; either loaf sugar or good preserving sugar, 10 lb. Extract the juice as directed in the two preceding recipes. Add to it the water and sugar, stir until the latter is dissolved, then turn the whole into a cask and bung closely, but provide the top of the cask with a vent peg. As soon as fermentation ceases tighten the vent peg and let the cask remain undisturbed in a moderately warm place for 12 months. At the end of this time rack off into dry bottles, cork them closely and seal the top with melted wax. The wine should be ready for use in about 3 months.

Damson Wine.—1.—Crush 20 lb. ripe damson plums; boil in 3 gal. water; press out the juice; add 6 lb. sugar; put in a barrel and let it ferment; then add after 2 weeks a little good brandy; bottle.

2.—One gal. of boiling water to every 8 lb. of bruised fruit, 2½ lb. of sugar to each gallon of juice. Well bruise the fruit and pour the boiling water on it; let it stand for

48 hours. Then strain the mixture into a cask and put in the sugar. When fermentation ceases fill up the cask and bung closely. Bottle in 10 months' time. It will be fit for use in a year, but improves with keeping. Time required, about 2 years.

3.—To each gallon of damsons add 1 gal. of boiling water. To each gallon of liquor obtained from these add 4 lb. of loaf sugar and ½ pt. of French brandy. Remove the stalks, put the fruit into an earthenware bowl, pour in the boiling water and cover with a cloth. Stir the liquid 3 or 4 times daily for 4 days, then add the sugar and brandy, and when the former is dissolved turn the whole into a clean dry cask. Cover the bunghole with a cloth, folded into several thicknesses, until fermentation ceases, then bung tightly and allow the cask to remain undisturbed for 12 months in a moderately warm place. At the end of this time it should be racked off into bottles. The wine may be used at once, but if well corked and stored in a dry place it may be kept for years.

Dandelion Wine.—Four qt. of dandelion flowers, 4 qt. of boiling water, 3 lb. of loaf sugar, 1 in. whole ginger, 1 lemon, the thinly pared rind of 1 orange, 1 tablespoonful of brewer's yeast or ¼ oz. of compressed yeast moistened with water. Put the petals of the flowers into a bowl, pour over them the boiling water, let the bowl remain covered for 3 days, meanwhile stirring it well and frequently. Strain the liquid into a preserving pan, add the rinds of the orange and lemon, both of which should be pared off in thin fine strips, the sugar, ginger, and the lemon previously stripped of its white pith, and thinly sliced. Boil gently for about ½ hour, and when cool add the yeast spread on a piece of toast. Allow it to stand for 2 days, then turn it into a cask, keep it well bunged down for 8 or 9 weeks, and bottle the wine for use.

Elderberry Wine.—1.—Gather the berries when quite ripe, on a dry day; pick them off the stems and bruise them with your hands. Strain the juice; let the liquor rest in glazed earthenware pans for 12 hours to settle.

Beverages—Alcoholic

Allow to every pint of juice 1½ pt. of water, and to every gallon of the mixed water and juice 3 lb. of good moist sugar. Put it over the fire in a large saucepan, and when it is ready to boil clarify it with the whites of 4 eggs. Let it boil for an hour, and when nearly cold put in some yeast to work it; pour it into the cask, reserving some of the liquor to fill up the cask with, as it sinks with working. If you have about 10 gal. or so, it should be fit to bottle off in 2 months' time after it has been closed down. Keep at least a year in bottle.

2.—Gather the berries when quite ripe, and in dry weather. Pick them clean; put them into a copper with ½ gal. of water, and keep up a slow fire until the berries sink; then strain the juice through a hair sieve, and to every gallon of it allow 3 gal. of soft water, and to every gallon of the mixed liquor 3 lb. of good moist sugar. Put back into the copper and boil for an hour, skimming thoroughly; draw off into a tube, and when it is about 70° put a toast, spread with yeast, into it, and let it work for 48 hours, or longer, if necessary; pour it, or draw it off, if you have a tap in your tub, as should be the case, into the cask which is to hold it; and if you have 18 gal. of liquor, add 1 oz. of cloves, 2 oz. of allspice, 2 oz. of Jamaica ginger, and 1 oz. of sweet almonds, all bruised. Bung very slightly until fermentation is quite over; then close down tightly and tap in 3 months.

3.—Old recipe: Put the ripe, picked-over berries into an earthen pot; put this into a copper with sufficient water to come up about two-thirds of the height of the pot, which is about as far as the berries should reach inside; be careful that no water touches them. Make a gentle fire, and keep the pot in the water till it is quite hot, then take it out. Pour the berries into a coarse cloth, strain the juice, and put it into a large saucepan; to every quart of juice allow 1 lb. of good moist sugar; let it boil, and skim well. It should boil until rather thick, then pour it into a jar. Put 60 lb. of raisins into a cask, and fill it up with water; let it stand for a fortnight; stir it well every day; then pour off the liquor into a clean cask that just holds it. It should stand until it has done hissing; then bung it down close, and stand until fine. To every gallon of this liquor allow ½ pt. of the elder syrup; mix well, and when it has fined down, rack off into another cask; bottle off after 3 months.

4.—Chop a quantity of Malaga (or other) raisins quite fine; allow 1 qt. of water to every lb. of raisins, and put raisins and water into an open tub; cover over with a double cloth and let it stand for 9 days, stirring up each day. Then draw off the liquor as long as it will run, and press the raisins to get out the remainder of the juice; mix all together in a barrel. To every gal. of liquor allow 1 pt. of the juice of the elderberries, prepared simply by mashing the berries with the hands and straining off the juice. Stop down close, and stand for 6 weeks; then draw off the fine liquor, and to every gal. add ½ lb. of moist sugar. Stand again until quite fine, and then bottle off. Keep in a cool cellar for use.

Elder Flower Wine.—1.—Gather the flowers on a dry day; remove all stalks, and to every quart of flowers allow 1 gal. of water and 3 lb. of loaf sugar; boil the sugar and water for ¼ hour; then pour it on the flowers and let it work for 3 days; then strain the wine carefully through a hair sieve, and put it into a cask. To every 5 gal. of wine add ½ oz. of isinglass (gelatine) dissolved in cider, and 3 eggs (whites only), beaten up; close up the cask, and stand six months before bottling off.

2.—Boil 18 lb. of powdered loaf sugar in 6 gal. of spring water; beat up the whites of 2 eggs, and add; skim very thoroughly, and put in ¼ peck of elder flowers, picked from their stems; take off the fire, and stir until cool; then add 4 tablespoonfuls of yeast and 6 spoonfuls of lemon juice, strained, and free from pips; mix well with the liquor by stirring twice daily for 4 days. Stone 6 lb. of Malaga (or other) raisins, and put them into a well cleaned out cask; pour the wine upon them. Stop up the cask closely, and keep it in a rather warm place.

If made in July or August, bottle off in February or March.

Fig Wine.—Figs are largely employed, especially in Algeria, for the production of fictitious wine. For this purpose, figs from Asia Minor are preferred, on account of their relative cheapness, and richness in sugar. When the fruit is treated with a suitable quantity of tepid water, acidified with tartaric acid, fermentation rapidly commences, resulting in the production of a vinous liquid of about 8% alcoholic strength, and so inexpensive that it defies all competition of genuine grape wine, Algerian or otherwise. Fig wine cannot be distinguished either by taste or the ordinary methods of analysis, from genuine grape wine, especially when it is mixed with a proportion of the latter. The detection of fig wine, however, is rendered comparatively easy by the fact that it contains mannitol. In order to separate the mannitol, 100 c.c. of fig wine are evaporated to a syrup, which is allowed to stand in a cool place for 24 hours. At the end of this time the residue will have solidified, well defined groups of crystals being formed. The crystals are washed with cold alcohol of 85% strength, in order to remove impurities. The residue is mixed with animal charcoal and extracted with boiling 85% alcohol, and filtered. The alcoholic solution yields on evaporation a crystalline mass of mannitol, which may be recognized by its physical and chemical properties. Certain white wines from the Gironde district, as well as raisin and some other wines, contain mannitol, but only to the extent of a few decigrams per liter; while fig wine contains from 6 to 8 grams per liter. By a determination of the mannitol it is possible to detect an adulteration of normal Algerian wine with ½ or even ¼ of fig wine.

Ginger Wine.—1.—Cold water, 3 gal.; loaf sugar, 9 lb.; whole ginger, bruised, ¼ lb.; raisins, ¼ lb.; lemons, strained juice and finely prepared rinds of 4; brewer's yeast, 1 good tablespoonful. Stone and halve the raisins, put them into a large preserving pan, or perfectly clean copper, with the water, sugar and ginger, bruised; boil for 1 hour, skimming frequently. Turn the whole into a large earthenware bowl or wooden tub, allow the liquid to stand until milk-warm, then stir in the yeast. On the following day put the preparation into a clean, dry cask, add the lemon juice, and bung lightly. Stir the wine every day for a fortnight, then tighten the bung. Let the wine remain undisturbed for 3 or 4 months, when it may be bottled for use.

2.—Water, 6 gal.; loaf sugar, 14 lb.; whole ginger, bruised, 6 oz.; Muscatel or other good raisins, 2 lb.; isinglass, ½ oz.; lemons, 6; brandy, 1 pt.(if possible). Remove the peel of the lemons as thinly as possible, and boil it with the water, sugar and ginger for half an hour. Meanwhile, stone and halve the raisins, put them into an earthenware bowl, pour the liquid over them when nearly cold, add the lemon juice and yeast. Stir it every day for a fortnight, then add the isinglass, previously dissolved in a little warm water, and drain into a clean, dry cask. Let the wine remain closely bunged for about 3 months, then bottle for use.

3.—This is an excellent stomachic, and is very popular in England as a cheap substitute for a grape wine: Sugar, 12 lb.; water, 3½ gal.; ginger, 4 oz. Boil them together for half an hour; when cooled to 75° add the rinds of 6 lemons and some good yeast; let it ferment for 10 or 14 days, then add 1 pt. of brandy (if convenient) and bottle it for use.

4.—To 9 gal. of water allow 27 lb. of loaf sugar, 9 lemons, 12 oz. of bruised ginger, 3 tablespoonfuls of yeast, 2 lb. of raisins, stoned and chopped, and 1 pt. of brandy. Boil together for 1 hour in a copper (let it previously be well scoured and beautifully clean) the water, sugar, lemon rinds and bruised ginger. Remove every particle of scum as it rises, and when the liquor is sufficiently boiled put it into a large tub or pan, as it must not remain in the copper. When nearly cold, add the yeast, which must be thick and very fresh, and the next day put all in a dry cask with the strained lemon juice and chopped raisins. Stir the wine every day for a fortnight; then add the brandy, stop the cask down by degrees, and in a few weeks it will be fit to bottle. Sufficient to make 9 gal. of wine. The best time for making this wine is either in March or September.

Gooseberry.—1.—Firm green gooseberries, 20 lbs.; hot water, 3 gal.; loaf sugar, 15 lb.; cream of tartar, 1½ oz. Top and tail the gooseberries, put them into an earthenware bowl or wooden tub, and pour over them the hot water. Let them soak for 24 hours, then bruise them well with a heavy wooden mallet or potato masher, and drain the juice through a fine hair sieve or jelly bag. Replace the skins in the vessel in which they were soaked, cover them with boiling water, stir and bruise well, so as to completely extract the juice, then strain through the sieve or bag. Mix this preparation with the juice, add the sugar, and boiling water to increase the liquid to 5 gal. Replace in the bowl or tub, stir in the cream of tartar, cover with a heavy woolen cloth, and allow the vessel to stand in a moderately warm place for 2 days. Now strain the liquid into a small cask, cover the bunghole with a folded cloth until fermentation ceases—which may be known by the cessation of the hissing noise—then bung closely, but provide the top of the cask with a vent peg. Make this wine in the beginning of June, before the berries ripen; let it remain undisturbed until December, then drain it off carefully into a clean cask. In March or April, or when the gooseberry bushes begin to blossom, the wine must be bottled and tightly corked. To insure its being clear and effervescing, the wine must be bottled at the right time, and preferably on a clear day.

Grape Wine.—1.—The grapes must be gathered and transported with as little injury as possible, and must be protected from dirt and injurious fermentation. Crush the well-matured fruit in a regular wine or cider mill, or gently mash it in any other receptacle by means of a wooden implement. It is absolutely necessary to use only sweet, clean containers or utensils. The best method for cleaning barrels, utensils, etc., is to scald them with boiling water several times and then rinse repeatedly with fresh cold water. Do not, under any circumstances, use a vinegar barrel. If a barrel is to be stored before using, it is well to sulphur it by suspending a little burning sulphur on a wire inside the bunghole until the burning sulphur is extinguished.

If a red wine is being made, the juice and crushed pulp are allowed to ferment together. For a white wine the pulp is pressed as dry as possible as soon as the grapes are crushed. This is usually accomplished by wrapping the pulp in cheesecloth and applying pressure by means of either a screw or a hand or power press.

The fermentation is allowed to proceed as rapidly as possible. If the temperature of the crushed grapes is below 60° F., they should be warmed before fermentation. The best temperature for fermentation depends on the kind of wine. Light white wines should not exceed 75° or 80° F. Heavy red wines, where high extract and tannin are desired, may be allowed to reach 85° or 90° F. When the fermentation of the grapes for red wine has slackened, the young wine is pressed from the pulp as completely as possible, and run into a barrel until it is almost full. Plug with cotton and allow to remain until still. This will require several weeks. The juice for the white wine is also put into a barrel and the fermentation allowed to proceed until still. During this initial fermentation much sediment or argols will settle to the bottom of the barrel. The still wine should be carefully siphoned off from this sediment after several months by means of a hose. The clear wine is then racked into a clean barrel, so that the barrel will be filled to the bung and about five gallons left over. The extra wine is put into a 5-gallon container, or bottled and used to "fill up" the shrinking contents of the barrel during its aging period.

Always keep the barrel full, as air spaces are unhealthy for wine. Wine is better after an aging period in wood of

Beverages—Alcoholic

about a year, if made in lots of over 50 gallons. At the end of this period the clear wine may be carefully siphoned directly into the bottle It will be possible to bottle or use the ordinary sour wine after a settling period of three or four months, but aging in wood makes a better wine.

2.—Ripe Grapes.—Mash sound, ripe grapes well with your hands, in an earthen pan, or, if not with your hands, with a perfectly tasteless stick of wood. Do not crush the seeds; strain the liquor into a cask, gently squeeze the pulp, pouring the remainder of the juice into the cask (strained). Let it stand aside for a fortnight, then draw it off into another cask, covering up the bunghole with a piece of slate till all fermentation has ceased. Bottle in 6 months, cork, and seal, and it will be drinkable in 12 months' time.

3.—Ten lb. fresh grapes are put into a large jar or crock, 3 qt. boiling water poured over them, and when the water is cool enough to permit of it, squeeze the grapes well with the hand. After allowing the jar to remain 3 or 4 days covered with a cloth, press out the grapes, then add 5 lb. of sugar. Allow it to remain for 1 week, skim and strain carefully, then bottle, corking loosely. After the fermentation is completed strain and seal tightly.

4.—Put 20 lb. of ripe grapes into a stone jar, and pour on 6 qt. of boiling water; when cooled sufficiently squeeze by hand. Cover jar with cloth, let stand for 3 days, then press out the juice; add 10 lb. crushed sugar. After standing a week, scum, strain and bottle, corking loosely. When fermentation is complete strain again and bottle, corking tightly. Lay on side in cool place.

5.—Sound, not overripe grapes; to each lb. allow 1 qt. of cold water; add to each gal. of liquid obtained from the grapes 3 lb. of loaf sugar, ¼ pt. of French brandy, and ¼ oz. of isinglass. Strip the grapes from the stalks, put them into a wooden tub or earthenware bowl, and bruise them well. Pour over them the water, let them stand for 3 days, stirring frequently, then strain through a jelly bag or fine hair sieve. Dissolve the sugar in the liquid, then pour the whole into a cask. Bung lightly for a few days until fermentation subsides, then add the isinglass, dissolved in a little warm water, and the brandy, and tighten the bung. Let the cask remain undisturbed for 6 months, then rack the wine off into bottles, cork and seal them securely, and keep for at least a year before using.

6.—*Hock, British Red.*—From cream of tartar, 1¼ oz; tartaric acid, ½ oz. (both in very fine powder); juices of the purple plum, ripe apples, and red beet, of each (warmed), 5 pt.; lemon juice, 1 pt.; with white sugar, 2½ lb. per gal.

Honey Wine (Metheglin).—1.—Three and a half lb. of honey, 1 qt. of white currant juice, 2 gal. of boiling water, 1-3 of an oz. of cream of tartar, 1 pt. of brandy.

Mix all together but the brandy, and stir until the honey is dissolved. Let it remain until fermentation ceases, then strain, add the brandy, bottle and cork securely.

2.—Or dissolve 4½ lb. of honey in 5 qt. of boiling water in which 1 oz. of hops has been simmered for 20 minutes, and, when cool, stir in 2 or 3 tablespoonfuls of yeast. When fermentation has ceased, strain into bottles and cork securely.

Kola.—Kola nuts, in coarse powder, 1 oz.; sherry wine, 30 oz. Macerate for 8 days, and filter. This wine may also be made with roasted kola nuts, which give a better tasting preparation, and it is none the worse for the addition of a little sugar.

Lemon Wine.—1.—Ten lemons, 4 lb. of loaf sugar, 4 qt. of boiling water, 1 tablespoonful of brewer's yeast. Remove the rinds of 5 lemons in thin fine strips, and place them in a wooden tub or earthenware bowl. Boil the sugar and water together for ½ an hour, then pour the syrup over the lemon-peel. When cool, add the strained juice of the 10 lemons, stir in the yeast, and let the vessel stand for 48 hours. At the end of this time, strain into a cask, which the wine must quite fill, bung loosely until fermentation ceases, then tighten the bung, and allow the cask to remain undisturbed for about 6 months before racking the wine off into bottles.

2.—To 4½ gal. of water allow the pulp and juice of 50 and the rinds of 25 lemons, 16 lb. of loaf sugar, ½ oz. of isinglass, 1 pt. of brandy (if convenient). Remove the rinds of 25 lemons in thin strips, remove from each lemon every particle of white pith, and cut them into slices. Put aside the pips, place the sliced lemon rind and lemons in a wooden tub or earthenware bowl, and pour over them the cold water. Stir frequently for 7 days, then strain into a cask and add the sugar. Bung loosely until fermentation ceases, then add the isinglass dissolved in a little water, and bung tightly for 6 months. At the end of this time add the brandy and rack the wine off into bottles.

Malmsey, British.—From sliced or grated parsnips, 4 lb.; boiling water, 1 gal.; when cold press out the liquid, and to each gal. add of cream of tartar, ½ oz.; and good granulated sugar, 3 lb.; ferment, rack, and add of brandy 3 to 5%. Good Malaga raisins may be substituted for the sugar.

Mead, or Honey Wine.—Take 10 gal. of water, 2 gal. of strained honey, with 2 or 3 oz. of white Jamaica ginger root, bruised, and 2 lemons cut in slices. Mix all together, and boil for half an hour, carefully skimming all the time. Five minutes after the boiling commences add 2 oz. of hops. When partially cold put it into a cask to work off. In about 3 weeks after working it will be fit to bottle. This is a wholesome and pleasant beverage, particularly grateful in summer, when drunk mixed with water.

Medicated Wines.—Dieterich, in a late issue of his *Pharmaceutische Manual*, gives a number of formulæ for the preparation of medicated wines. Few, if any, of these can be regarded as tipples, but all are peculiar for the fact that the wine from which they are made is detannated. We give a selection of the more important formulæ for articles which should be salable if put up in attractive form and brought before customers in a nice way.

1.—*Cascara Sagrada Wine.*—Wine gelatine, in strips, 15

gr.; distilled water, 2½ dr.; dissolve by the aid of heat, and add to sherry wine, 28 oz. Shake well, set aside for some time, then add: Tasteless fluid extract of cascara sagrada, 1½ oz.; sugar, 1½ oz. Set aside in a cool place for 8 days, and filter. A similar wine, not free from the bitter principle of the bark, may be made by macerating 1½ oz. of cascara sagrada and 1½ oz. of sugar in 30 oz. of sherry for 8 days, and filtering. A *Rhamnus frangula* wine can be made in the same way.

2.—Cinchona Wine.—a.—White gelatine, 15 gr.; distilled water, 2½ dr.; sherry wine, 18 oz. Detannate in the manner directed above, and then add: Simple syrup, 6 oz.; tincture of cinchona, 6 oz. After 8 days, filter.

b.—May also be made with red wine, or direct from the bark, the quantities being: Gelatine, 15 gr.; distilled water, 2½ dr.; sherry wine, 30 oz.; cinchona bark, in coarse powder, 10 dr.; sugar, 1½ oz. Macerate for 8 days, and filter. In this case care must be taken to have the gelatine and wine reaction complete before adding the cinchona; otherwise the alkaloid may be thrown out by the tannin of the wine.

3.—Improved Quinine Wine.—Gelatine, 15 gr.; distilled water, 2½ dr.; dissolve, and add to sherry wine, 29½ oz. Shake, and set aside to clear; then add the following solution: Hydrochlorate of quinine, 30 gr.; dilute hydrochloric acid, 30 drops; water, ½ oz. After a week filter. This is double the strength given by Dieterich.

Moselle.—British Sparkling Moselle.—From rich cider apples (carefully peeled and garbled), pressed with ¼ of their weight of white plums (previously stoned), and the juice fermented with 2½ lb. double refined sugar per gal., as champagne.

2.—*Mulberry.*—Ripe mulberries, ripe apples, equal quantities; sugar or honey, 1 lb. to the gal. Express the juice, put it into a cask, and add the sugar; ferment with yeast, 1 qt. to every hhd.; catechu, ½ lb.; red argol, ½ lb.

Mulled Wine.—Take ¼ oz. bruised cinnamon, ½

Beverages—Alcoholic

nutmeg, grated, and 10 bruised cloves. Infuse them in ½ pt. boiling water for an hour, strain, and add ½ oz. white sugar. Pour the whole into 1 pt. hot port or sherry wine. This is a good cordial and restorative in low stages of fever, or in the debility of convalescence from fevers.

1.—The juice of 50 oranges, 15 lb. of loaf sugar, 4 gal. of water, the whites and shells of 3 eggs, 1 pt. of French brandy, 3 tablespoonfuls of brewer's yeast. Dissolve the sugar in the water, add the whites and crushed shells of the eggs, bring to the boil, and simmer gently for 20 minutes. Let it stand until nearly cold, then strain through a jelly bag, add the strained orange juice and yeast, and leave the vessel covered for 24 hours. Pour into a cask, bung loosely until fermentation subsides, then tighten the bung, and allow the cask to remain undisturbed for 3 months. At the end of this time rack it off into another cask, add the brandy, let it remain closely bunged for 12 months, then bottle for use.

2.—The oranges must be perfectly ripe. Peel them into halves, crosswise of the cells; squeeze into a tub. The press used must be so close that the seeds cannot pass into the must. Add 2 lb. white sugar to each gal. sour orange juice, and 1 qt. water to each gal. of the mixed sugar and juice. Close fermentation is necessary. The resultant wine is amber-colored, and tastes like dry hock, with the orange aroma. Vinegar can be made from the refuse, and extract from the peels.

Peach.—Take of cold soft water, 18 gal.; refined sugar, 25 lb.; honey, 6 lb.; white tartar, in fine powder, 2 oz.; peaches, 60 or 80 in number. Ferment, then add 2 gal. brandy (if obtainable). This will make 18 gal. The first division is to be put into the vat, and the day after, before the peaches are put in, take the stones from them, break them and the kernels, then put them and the pulp into the vat.

Port (Imitation).—1.—Ripe fruit, 4 lb.; clear soft water, 1 gal.; sugar, 3 lb.; cream of tartar, dissolved in boiling water, 1½ oz.; brandy, 2 to 3%; flavoring as required.

Wines and Wine Making

The addition of an equal quantity of fruit and sugar increases the strength.

2.—Add to 10 gal. prepared cider, 2 gal. genuine port wine, 2 qt. best cognac brandy, 1 pt. simple syrup, 1 lb. bruised raisins, 1 oz. tincture kino, ½ oz. extract rhatany, 3 qt. proof spirits. Allow it to stand for 2 weeks, rack, fine, and repeat, if necessary. Keep the wine cool.

3.—Strong old cider, 6 gal.; elderberry juice, 4 gal.; sloe juice, 3 gal.; sugar, 28 lb.; powdered extract of rhatany, 1 lb.; at time of racking add brandy, ½ gal.; good port wine, 2 gal.

Quinine Wine.—Break into small pieces 1 oz. of sulphate of quinine and put it into a glass jar with 2 oz. of 90% alcohol; let the quinine infuse for 24 hours; add 1 qt. of claret, and let it remain thus for 12 days; then filter the wine through a felt bag, and bottle for use. The above quantity of quinine may be dissolved, without the addition of alcohol, in any of the following wines: Madeira, Marsala, Malaga, Lunel, or Alicante.

Raisin Wine.—1.—To each lb. of raisins allow 1 gal. of cold water, 2 lb. of good preserving sugar, 1 tablespoonful of yeast. Strip the raisins from the stalk, put them into a large boiler or clean copper, with the water, simmer gently for about 1 hour, then rub them through a sieve. Dissolve the sugar in the liquid, and add the raisin pulp and the yeast, let the vessel stand covered for 3 days, then strain the liquid into a cask. Bung loosely until fermentation ceases, then tighten the bung, and allow the cask to stand for at least 12 months before racking the wine off into bottles.

2.—With Cider.—Good cider, 8 gal.; Malaga raisins, 15 lb.; French brandy, 1 bottle; sugar candy, 3 oz.; the rind of 3 lemons. Strip the raisins from the stalks, halve them, put them into a 9-gal. cask, and pour over them the cider. Bung lightly for 5 or 6 days, then tighten the bung and let the cask stand for 6 months.

Raspberry Wine.—1.—Ripe raspberries, 10 qt.; boiling water, 10 qt.; good preserving sugar, 6 lb.; brewer's yeast,

Beverages—Alcoholic

2 tablespoonfuls; French brandy, 1 pt (if obtainable); isinglass, ¼ oz. Prepare the fruit in the usual way, put it into an earthenware or wooden vessel, pour over it the boiling water, and let it remain covered until the following day. Pass both liquid and fruit through a fine hair sieve, let it stand for 24 hours, then strain it carefully, without disturbing the sediment, into another vessel. Add the sugar, stir in the yeast, and as soon as the sugar is dissolved turn the whole into a clean, dry cask. Cover the bunghole with a folded cloth until fermentation subsides, then bung it closely. Let it stand for 1 month, rack it off into a clean cask, add the brandy (if on hand), and isinglass dissolved in a little warm water, bung tightly, and allow it to remain undisturbed for 12 months. At the end of this time rack it off into bottles, cork them securely, store for 12 months longer, and the wine will be ready for use.

2.—Put 6 qt. of ripe raspberries into an earthenware or wooden vessel, bruise them well with a heavy wooden spoon, and pour over them 6 qt. of cold water. Let them stand until the following day, stirring them frequently, then strain the liquid through a jelly bag or fine hair sieve, and drain the fruit thoroughly, but avoid squeezing it. Measure the liquid; to each qt. add 1 lb. loaf sugar; stir occasionally until dissolved, then turn the whole into a cask. Bung loosely for several days, until fermentation ceases, then tighten the bung; let it remain thus for 3 months, and bottle for use.

Raspberry and Currant Wine.—Six qt. of raspberries, 4 qt. of red currants, 10 qt. of water, 10 lb. of good preserving sugar, 1 pt. of French brandy (if obtainable). Strip the red currants from the stalks, put them into a large earthenware or wooden vessel, and pour over them the water (which must have been previously boiled, and allowed to become quite cold). On the following day crush the red currants with a wooden mallet or potato masher, add the raspberries, and allow the whole to stand until the following day. Strain the liquid through a jelly bag or fine hair sieve, and drain the fruit thoroughly, but do not squeeze it. Stir in the sugar, and when quite dissolved turn the wine into a clean, dry cask. Bung loosely until fermentation has entirely subsided, then tighten the bung, and allow the cask to remain undisturbed for 3 months. At the end of this time rack the wine off carefully, straining that near the bottom of the cask repeatedly until quite clear. Scald and drain the cask, replace the wine, add the brandy (if convenient), bung lightly, let it remain 2 months longer in the cask, and then bottle.

Rhubarb Wine.—1.—Rhubarb, 25 lb.; cold water, 5 gal.; to each gal. of liquid thus obtained add 3 lb. of either loaf or good preserving sugar and the juice and very thinly pared rind of 1 lemon; to the whole add 1 oz. of isinglass. Wipe the rhubarb with a damp cloth and cut it into short lengths, leaving on the peel. Put it into an earthenware or wooden vessel, crush it thoroughly with a wooden mallet or heavy potato masher, and pour over it the water. Let it remain covered for 10 days, stirring it daily; then strain the liquor into another vessel, add the sugar, lemon juice and rind, and stir occasionally until the sugar is dissolved. Now put it into a cask, and add the isinglass, previously dissolved in a little warm water; cover the bunghole with a folded cloth for 10 days, then bung securely, and allow it to remain undisturbed for 12 months. At the end of this time rack off into bottles and use.

2.—Rhubarb, 20 lb.; cold water, 5 gal.; loaf or good preserving sugar, 12 lb.; French brandy, 1 pt.; barley sugar, ½ lb.; isinglass, ½ oz.; the rind of 2 oranges; the rind of 2 lemons. Wipe the rhubarb with a damp cloth, slice it thinly, put it into a large earthenware or wooden vessel, pour over it the water, and let it stand, closely covered, for 4 days. Strain the liquid through a jelly bag or fine sieve, pressing the pulp as dry as possible without allowing any of it to pass through the sieve. Add the sugar, stir occasionally until dissolved, then turn the preparation into a cask and cover the bunghole with a folded cloth. As soon as fermentation subsides add the

Beverages—Alcoholic

brandy. Bung the cask securely, and allow it to remain undisturbed for 3 months. Rack the wine into a clean, dry cask, add the very finely pared rind of the oranges and lemons, the barley sugar, finely powdered, and the isinglass dissolved in a little warm water. Bung the cask securely, store in a cool, dry place for at least 12 months, then bottle, cork securely, store for 6 months longer, when the wine will be ready for use.

Sherry Wine (Imitation).—1.—To each gal. of strong raisin wine can be added, when racking, 1 orange and 2 bitter almonds, both sliced. By omitting the almonds and adding 2 or 3 green citrons to each 10 gal., this forms British Madeira:

2.—From Sour Grapes.—The way an imitation sherry is made in England is to mix equal quantities of new cider and honey, and evaporate to a density so that a fresh egg will float so as to be half immersed. The liquid is then cooled and kept in a stone vessel at a temperature of from 60 to 67° F., until in about 12 or 14 days the peculiar smell of the fermentation is strongly established; then the liquid is put into a barrel, closed up, and placed in a cool cellar to settle; after 3 or 4 days it will be cleared; it is then bottled, and six weeks later is fit for drinking. We believe that grape juice may be used in place of cider, but if too acid, sugar and water would only make a kind of lemonade, and spoil the sherry taste, which is not acid. Sugar does not destroy this, but sulphite of lime is the proper material (not sulphate).

Strawberry Wine.—Take of cold, soft water, 7 gal.; cider, 6 gal.; strawberries, 6 gal. Ferment. Mix raw sugar, 16 lb.; red tartar, in fine powder, 3 oz.; the peel and juice of 2 lemons; then add 2 or 3 qt. of brandy. This will make 18 gal.

Yeast Wine.—Pour 100 parts of water in which 12 to 14 parts of white loaf sugar have been dissolved on to 40 parts of fresh yeast, and allow the whole to ferment at 41° F. The fermented wine is drawn off from the yeast, and may be further fortified by the addition of spirits.

Chapter XX.

MIXED DRINKS

Apple Champagne Syrup

APPLE syrup, 3 pt.; pear syrup, 3 pt.; Johannisberger wine, 20 oz.; cognac brandy, 8 oz.; citric acid solution (10%), 1 oz.; ginger essence, soluble, 1 oz.; safflower tincture, 6½ dr.; mucilage of acacia, 5 dr.; apple ether essence, 1 dr.

Apple Toddy

Hot soda mug. Sugar, ½ tablespoonful; baked apple, ½; applejack, 1 wineglass; fill balance with hot water; mix well, using a spoon; grate nutmeg on top.

Bishop

1.—Port or sherry, 1 bottle; lemons, 2; loaf sugar, 2 oz.; water, 1 tumbler; spice to taste. Stick 1 lemon with cloves, and roast or bake it; boil the spice in the water, boil up the wine, take off some of the spirit with a lighted paper, add the water and the roasted lemon, and let the preparation stand near the fire for a few minutes. Rub the sugar on the rind of the other lemon, put it into a bowl, strain, and add half the juice of the lemon; pour in the wine, and serve as hot as possible.

2.—To 2 bottles of claret add ¼ lb. of loaf sugar, the thin yellow rind of an orange, and 6 cloves; make all hot, but do not allow it to boil; then strain it through a sieve into a bowl and ice.

Beverages—Alcoholic

Blackberry Beverage

To each lb. of fruit allow 1 lb. of loaf or preserving sugar and 1 tablespoonful of cold water; brandy. Place the fruit, sugar and water in a large jar with a close-fitting cover, stand the jar in a saucepan of boiling water, and cook gently for 2 hours. Strain the juice, measure it, put it into a preserving pan or stew-pan (preferably an enameled one), and boil gently for 20 minutes, skimming carefully meanwhile. To each pint of syrup add a small glass of brandy; let the whole become quite cold, then bottle for use.

Brandy Mint Julep

Brandy, 1 wineglass; sugar, 1 lump; fresh mint, 1 of 2 small sprigs; orange, 1 thin slice; pineapple, 1 thin slice; crushed ice. Put the lump of sugar into a glass, and dissolve it in a few drops of cold water; add the brandy, mint, and a little crushed ice. On the top place a small piece of orange and a small piece of pineapple, and serve:

Note.—Gin or whiskey mint julep may be made by substituting these spirits for the brandy.

Brandy Smash

Water, 1 tablespoonful; white sugar, ½ tablespoonful; brandy, 1 wineglass; fill the tumbler two-thirds full of shaved ice, put in 2 sprigs of mint; put 2 small pieces of orange on top.

Catawba Syrup

1.—Simple syrup, 1 pt.; Catawba wine, 1 pt.

2.—Catawba wine, 2 qt.; citric acid, 2 oz.; simple syrup, 2 gal.

Champagne

1.—Tart wine, 2 pt.; brandy, 2 oz.; sherry, 1 oz.; granulated sugar, 3 lb. Dissolve the sugar without heat.

2.—Tart wine (California will answer), 2 qt.; cognac, 4 oz.; sherry, 2 oz.; granulated sugar, 6 lb. Dissolve the sugar in the wine without heat.

Mixed Drinks

3.—*Phosphate.*—Champagne syrup, 1 oz.; phosphate, three dashes; orange cider, 2 oz.; add a dash of cream, and stir while filling with hot soda.

Cherry Bounce

1.—To 6 gal. cherry juice add: 80% spirit, 15 gal.; Catalonia or Marseilles wine, 15 gal.; essence noyau 1½ oz.; cinnamon, ground, and infused in ¼ gal. of water, ¼ lb.; cloves, ground, and infused in ¼ gal. of water, ¼ lb.; mace, infused in ½ pt. 95% alcohol, ¾ oz. Mix all the above ingredients in a clean barrel, and add 30 gal. sugar syrup, 13° Réaumur. Stir up all the ingredients well together, and filter after 4 or 5 days. Make the color a little darker with sugar coloring, and to give a good shade add a little archil.

2.—Cherries, 12 lb.; to each gal. of juice obtained from them allow 4 lb. of sugar; ground mace, ½ teaspoonful; ground allspice, ¼ teaspoonful; brandy, 1 qt.; rum, 1 qt. Remove the stones, place the fruit in a large jar, and stand the jar in a saucepan containing boiling water. Cook gently until all the juice is extracted, strain it, and measure it into a preserving pan. Add sugar, mace and allspice in the proportions stated above, and simmer the ingredients until the scum ceases to rise. When cold add the spirits, and bottle for use.

Claret

1.—To 1 qt. of orangeade add a bottle of claret, and freeze as for iced coffee.

2.—Make syrup as egg phosphate, only use claret syrup. One ounce of the wine may be added if desired.

3.—Make an egg phosphate in the usual manner, and add 1 tablespoonful of claret before serving.

4.—Use claret concentrated syrup, diluting 1 qt. concentrated syrup with 3 qt. plain syrup. Put into a phosphate glass 1½ oz. fountain syrup, add a dash of phosphate, draw soda of sufficient quantity into another glass, pour into glass that contains the syrup, and serve. Claret is a flavor that lends itself specially well to blends and mixtures, like claret mint, claret lemonade, claret pineapple, etc.

Coca

1.—Coca wine, 1 oz.; calisaya elixir, 1 oz.; orange syrup, 6 oz.

2.—Coca wine, 1 oz.; orange syrup, 3 oz.

3.—Fluid extract coca, 2 oz.; fuller's earth, ½ oz. Mix, then add: Claret wine, 24 oz.; port wine 4 oz.; simple syrup, 3 oz. Mix, and filter.

4.—*Cognac.*—Wine of coca, 1 pt.; pure cognac brandy, 8 oz.; strong extract of vanilla, 2 oz.; strong extract of rose, 1 oz.; cane sugar or rock candy syrup, enough to make 1 gal.

5.—*White Wine.*—Wine of coca, 1 pt.; old white wine 2 pt.; cane sugar or rock candy syrup, 5 pt.

Coffee

Coffee syrup, 2 oz.; brandy, 4 dr.; cream, 2 oz.; 1 egg.

Cups

Apple.—Slice 3 or 4 large apples, without paring, barely cover them with boiling water, and let the water stand covered until cold. Strain, add 1 pt. of cider sweeten to taste, pour over crushed ice, and serve.

Bacchus.—Champagne, ½ bottle; sherry, ½ pt.; brandy, ⅛ pt.; noyau, 1 liqueur glass; castor sugar, 1 tablespoonful; seltzer or soda water, 1 bottle; a few balm leaves; ice. Put the champagne, sherry, brandy, noyau, sugar and balm leaves into a jug, let it stand for a few minutes, then add a few pieces of ice and the mineral water, and serve at once.

Burgundy.—Burgundy, 1 bottle; port, ½ bottle; soda water, 2 bottles; chartreuse, 1 liqueur glass; juice of 2 oranges; juice of 1 lemon; a few thin slices of cucumber; 1 or 2 sprigs of fresh lemon thyme; 1 tablespoonful of castor sugar. Put all the ingredients, except the port wine, into a large glass jug, surround it with rough pieces of ice, cover closely, and let it remain thus for 1 hour. Just before serving add the port wine.

Champagne.—1.—Champagne, 1 bottle; brandy, 1 liqueur glass; seltzer or soda water, 2 bottles; maraschino, ½ teaspoonful; a few fine strips of lemon peel. When the time permits, it is much better to ice the liquor which forms the basis of a "cooling cup" than to reduce the temperature by adding crushed ice. Place the champagne and seltzer water in a deep vessel, surround them with ice, cover them with a wet woolen cloth, and let them remain for 1 hour. When ready to serve, put the strips of lemon rind into a large glass jug, add the maraschino and liqueur brandy, pour in the soda water, and serve at once.

2.—Parisian.—Champagne, 1 bottle; seltzer water, 2 bottles; Swiss absinthe, 1 tablespoonful; lump sugar, 1 dessertspoonful; cucumber, a few thin slices; verbena, 2 or 3 sprigs, when procurable. Cool the champagne and seltzer water as directed in the preceding recipe. Place the rest of the ingredients in a large glass jug, and when ready to serve add the iced champagne and seltzer water.

Cider.—Cider, 1 bottle; soda water, 1 bottle; brandy, 1 liqueur glass; cucumber and lemon rind, a few thin strips; lemon juice, a dessertspoonful; castor sugar, 1 dessertspoonful, or to taste. Surround the cider and soda water with rough ice, and let them cool for half an hour. Put the brandy, cucumber and lemon rind, lemon juice and sugar, into a large jug, add the iced cider and soda water, and serve at once.

Claret.—1.—Claret, 1 bottle; sherry, 1 wineglassful; brandy, noyau and maraschino, each 1 wineglassful; thin rind of 1 lemon; 2 or 3 springs of mint; loaf sugar, to taste; seltzer or soda water, 1 large bottle. Put the claret, lemon rind, and 1 or 2 tablespoonfuls of loaf sugar into a large jug, cover, and let it stand embedded in ice for 1 hour. Add the rest of the ingredients, and serve.

Beverages—Alcoholic

A few strips of cucumber peel may be used instead of mint.

2.—Put 1 bottle of claret into a glass jug, add a few thin strips of lemon and cucumber rind, cover, and let the jug stand embedded in ice for 1 hour. Before serving, add 2 glasses of Curaçoa and 1 bottle of soda water, and sweeten to taste.

3.—Claret, 1 bottle; soda water, 1 bottle; iced water, ½ tumblerful; ½ lemon, sliced; put in small lumps of ice, and sweeten with sugar. Or claret and champagne cup: claret or champagne, 1 bottle; sherry, 1 large wineglassful; seltzer water, ½ tumblerful; balm and borage; peel of lemon, very thin; 1 slice of cucumber, to be sweetened to taste and highly iced.

Hock.—1.—Hock, 1 bottle; old brandy, 1 liqueur glassful; Curaçoa or Bénédictine, ½ liqueur glassful; seltzer or soda water, 2 bottles; few strips of lemon peel; a little borage. Stand the wine, seltzer or soda water in a deep vessel, surround them with rough ice, and let them remain for an hour. Have the rest of the ingredients ready, in a glass jug, pour in the wine, add the mineral water, and serve at once.

2.—Hock, 1 bottle; seltzer or soda water, 1 bottle; Curaçoa, 1 glassful; lemon juice, 1 tablespoonful; lemon rind, a few fine strips; cucumber rind, a few fine strips; castor sugar, a teaspoonful, or to taste. Put all these ingredients, except the mineral water, into a glass jug, surround it with ice, cover closely, and let it remain for half an hour. Just before serving add the mineral water, which must previously be iced.

Loving Cup.—Champagne, 1 bottle; Madeira, ½ bottle; French brandy, ¼ pt.; water, 1½ pt.; loaf sugar, ¼ lb.; lemons, 2; balm, a few leaves; borage, 2 or 3 sprigs. Rub the peel off one lemon with some lumps of sugar, then remove every particle of pith, also the rind and pith of the other lemon, and slice them thinly. Put the balm, borage, the sliced lemons and all the sugar into a jug, add the water, Madeira and brandy, cover, surround

Mixed Drinks

with ice, and let the mixture remain thus for about 1 hour. Also surround the champagne with ice, and add it to the rest of the ingredients when ready to serve.

Moselle.—Moselle, 1 bottle; Curaçoa, 2 glassfuls; seltzer or soda water, 1 bottle; the juice and thin rind of 1 lemon; a few thin slices of cucumber; castor sugar, 1 tablespoonful, or to taste; crushed ice. Put the lemon rind and lemon juice, the sugar, cucumber, Curaçoa and wine into a jug, let it stand, covered, for 15 or 20 minutes, then add the mineral water and a little crushed ice, and serve at once.

Sauterne.—Sauterne, 1 qt. bottle; Apollinaris, 1 pt. bottle; brandy, 1 wineglassful; Curaçoa, 1 wineglassful; juice of 1 lemon; 1 lemon, thinly sliced; 1 orange, thinly sliced; cucumber rind, 2 pieces; mint, a few small sprigs; crushed ice. Put all the above mentioned ingredients, except the mint and ice, into a large jug, surround it with ice, and let it stand for 1 hour. Serve with small sprigs of mint floating on the top. If liked, a little loaf sugar may be added, and, if more convenient, the cup may be cooled by adding 2 or 3 tablespoonfuls of crushed ice, instead of surrounding it with ice.

Wine.—Champagne (iced), 1 pt.; good claret, 1 pt.; Apollinaris, 1 pt.; brandy, 1 wineglassful; Curaçoa, 1 wineglassful; orange, sliced, 1; lemon, sliced, 1; cucumber rind, 2 pieces; green mint; ice. Put all these ingredients into a large glass jug, adding 2 or 3 tablespoonfuls of crushed ice. If liked, a little loaf sugar may be added. The cup is served with small sprigs of mint floating on its surface.

California Cup.—White wine, 1 bottle; sherry, 1 glassful; soda or seltzer water, 1 bottle; fresh or preserved pineapple, cut into sections, 3 or 4 slices; lemon (the juice and thin rind), 1; loaf sugar, 1 dessertspoonful, or to taste; ice. Strain the lemon juice into a large glass jug, add the sugar, lemon rind, pineapple, wine, a few lumps of ice, and lastly the soda water. Serve at once.

Beverages—Alcoholic

Egg Flip

Beer, 1 pt.; eggs, 5; sugar, 2 oz.; nutmeg and ginger, sufficient. Break the eggs into half of the beer, add the sugar, and beat well together; then place it in a clean warmer and heat it over the fire to nearly the boiling point, stirring it all the time; but do not let it boil. Next add the other portion of the beer and the spices, and mix well together. Some persons add a glassful of spirits. Care must be taken not to let it boil, as if it does the eggs will separate.

Egg Nog

1.—Take the yolks of 8 eggs, and beat with them 6 large spoonfuls of pulverized loaf sugar; when this is a cream add the third part of a nutmeg, grated; into this stir 1 tumblerful of good brandy and a wineglassful of good Madeira wine; mix them well together; have ready the whites of the eggs, beaten to a stiff froth, and beat them into the mixture; when all are well mixed add 3 pt. of rich milk.

2.—Put 1 tablespoonful of sherry or brandy into a tumbler, add 1 tablespoonful of cream and a little sugar, and mix well. Whisk the white of 1 egg to a stiff froth, stir it lightly into the contents of the tumbler, and serve.

3.—Beat 1 egg in a cup add 1 tablespoonful of brandy and 1 small teaspoonful of castor sugar, and mix well. Strain into a tumbler, stir in 1-3 pt. of milk, and serve.

4.—*Hot.*—a.—Beat the yolk of 1 egg and 1 tablespoonful of castor sugar well together, then stir in 1 tablespoonful of brandy or whiskey. Bring 1 pt. of milk to boiling point, then pour it over the mixed ingredients, stir well, and serve.

b.—Plain syrup, ¾ oz.; brandy, ½ oz.; whiskey, ¾ oz.; Angostura bitters, 3 drops; 1 egg. Put in shaker and beat well. Strain in 10-oz. mug and fill with hot milk; finish with whipped cream and nutmeg.

c.—Break fresh egg into shaker. Shake well, and pour into 5-oz. bouillon cup. Add dashes of whiskey and sherry and 1 teaspoonful of sugar. Sprinkle a little cinnamon before drawing hot milk. Serve with two 5-o'clock tea cakes.

d.—Plain syrup, ¾ oz.; brandy, ½ oz.; Angostura bitters, 3 drops; 1 egg. Put in shaker and beat well. Strain in 10-oz. mug and fill with hot milk; finish with whipped cream and nutmeg.

Gin

Cocktail.—Good unsweetened gin, 1 wineglassful; rock-candy syrup, 10 drops; orange bitters, 10 drops; lemon peel, small piece; crushed ice. Half fill a tumbler with small pieces of ice, pour over it the gin, add the syrup and bitters, then cover and shake well. Strain into a small glass, place a small piece of lemon peel on the top, and serve.

Rickey.—Gin, 1 wineglassful; lemon or lime juice, 1 dessertspoonful; seltzer water; ice. Place a small block of ice at the bottom of a deep champagne glass, strain over it the lemon juice, add the gin, fill up with seltzer water, and serve.

Note.—Any other spirit may be used instead of gin, and would, of course, give its name to the compound. Use fresh limes in season.

Golden Fizz

Claret syrup, 2 oz.; Holland gin, ¼ oz.; lemon juice, 8 dashes; yolk of 1 egg.

John Collins

Gin, 1 glassful; soda water, iced, 1 bottle; sugar, 1 level teaspoonful; lemon juice, 1 tablespoonful; lemon, 2 or 3 thin slices; crushed ice. Half fill a tumbler with ice, pour over it the gin and lemon juice, add the sugar, cover with a small plate, and shake well. Strain into another tumbler, add the soda water, 1 tablespoonful of crushed ice, and the sliced lemon, then serve.

Beverages—Alcoholic

Kola

1.—Fluid extract kola, 1 fl.oz.; elixir coca, 2 fl.oz.; extract vanilla, 2 fl.dr.; essence rose, 2 fl.dr.; essence cinnamon, 2 fl.dr.; syrup, to make 2 pt.

2.—Powdered kola, 2 oz.; glycerine, 14 fl.dr.; alcohol, 10 fl.dr.; alcohol, 10 fl.dr.; cinnamon water, 6 fl.oz.; essence vanilla, 1 fl.dr.; tincture orange, 1 fl.oz.; syrup, 5 fl.oz. Macerate for a week, and then filter.

3.—Kola nuts, roasted, 1 oz.; essence vanilla, 1 dr.; syrup, 2 oz.; sherry wine, to make 1 pt.

4.—Roasted kola, No. 20, powdered, 1 part; sherry wine, 50 parts. Macerate for a week, express, and after allowing the product to stand several days, filter. If a sweet wine is desired, replace 2 parts of the sherry wine by the same quantity of sugar. It is preferable to employ detannated sherry wine, for the reason that the tannin contained in ordinary sherry wine is apt to gradually precipitate the proximate principles of the kola in the finished wine; and thus the latter is likely to become progressively weaker with age.

5.—Shaved ice, ¼ glassful; kola wine, calisaya elixir, ginger ale syrup, of each ½ oz.; liquid phosphate, three dashes; plain soda, 1 glassful, using both streams. Stir and serve.

Manhattan Cocktail

Vermouth, ½ wineglassful; whiskey, ½ wineglassful; simple syrup, 30 drops; Angostura bitters, 10 drops; Curaçoa, 6 drops; a little shaved ice; lemon peel, 1 small strip. Put all the ingredients, except the lemon rind, into a large tumbler, cover the top closely, shake well, and strain into a wineglass. Place the strip of lemon peel on the top, and serve.

Martini Cocktail

Good, unsweetened gin, ½ wineglassful; Italian vermouth, ½ wineglassful; rock-candy syrup, 6 drops; orange bitters, 12 drops; lemon peel, 1 small piece;

Mixed Drinks

crushed ice. Half fill a tumbler with crushed ice, pour over it all the liquids, shake well, then strain into a glass, and serve with a small piece of lemon peel floating on the surface.

Note.—For dry cocktails use French vermouth, and be sparing of bitters.

May Drink

Hock type, or other white wine, 1 bottle; water, ½ pt.; sugar, 1 or 2 tablespoonfuls; lemon (the juice and thin rind), 1; black currant leaves a small handful; crushed ice. Put the sugar, lemon rind and lemon juice, black currant leaves, into a jug, add the water and wine, and let it stand, covered and surrounded with ice, for at least ½ hour. Strain into a glass jug, add a few sprigs of mint, then serve.

Metheglin

From honey, 1 cwt.; warm water, 24 gal.; stir well until dissolved; the next day add of yeast, 1 pt., and hops, 1 lb., previously boiled in 1 gal. of water, along with water, q. s. to make the whole measure 1 bbl.; mix well, and ferment the whole with the usual precautions adopted for other liquors. It contains, on the average, from 7 to 8% alcohol.

Mint Julep

1.—This is made precisely in the same manner as sherry cobbler, except that you use brandy instead of wine, and you add to your fruits 3 or 4 sprigs of fresh spearmint. Decorate the top with sprigs of mint instead of flowers.

2.—Loaf sugar, 4 cubes; extract mint, 10 drops; prepared milk, 1 dessertspoonful; hot soda, sufficient to fill cup; whipped cream, 1 tablespoonful; grated nutmeg, q. s.

3.—Make a syrup of 1 qt. of water and 1 lb. of sugar Break up 1 doz. sprigs of mint and soak them in 1½ cupfuls of boiling water, in a covered bowl, for 5 minutes. Then strain, and add the flavored water to the syrup. Turn in the juice of 8 oranges, 8 lemons, ½ pt. of strawberry juice and 1 pt. of claret. Serve with ice in the punch bowl, adding enough ice-water to dilute properly. Fresh mint leaves and berries should float on top of the bowl and in the individual cups.

Mulled Ale

Good ale, 1 qt.; rum or brandy, 1 glassful; loaf sugar, 1 tablespoonful; ground cloves, a pinch, grated nutmeg, a pinch; ground ginger, a good pinch. Put the ale, sugar, cloves, nutmeg and ginger into an ale warmer or stewpan, and bring nearly to boiling point. Add the brandy, and more sugar and flavoring, if necessary, and serve at once.

Mulled Claret

Heat 1 pt. of claret nearly to boiling point, add ½ pt. of boiling water, sugar, nutmeg and cinnamon to taste, and serve hot. Any kind of wine may be mulled, but port and claret are those usually selected for the purpose.

Negus

Port wine, ½ pt.; boiling water, ½ pt.; lemon, 2 or 3 thin slices; sugar and nutmeg to taste. Heat the wine in a stewpan, but do not allow it to boil. Put the slices of lemon, a pinch of nutmeg, and 4 or 5 lumps of sugar into a jug, pour in the boiling water, stir gently until the sugar is dissolved, then add the hot wine, and serve at once.

Perry

A fermented liquid, prepared from pears, in the same way as cider is from apples. The reduced pulp must not be allowed to remain long without being pressed. In the cask, perry does not bear changes of temperature so well as cider. It is, therefore, advisable, if at the end of the succeeding summer it be in sound condition, to bottle it, when it will keep perfectly well. The red, rough-tasted sorts of pears are principally used for making perry. They should be quite ripe, without, however, approaching to mellowness or decay. The best perry contains about 9% of absolute alcohol; ordinary perry, from 5 to 7%. Perry is a very pleasant-tasted and wholesome liquid. When bottled, champagne fashion, it is said to frequently pass for champagne without the fraud being suspected.

Pineapple Julep

Pineapple, either fresh or preserved, 1; sparkling Moselle, 1 bottle; gin, 1 gill; raspberry syrup, 1 gill; maraschino, ½ gill; oranges (juice of), 2; crushed ice, 1 lb. Slice the pineapple rather thinly, and divide each slice into 8 sections. Put all the liquids into a glass jug or bowl, add the ice and prepared pineapple, and serve.

Purl

To warm ale or beer add bitters, 1 glassful, or q. s. Some add spirit.

Sangaree

One-third of wine in water, with sugar and nutmeg to the taste.

Frozen.—Nothing can be more refreshing at the dinner table in hot weather than claret or port wine made into sangaree, with proportions of water, sugar and nutmeg as taste shall direct, then frozen, with the addition of a few whites of egg, beaten to a froth. Send to table exactly as you would Roman punch.

Shandy Gaff

Equal quantities of cold ale or beer and good ginger ale. Empty the bottles into a jug in which some lumps of ice have been broken, and serve when quite cold.

Sherry Cobbler

1.—Sherry, ¼ pt.; orange juice, 1 teaspoonful; fine white sugar, 1 teaspoonful; crushed ice. Half fill a large tumbler with ice, pour over it the sherry and orange juice, cover, and shake well. Strain into another tumbler containing the sugar, stir well, and serve with straws.

2.—Sherry, ½ pt.; soda water, 1 bottle; Curacoa, 1 glassful; loaf sugar, 1 tablespoonful; crushed ice. Dissolve the sugar in the sherry, and add the liqueur and soda. Put the preparation into tumblers; to each add a few small pieces of ice, and serve. Beverages of this description are usually drunk through straws, but it is merely a matter of taste.

3.—Take sugar, 1 tablespoonful; orange, 2 or 3 slices; sherry, 2 wineglassfuls. Fill the tumbler with shaved ice, and shake well.

4.—To 1 pt. good sherry add an equal measure of heavy simple syrup and one lemon cut in very thin slices. Allow the syrup to stand a few hours; strain through a sieve, and bottle for use.

5.—White syrup, 3 pt.; sherry, 1 qt. Add 1 lemon, cut in thin slices. Macerate for 12 hours, and strain.

6.—*Egg Flip.*—Sherry, 1 glassful; 1 egg; loaf sugar, 1 teaspoonful, or to taste; nutmeg; crushed ice. Beat the egg well, add the sugar, sherry, and a little crushed ice, shake well until sufficiently cooled, then strain into a small glass, and serve.

Note.—Port wine, or any spirit, may replace the sherry, and the liquor used would, of course, give its name to the "flip."

7.—*Frappé.*—Add 1 pt. of sherry wine to every qt. of lemon water-ice.

Shrub

Rum, ½ gal.; orange juice, ¾ pt.; lemon juice, ½ pt.; lemons, peel of 2; loaf sugar, 2 lb.; water, 2½ pt. Slice the lemon peel very thinly and put it, with the fruit juice and spirit, in a large covered jar. Let it stand for 2 days, then pour over it the water in which the sugar has been dissolved, take out the lemon peel, and leave it for 12 days before using.

Mixed Drinks

Silver Fizz

Gin, 1 wineglassful; juice of ½ lemon; white of 1 egg; icing sugar, 1 teaspoonful; carbonate of soda, a pinch; pounded ice. Fill a tumbler 3 parts full with pounded ice, pour over this the gin and lemon juice, then add the white of egg, beaten to a stiff froth. Shake well, then strain into another tumbler containing the icing sugar and carbonate of soda, and serve at once.

Silver Sour

Lemon juice, 1 dessertspoonful; unsweetened gin, 1 wineglassful; egg, white of 1; loaf sugar, 1 teaspoonful; crushed ice. Put the white of an egg into a tumbler, beat it slightly, then add the lemon juice, gin, sugar, and a heaped tablespoonful of crushed ice. Cover, and shake well until sufficiently cooled, then strain into a small glass, and serve.

Sloe Gin

1.—Half fill clean, dry wine bottles with sloes. Add to each 1 oz. of crushed barley sugar, a little noyau, or 2 or 3 drops of essence of almonds. Fill the bottles with good unsweetened gin, cork them securely, and allow them to remain in a moderately warm place for 3 months. At the end of this time strain the liqueur through fine muslin or filtering paper until quite clear. then bottle it. cork securely, and store for use.

2.—*Cocktail.*—Half fill a tumbler with broken ice, pour over it ½ wineglassful each of sloe gin and unsweetened gin and 10 drops of orange bitters, cover the top of the glass, and shake it well. When sufficiently cooled, strain it into a small glass, and serve with a small piece of lemon peel floating on the top.

Solferino

Brandy, 1 pt.; simple syrup, 2 pt.

Beverages—Alcoholic

Whiskey Cocktail

Half fill a tumbler with crushed ice, pour over it 1 wineglassful of whiskey, 15 drops of rock-candy syrup and 10 drops of Angostura bitters, cover, and shake well, then strain into a small glass. Place a very small piece of lemon peel on the top and serve.

Note.—Brandy cocktail may be made by substituting a wineglassful of good French brandy for the whiskey.

Whiskey Sour

Rock-candy syrup, 1 dessertspoonful; whiskey, 1 wineglassful; lemon juice, and pineapple, 1 thin, small piece; crushed ice. Strain 1 dessertspoonful of lemon juice into a tumbler, add 1 dessertspoonful of rock-candy syrup and 1 wineglassful of whiskey, and a heaped tablespoonful of crushed ice, and shake well. Strain into a small glass, and serve with thin slices of orange and pineapple floating on the top.

Note.—Brandy or any other spirit may be substituted for the whiskey, the name being changed accordingly.

Chapter XXI.

PUNCHES

Punch

PUNCH is a beverage made of various spirituous liquors or wine, hot water, the acid juice of fruits, and sugar. It is considered to be very intoxicating, but this is probably because the spirit, being partly sheathed by the mucilaginous juice and the sugar, its strength does not appear to the taste so great as it really is. Punch, which was almost universally drunk among the middle classes about 50 or 60 years ago, has almost disappeared from our domestic tables, being superseded by wine. There are many different varieties of punch. It is sometimes kept cold in bottles, and makes a most agreeable summer drink.

1.—Lemons, juice of 3 or 4; lemons, yellow peel of 1 or 2; lump sugar, ¾ lb.; boiling water, 3½ pt.; infuse ½ hour, strain, add porter, ½ pt.; rum and brandy, of each, ¾ to 1 pt. (or either, alone, 1½ to 2 pt.); and add more warm water and sugar, if desired weaker or sweeter.

2.—Water, 3 pt.; sugar, 1½ lb.; raspberry juice, 1 pt.; lemons, juice of 2; 1 orange; mace, 1 blade; cinnamon, 1 small stick; cloves, 8; claret, 1 pt.; brandy, 1 pt.; French cherries, 3 oz. Put the cherries to soak in a little of the brandy, and afterward cut them in quarters. Crush the spices, and add them and the grated rind of 1 lemon, and 1 orange to the sugar and water; boil up once and set aside to cool. Strain the syrup and add the lemon, orange and raspberry juices, then freeze. When partly frozen add the claret and brandy; freeze a few

Beverages—Alcoholic

minutes longer, then mix in the cut cherries, and finish. The well-whisked whites of 2 eggs may be worked in when the cherries are added, if desired. Color pink or very light red.

3.—Brandy, ½ pt.; rum, ½ pt.; boiling water, 1 pt.; loaf sugar, 2 or 3 oz.; 1 large lemon; ground cinnamon, a pinch; grated nutmeg, a pinch. Remove the rind of the lemon by rubbing it with some of the sugar. Put the whole of the sugar, cinnamon, cloves, brandy, rum and boiling water into a stewpan, heat gently by the side of the fire, but do not let it approach boiling point. Strain the lemon juice into a punch bowl, add the hot liquid, and serve at once.

4.—Very old ale, 1 qt.; boiling water, 1 pt.; rum, ¼ pt.; whiskey, ¼ pt.; gin, ¼ pt.; 1 lemon, thinly sliced, sugar to taste; ground cinnamon, a pinch; ground cloves, a pinch; grated nutmeg, a pinch. Put all these ingredients into a large stewpan and bring nearly to boiling point. Strain into a punch bowl, add a few fresh thin slices of lemon, and serve.

Arrack Punch, Imitation

Two or three preserved tamarinds, dissolved in a bowl of any kind of punch, will impart to it a flavor closely resembling arrack.

Brandy

1.—To 1 pt. cognac brandy, ½ pt. of Jamaica rum, ½ pt. of peach brandy, add 2 lb. white sugar, 1 gill of lemon and 1 gill of lime juice; mix all well together, and add ice equal to 2 qt. of water; cut 2 lemons into thin slices, peel and slice thin 1 pineapple; add these to the punch, and let stand, to ripen and blend, for 1 hour before using.

2.—To 1 teaspoonful of raspberry syrup add 1 tablespoonful of white sugar, 1 wineglassful of brandy, the same quantity of water, a small piece of lemon, 2 slices of orange, 1 piece of pineapple. Fill the tumbler with

Punches

---

shaved ice, shake well, and dress the top with berries in season; sip through a straw.

3.—Take 3 doz. lemons, chip off the yellow rinds, taking care that none of the white underlying pith is taken, as that would make the punch bitter, whereas the yellow portion of the rinds is that in which the flavor resides, and in which the cells are placed containing the essential oil. Put this yellow rind into a punch bowl, add to it 2 lb. of lump sugar, stir the sugar and peel together with a wooden spoon or spatula for nearly half an hour, thereby extracting a greater quantity of the essential oil. Now add boiling water, and stir until the sugar is completely dissolved. Squeeze and strain the juice from the lemons and add it to the mixture; stir together and taste it; add more acid or more sugar, as required, and take care not to render it too watery. "Rich of the fruit and plenty of sweetness," is the maxim. Now measure the sherbet, and to every 3 qt. add 1 pt. of cognac brandy and 1 pt. of old Jamaica rum, the spirit being well stirred as poured in. This punch may be bottled, and kept in a cold cellar; it will be found to improve with age.

Burgundy

Burgundy wine, 2 oz.; orange syrup, 1 oz. Fill a 12-oz. glass with crushed ice, draw coarse stream to fill glass. Decorate with slice each of pineapple and orange. Serve with straws.

Catawba

Lemon syrup, 1 oz.; juice of half a lemon; Catawba wine, 2 oz.; shaved ice, ¼ glassful. Mix in 14-oz. straight lemonade glass. Decorate with pineapple and cherries.

Chatham Artillery Punch

Catawba wine, 1 gal.; New England rum, 1 qt.; whiskey, 1 qt. Cut up and add 6 pineapples, 12 oranges, and strawberries q. s., and allow to stand or draw one night. When

Beverages—Alcoholic

ready to use, 1 doz. qt. bottles of champagne are needed to give tone and bead. A Southern drink, which is *very intoxicating*, and should be avoided.

Cider

Cider, iced, 1 qt.; seltzer or soda water, iced, 1 bottle; brandy, 1 wineglassful; sugar, 2 oz., or to taste; 1 lemon, thinly sliced. Mix all the ingredients together in a glass jug, and serve in small glasses.

Claret

1.—To a large punch bowl half filled with broken ice, add 2 lb. of pulverized sugar, 6 oranges cut crosswise into thin slices, 6 bottles of claret, and 1 bottle of champagne; mix well together and let stand for 1 hour before using.

2.—Take 1 tablespoonful of sugar, a small slice of lemon, 2 or 3 slices of orange. Fill the tumbler with shaved ice, and then pour in the claret, shake well, and ornament with berries in season. Place a straw in the glass.

3.—Take 1½ tablespoonfuls of sugar, 1 slice of lemon, 2 or 3 slices of orange. Fill the tumbler with shaved ice, pour in the claret, and shake well.

4.—Claret syrup, ½ oz.; orange, 1 slice; lemon, 1 slice; shaved ice, ¼ glassful. Fill 12-oz. glass with coarse stream, stir, decorate with fruit, and serve with straws.

Cold Punch

1.—Rum, 1 bottle; Curaçoa, 2 small glassfuls; white wine, 1 bottle; powdered sugar, ½ lb.; 1 large lemon; water, ½ pt.; ice. Put the sugar and lemon rind into a bowl with the water; when dissolved, add the spirits, the wine, and the juice of the lemon. Break some ice into the bowl before serving.

2.—Arrack, port wine, water, of each 1 pt.; lemons, juice of 4; sugar, 1 lb.; mix.

Punches

Cream Punch

Pare off the rind of four large lemons, and steep it for 24 hours in 1 qt. brandy or rum; then mix it with the juice of the lemons, 1½ lb. of sugar, 3½ pt. of boiled water, and about 2-3 of a can of evaporated cream; mix well, and strain the whole through a jelly bag. You may either use it at once, or make a large quantity and bottle it.

East India Punch

Brandy, ½ pt.; port wine, 1 pt.; syrup, simple, 1 pt.; lime-juice syrup, ½ pt.; seltzer water, iced, 1 bottle; arrack, ½ gill; lemons, the thinly pared rinds of 2; syringa, 2 or 3 sprigs; crushed ice, 1 breakfast-cupful; sugar to taste. Soak the lemon rind in the brandy for 3 hours, then strain, add the rest of the ingredients, and serve.

Gin Punch

1.—To ½ pt. of old Holland gin add 1 gill of maraschino, the juice of 2 lemons, and the yellow rind of 1, previously infused in the gin, 2 gills of simple syrup or 4 oz. of pulverized sugar, and 1 qt. of seltzer water. Mix well, and freeze to a semi-solid.

2.—Lemon, yellow peel and juice of 1; gin, ¾ pt.; water, 1¾ pt.; sherry, 1 glassful.

Hot Punch

Rum, ½ pt.; brandy, ½ pt.; sugar, ¼ lb.; 1 large lemon; nutmeg, ½ teaspoonful; boiling water, 1 pt. Rub the sugar over the lemon until it has absorbed all the yellow part of the skin; then put the sugar into a punch bowl; add the lemon juice (free from pips), and mix these two ingredients well together. Pour over them the boiling water, stir well together, add the rum, brandy and nutmeg, mix thoroughly, and the punch will be ready to serve. It is very important in making good punch that all the ingredients are thoroughly incorporated; and to

Beverages—Alcoholic

insure success, the process of mixing must be diligently attended to.

Iced

Champagne or white wine, 1 qt.; arrack, 1 pt.; lemons, juice and yellow peel of 6; white sugar, 1 lb.; soda water, 1 or 2 bottles; ice as cream.

Manhattan

Powdered sugar, 1 tablespoonful; sweet milk, 2 oz.; 1 egg; vermouth, 1/4 oz.; whiskey, 3/4 oz.; Angostura bitters, 1 dash. Cracked ice to fill glass. Shake well, and strain in 7-oz. goblet. Grate nutmeg on top. Serve with straws.

Maraschino Fruit Punch

Whole cherries, 1 qt.; maraschino cordial, 2 oz.; sliced oranges, 8; sliced lemons, 4; pineapple cubes, 8 oz.; brandy, 4 oz.; juice of 6 lemons; juice of 6 oranges; water, 1 1/2 gal. Sweeten and color to suit taste. Mix all ingredients; serve from punch bowl, with the addition of cracked ice.

Milk Punch

1.—Fill a tumbler about 1/4 full of evaporated cream, put in a tablespoonful of powdered sugar, about as much liquor (or sherry, if preferred) as cream, then fill the tumbler with cracked ice and shake well.

2.—Take sugar, 1 tablespoonful; water, 2 tablespoonfuls; brandy, 1 wineglassful; Santa Cruz rum, 1/2 wineglassful; shaved ice, 1-3 tumblerful. Fill with milk and shake well; grate a little nutmeg on top.

3.—Yellow rinds of 2 doz. lemons; steep for 2 days in rum or brandy, 2 qt.; then add spirit, 3 qt. more; hot water, 3 qt.; lemon juice, 1 qt.; loaf sugar, 4 lb.; 2 nutmegs, grated; boiling milk, 2 qt. Mix and in 2 hours strain through a jelly bag.

4.—*Syrup.*—a.—Simple syrup, 1 pt.; brandy, 8 oz.; Jamaica rum, 8 oz.; cream, 1 pt.

Punches

b.—To 1 pt. heavy syrup add ½ pt. each of brandy and Jamaica rum; flavor with 2 teaspoonfuls of an extract prepared by macerating 2 oz. of ground nutmegs in 8 oz. of alcohol. The syrup is first to be poured into the glass in the proper quantity and ordinary cream syrup added before drawing the soda water.

c.—Brandy, 4 vol.; Jamaica rum, 4 vol.; condensed milk, 1 vol.; syrup, 8 vol.

d.—Rock-candy syrup, 2 pt.; brandy, 8 oz.; Jamaica rum, 6 oz.; cream, 1½ pt.

Norfolk

French brandy, 20 qt.; yellow peels of 30 oranges and 30 lemons; infuse for 12 hours; add cold water, 30 qt.; lump sugar, 15 lb.; and the juice of the oranges and lemons; mix well, strain through a hair sieve, add new milk, 2 qt., and in 6 weeks bottle. Keeps well. (Can be made on small scale.)

Orgeat Punch

Orgeat syrup, 12 dr.; brandy, 1 oz.; juice of 1 lemon.

Princes'

Put into a freezing can a bottle of sparkling champagne, 1 gill of maraschino, ½ pt. of strawberry syrup, the juice of 6 oranges, the yellow rind of 1 rubbed on sugar.

Raspberry

As Norfolk, but using raspberry juice or vinegar for oranges or lemons.

Regent's

Pare off the thin yellow rinds from 4 oranges and 4 lemons; express the juice from the same fruit and strain it; add to it the yellow rinds, with 2 sticks of cinnamon broken up, ½ doz. cloves and a dessertspoonful of vanilla sugar. Simmer these ingredients very slowly for ½ hour in 1 qt. of simple syrup. Express the juice from 1½ doz.

Beverages—Alcoholic

of lemons and add it to the decoction. Then make a strong infusion of the finest green tea and add it to the mixture. After which add equal portions of old Jamaica rum and cognac brandy, according to the strength required. Mix all well together, strain through a hair sieve, put it into a freezer and make very cold.

Roman

French brandy, 4 oz.; best Jamaica rum, 4 oz.; extract vanilla, ¼ oz.; fruit acid, ¼ oz.; syrup, 1 gal.

Tea

1.—Strong hot green tea, lemon juice and capillaire, of each 1½ pt.; rum, brandy, arrack and Curaçoa, of each 1 pt.; champagne, 1 bottle. Mix and slice a pineapple into it.

2.—Hot tea, 1 qt.; arrack, ½ bottle; white sugar, 6 oz.; juice of 8 lemons; yellow rinds of 4 lemons.

Wine

Sugar, 1 lb.; yellow peel of 3 lemons; juice of 9 lemons; arrack, 1 pt.; port or sherry wine, hot, 1 gal.; cinnamon, ¼ oz.; nutmeg, 1 dr.

Whiskey

1.—To 1 wineglassful of whiskey add 2 wineglassfuls of hot water and then sugar to taste. Dissolve the sugar well with 1 wineglassful of the water, then pour in the whiskey and add the balance of the water; sweeten to taste and put in a small piece of lemon rind or a thin slice of lemon.

2.—Scotch whiskey, 1 bottle; boiling water, 1 qt.; loaf sugar, ½ lb.; the juice and finely pared rinds of 3 lemons. Pour the boiling water over the sugar, lemon rinds and juice. Let it remain until cold, then strain into a punch bowl. Add the whiskey, place the bowl in a large vessel,

Punches

surround it with ice, cover and let it stand thus for at least 1 hour before serving.

3.—Whiskey, 1 wineglassful; lemon juice, 1 dessertspoonful; loaf sugar, 1 teaspoonful; orange, 1 thin slice; pineapple, 1 thin small piece; crushed ice. Put a heaped tablespoonful of crushed ice into a glass, pour over it the whiskey and lemon juice, add the sugar and shake well until sufficiently cooled. Strain into a small glass and serve with the orange and pineapple floating on the surface.

AS this book goes to press there is much uncertainty as to what laws will be promulgated or enforced. Therefore some of the formulas call for brandy and other liquors which can be obtained without question up to July 1, 1919, and possibly afterwards. Some people have laid in a supply of materials, not for a rainy day, but for a more or less drastic period of abstinence. This will enable them to make many of the preparations that their less well-heeled neighbors cannot expect to emulate. This book is written for all, and is without prejudice of any kind.

METRIC MEASURES.

Measures.		Metric to Customary.	Customary to Metric.
LENGTHS	1 Millimeter = 0.03937 inch 1 Centimeter = 0.3937 " 1 Meter = 39.37 " 1 " = 3.28083 feet 1 " = 1.093611 yards 1 Kilometer = 0.62137 mile	1 Inch = 25.4001 millimeters 1 " = 2.54001 centimeters 1 Foot = 0.0254 meter 1 Yard = 0.304801 " 1 Mile = 0.914402 " 1 Mile = 1.60935 kilometers	
AREAS	1 Square Millimeter = 0.00155 square inch 1 " Centimeter = 0.1550 " " 1 " Meter = 10.764 feet 1 " " = 1.1960 yards 1 " Kilometer = 0.3861 mile 1 Hectare = 2.471 acres	1 Square Inch = 645.16 square millimeters 1 " " = 6.452 " centimeters 1 " Foot = 0.0929 " meter 1 " Yard = 0.8361 " " 1 " Mile = 2.5900 " kilometers 1 Acre = 0.4047 hectares	
VOLUMES	1 Cubic Millimeter = 0.000061 cubic inch 1 " Centimeter = 0.0610 " " 1 " Meter = 35.314 " feet 1 " " = 1.3079 " yards	1 Cubic Inch = 16.3872 cubic millimeters 1 " " = 16.3872 " centimeters 1 " Foot = 0.02832 " meter 1 " Yard = 0.7645 " "	
CAPACITY — Liquid	1 Liter = 1.05668 quarts 1 " = 0.26417 gallon 1 Liter = 0.9081 quart	1 Quart = 0.94636 liter 1 Gallon = 3.78543 liters 1 Quart = 1.1012 "	
Dry	1 Decaliter = 1.1351 pecks 1 Hectoliter = 2.83774 bushels	1 Peck = 8.80982 decaliter 1 Bushel = 0.35239 hectoliter	
MASSES — Avoirdupois	1 Gram = 15.4324 grains 1 " = 0.03527 ounce 1 Kilogram = 2.20462 pounds 1 " = 2.67923 "	1 Grain = 0.06480 gram 1 Ounce = 28.3495 " 1 Pound = 0.45359 kilogram 1 Pound = 31.10348 grams	
Troy	1 Gram = (see above) 1 Kilogram = (see above)	1 Ounce = (see above) 1 Pound = 0.37324 kilogram	
Apothecaries	1 Gram = 0.2705 dram 1 " = 0.8115 scruple	1 Dram = 3.6967 grams 1 Scruple = 1.2322 "	

224

INDEX

INDEX

A

Acid Phosphates, 100.
Acid Taste in Wines, 160.
Age of Wines, 160.
Alcoholizing Wines, 160.
Allspice, Extract, 1.
Almonds, Extract, 1.
Angelica, Extract, 2.
Anise, Extract, 2.
Apollinaris Lemonade, 88.
Apple Champagne Syrup, 197.
Apple, Extract, 2.
Apple Syrup, 29.
Apple Toddy, 197.
Apple Wine, 174.
Apricot, Extract, 3.
Apricot Phosphate, 101.
Apricot Syrup, 29.
Apricot Wine, 175.
Arrack Punch, 214.
Arrowroot, 128.

B

Bacchus Cup, 200.
Banana Cream, 64.
Banana, Extract, 3.
Banana Syrup, 29.
Barley Water, 128.
Beef, Hot, 115.
Beer Tonic, 55.
Bergamot Essence, 3.
Birch Beer, 55.
Birch Essence, 3.
Bishop, 197.
Blackberry Beverage, 198.
Blackberry Essence, 4.
Blackberry Frappé, 66.
Blackberry Syrup, 30.
Blackberry Wine, 176.
Blueberry Essence, 4.
Boiled Lemonade, 88.
Bottling Cider, 136.
Bottling Wines, 161.
Bran Tea, 129.
Brandy Mint Julep, 198.
Brandy Punch, 214.
Brandy Smash, 198.
Burgundy Cup, 200.
Burgundy Punch, 215.

C

Cacao Essence, 4.
Calamus Essence, 4.
California Cup, 203.
Calisaya, 61.
Calisaya Phosphates, 101.
Calisaya Tonic, 115.
Calisaya Tonic Syrup, 30.
Capillaire Syrup, 30.
Caraway Essence, 5.
Cardamom Extract, 5.
Cassia Extract, 5.
Catawba Champagne, 176.
Catawba Punch, 215.
Catawba Syrup, 198.
Catechu Extract, 5.
Cedrat Essence, 5.
Celery Cocoa Cream, 84.

227

Index

Celery Extract, 5.
Celery Phosphate, 101.
Celery Syrup, 30.
Cellaring Wines, 162.
Champagne, 150, 198.
Champagne Cider, 137.
Champagne Cup, 201.
Chatham Artillery Punch, 215.
Checkerberry, Hot, 116.
Cherry Bounce, 199.
Cherry Cider, 138.
Cherry Cream, 84.
Cherry Extract, 5.
Cherry, Hot, 124.
Cherry Malt, 94.
Cherry Phosphate, 101.
Cherry Sundae, 112.
Cherry Syrup, 30.
Cherry Wine, 177.
Chicken Cream, 116.
Chocolate Cream, 64, 84.
Chocolate Frappé, 66.
Chocolate, Hot, 116.
Chocolate Phosphate, 102.
Chocolate Sundae, 112.
Chocolate Syrup, 32.
Chop Suey, 113.
Cider—Artificial, 135.
Cider—Canning, 137.
Cider—Cheap, 138.
Cider Cup, 201.
Cider Punch, 108, 216.
Ciders, 131.
Cinchona Extract, 6.
Cinchona Syrup, 34.
Cinchona Wine, 191.
Cinnamon Extract, 7.
Cinnamon Syrup, 34.
Citron Essence, 7.
Clam Beverages, 119.
Clam Juice, 64.
Claret, 63.
Claret Cup, 201.
Claret Drinks, 199.
Claret Glacé, 75.
Claret Lemonade, 89.

Claret Punch, 108, 216.
Clarification of Wines, 162.
Clearing Cider, 139.
Clove Essence, 7.
Coca Drinks, 200.
Coca Malt, 94.
Coca Phosphate, 102.
Coca Syrup, 34.
Coca-Vanilla Syrup, 34.
Coca Wine, 178.
Cocktails, 205, 206.
Cocoa Essence, 7.
Cocoa Malted Milk, 97.
Cocoa Mint, 63.
Coffee Cream, 65.
Coffee Drink, 63.
Coffee Extract, 7.
Coffee Extract, Hot, 120.
Coffee Frappé, 67.
Coffee Malted Milk, 97.
Coffee Punch, 108.
Coffee Syrup, 35.
Coffee Syrup, Alcoholic, 200.
Cold Punch, 216.
Coloring Matters, 164.
Cordial, 92.
Cowslip Wine, 178.
Crab Apple Tonic, 35.
Cranberry Phosphate, 102.
Cream Puff, 84.
Cream Punch, 217.
Cream Syrup, 36.
Creamade, 84.
Crushed Fruit Glacé, 75.
Cucumber à la Surprise, 85.
Cups, 200.
Currant Cream, 63.
Currant Essence, 9.
Currant Syrup, 36.
Currant Wine, 179.

D

Damson Wine, 180.
Dandelion Root Beer, 56.
Dandelion Wine, 181.
Date Sundae, 113.

Index

Decanting Wines, 166.
Detannation of Wines, 166.
Detartarization of Wines, 167.
Diabetic Lemonade, 89.

E

Earthiness of Wines, 164.
East India Punch, 217.
Egg Beverage, 121.
Egg Chocolate, 63.
Egg Drinks, 61.
Egg Flip, 204, 210.
Egg Lemonade, 89.
Egg Malted Milk, 97.
Egg Nog, 204.
Egg Phosphate, 102.
Egg Sour, 61.
Elderberry Wine, 181.
Elderflower Wine, 183.
Essences and Extracts, 1.

F

Fancy Syrup, 36.
Fermentation of Grape Juice, 76.
Fig Soufflé, 85.
Fig Wine, 184.
Filtration of Bottled Wines, 169.
Fining Wines, 169.
Flatness of Wines, 170.
Foam Extract, 9.
Foam Syrup, 37.
Frappés, 66.
Frozen Phosphate, 102.
Fruit Blend, 63.
Fruit Cream, 85.
Fruit Essences, 9.
Fruit Juice Preservation, 37.
Fruit Lemonade, 90.
Fruit Malt, 95.
Fruit Phosphate, 102.
Fruit Punch, 108.
Fruit Punch Syrup, 39.

G

Gin Cocktail, 205.
Gin Punch, 217.
Ginger Ale, 69.
Ginger Beer, 71.
Ginger Essence, 10.
Ginger, Hot, 122.
Ginger Mint, 73.
Ginger Phosphate, 103.
Ginger Syrup, 39.
Ginger Wine, 184.
Gingerade, 73.
Glacés, 75.
Golden Fizz, 61, 205.
Gooseberry Essence, 11.
Gooseberry Wine, 186.
Grape Egg Phosphate, 61.
Grape Essence, 11.
Grape, Hot, 122.
Grape Juice, 76.
Grape Juice Formulas, 80.
Grape Juice—Home Manufacture, 77.
Grape Phosphate, 103.
Grape Punch, 109.
Grape Syrup, 40.
Grape Wine, 186.
Grenadine, 40.

H

Hock Cup, 202.
Hock and Claret Syrup, 41.
Honey Wine, 189.
Hop Beer, 56.
Hot Beverages, 115.
Hot Punch, 217.

I

Ice Cream Beverages, 83.
Ice Cream Cantaloupe, 83.
Ice Cream Malted Milk, 98.
Ice Cream Shake, 85.
Iced Punch, 218.
Imitation Champagne, 176.

Index

Imitation Wines, 157.
Imperial Syrup, 41.
Improving Cider, 139.
Iron Malt, 95.

J

Java Tonic, 41.
John Collins, 205.

K

Kola, 206.
Kola, Hot, 122.
Kola Malt, 95.
Kola Phosphate, 103.
Kola Wine, 189.

L

Lemon, 87.
Lemon Beer, 57.
Lemon Essence, 12.
Lemon Frappé, 67.
Lemon, Lime, Mint, etc., 87.
Lemon Phosphate, 103.
Lemon Sour, 62.
Lemon Squash, 90.
Lemon Syrup, 41.
Lemon Wine, 189.
Lemonade, 62.
Lemonade for Sick, 129.
Lemonade, Hot, 123.
Lemonade Powder, 91.
Licorice Syrup, 42.
Lime Essence, 13.
Lime, Hot, 123.
Lime Lemonade, 91.
Linseed Tea, 129.
Loving Cup, 202.

M

Mace Extract, 13.
Maidenhair Syrup, 30.
Malmsey, 190.
Malt Beverages, 94.
Malt Extract, 13.
Malt Wine Cordial, 95.
Malted Milk, 96.
Malted Milk, Hot, 98, 123.
Malted Milk Syrup, 42.
Maple Cream, 85.
Marshmallow Cream, 85.
Mead, 98, 190.
Mead Essence, 13.
Medicated Wines, 190.
Mellowing Wines, 172.
Melon Essence, 14.
Metheglin, 189, 207.
Metric System, 224.
Milk Lemonade, 90.
Milk Punch, 219.
Mineral Milk, 65.
Mint Drink, 65.
Mint Julep, 207.
Mint Phosphate, 104.
Mint Punch, 109.
Mint Syrup, 43.
Mixed Drinks, 197.
Mock Turtle Bouillon, 124.
Molasses Beer, 57.
Moselle Cup, 203.
Moselle Wine, 191.
Mulberry Wine, 191.
Mulled Ale, 208.
Mulled Claret, 208.
Mulled Wine, 191.
Manhattan Cocktail, 206.
Manhattan Punch, 218.
Maple Beer, 57.
Maple Frappé, 67.
Maple Syrup, 42.
Maraschino Fruit Punch, 218.
Marshmallow Syrup, 43.
Martini Cocktail, 206.
Maturation of Wines, 171.
May Drink, 207.

N

Nectar Syrup, 44.
Nectarine Essence, 14.
Negus, 208.

Index

Non-Alcoholic Beers, 55.
Norfolk Punch, 219.
Nut Bamboo Soufflé, 85.
Nut Fruit Syrup, 45.
Nut Sundae, 113.
Nutmeg Essence, 14.
Nuts for Beverages, 44.

O

Oatmeal Water, 129.
Orange Cider, 139.
Orange Cream, 86.
Orange Drink, 63.
Orange Egg Phosphate, 62.
Orange Essence, 14.
Orange Frappé, 67.
Orange, Hot, 124.
Orange Lemonade, 92.
Orange Malted Milk, 98.
Orange Phosphate, 104.
Orange Punch, 110.
Orange Syrup, 45.
Orgeat Punch, 219.
Orgeat Syrup, 46.
Ottawa Beer, 57.
Oyster Broth, 124.

P

Peach Cream, 86.
Peach Drink, 65.
Peach Essence, 14.
Peach Syrup, 47.
Peach Wine, 192.
Pear Essence, 15.
Pear Syrup, 47.
Peppermint Essence, 15.
Pepsin, Hot, 125.
Pepsin Lemonade, 92.
Pepsin Phosphate, 105.
Perry, 208.
Phosphate, 62.
Phosphated Syrup, 47.
Phosphates, 100.
Phosphates, Hot, 124.
Pineapple Cider, 138.

Pineapple Cream, 86.
Pineapple Egg Phosphate, 62.
Pineapple Essence, 16.
Pineapple Frappé, 67.
Pineapple Glacé, 75.
Pineapple Julep, 209.
Pineapple Lemonade, 90.
Pineapple Phosphate, 105.
Pineapple Punch, 110.
Pineapple Sundae, 114.
Pineapple Syrup, 47.
Pistachio Essence, 17.
Pistachio, Hot, 125.
Pistachio Punch, 110.
Pistachio Syrup, 48.
Plum Essence, 17.
Pomegranate Essence, 17.
Pop, 73.
Port Wine—Imitation, 192.
Preservation of Lemon Juice, 91.
Preserving Cider, 141–142.
Princes' Punch, 219.
Prune Syrup, 48.
Punch, 64.
Punches, 107, 213.
Purl, 209.

Q

Quince Cider, 142.
Quince Essence, 17.
Quince Flip, 64.
Quinine Wine, 193.

R

Racking Wines, 172.
Raisin Cider, 142.
Raisin Wine, 193.
Raspberryade, Hot, 125.
Raspberry Essence, 18.
Raspberry Lemonade, 93.
Raspberry Phosphate, 105.
Raspberry Punch, 110, 219.
Raspberry Sour, 62.
Raspberry Syrup, 49.

Index

Raspberry Wine, 193.
Raspberry and Currant Wine, 194.
Red Coloring for Soda Water Syrups, 28.
Regents' Punch, 219.
Rhubarb Extract, 18.
Rhubarb Wine, 194.
Rice Water, 130.
Ripening Wines, 172.
Roman Punch, 220.
Root Beer, 58.
Root Beer Essence, 19.
Ropiness in Wines, 173.
Rose Cream, 64.
Rose Essence, 19.
Rose Mint, 64.
Rose Syrup, 50.
Royal Muscadine, 50.

S

Sago Water, 130.
Sandwiches—Cream, 86.
Sangaree, 50, 209.
Sarsaparilla Beer, 58.
Sarsaparilla Essence, 19.
Sarsaparilla Syrup, 50.
Sassafras Essence, 19.
Sauterne Cup, 203.
Seltzer Lemonade, 91.
Shandy Gaff, 209.
Sherbet, 64, 65, 93.
Sherbet Syrup, 51.
Sherry Cobbler, 209.
Sherry Flip, 64.
Sherry Wine, 196.
Shrub, 210.
Sick, Beverages for the, 128.
Silver Fizz, 62, 211.
Silver Sour, 211.
Simple Syrup, 51.
Sloe Gin, 211.
Solferine, 211.
Sour Wine, 174.
Sparkling Cider, 143.
Spearmint Extract, 20.

Spice Extract, 20.
Spruce Beer, 59.
Spruce Extract, 20.
Strawberry Drink, 64, 65.
Strawberry Extract, 20.
Strawberry Phosphate, 105.
Strawberry Punch, 111.
Strawberry Sundae, 114.
Strawberry Syrup, 51.
Strawberry Wine, 196.
Sundaes, 112.
Sundaes, Hot, 125.
Syrups, 24, 98, 117, 118.

T

Tangerine Phosphate, 106.
Tea, 126.
Tea Extract, 21.
Tea Frappé, 68.
Tea Punch, 220.
Tea Syrup, 53.
Toast Water, 130.
Tomato, Hot, 127.
Tonic Beer Essence, 21.
Tonka Essence, 21.
Tutti-Frutti Punch, 111.
Tutti-Frutti Sundae, 114.

V

Vanilla Essence, 22.
Vanilla Syrup, 53.
Vichy à la Egg, 62.
Vichy and Lime, 92.
Violet Cream, 64.
Violet Syrup, 54.

W

Watermelon Sundae, 114.
Whipped Cream, 54.
Whiskey Cocktail, 212.
Whiskey Punch, 220.
Whiskey Sour, 212.
White Spruce Beer, 60.

Index

Wine Cup, 203.
Wine Punch, 220.
Wines, 145.
Wines, Management of, 160.
Wines—To Lay Down, 170.
Wine, To Sweeten, 173.

Wintergreen Essence, 23.
Wintergreen Syrup, 54.

Y

Yeast Wine, 196.

THE END

www.ingramcontent.com/pod-product-compliance
Lightning Source LLC
Chambersburg PA
CBHW011954150426
43199CB00019B/2864